The Philosophy of Forgiveness - Volume I
Explorations of Forgiveness: Personal, Relational, and Religious

Edited by
Court D. Lewis
Owensboro Community & Technical College

Authors

Jennifer Mei Sze Ang
Singapore Institute of Management University

Raja Bahlul
Doha Institute

Margaret Betz
West Chester University and Rutgers University

Gregory L. Bock
Philosophy and Religion, University of Texas

Christopher Cowley
University College Dublin, Ireland

Rebecca Dew
University of Hawaii, Manoa

Alexis Elder
University of Minnesota Duluth

William C. Gay
University of North Carolina at Charlotte

Christopher Ketcham
University of Texas at Austin

Man-to Tang
Chinese University of Hong Kong

Vernon Series in Philosophy of Forgiveness

Copyright © 2017 Vernon Press, an imprint of Vernon Art and Science Inc, on behalf of the author.

All rights reserved. No part of this publication may be reproduced, stored in a retrieval system, or transmitted in any form or by any means, electronic, mechanical, photocopying, recording, or otherwise, without the prior permission of Vernon Art and Ascience Inc.

www.vernonpress.com

In the Americas:
Vernon Press
1000 N West Street,
Suite 1200, Wilmington,
Delaware 19801
United States

In the rest of the world:
Vernon Press
C/Sancti Espiritu 17,
Malaga, 29006
Spain

Vernon Series in Philosophy of Forgiveness

Library of Congress Control Number: 2016944316

ISBN: 978-1-62273-082-7

Product and company names mentioned in this work are the trademarks of their respective owners. While every care has been taken in preparing this work, neither the authors nor Vernon Art and Science Inc. may be held responsible for any loss or damage caused or alleged to be caused directly or indirectly by the information contained in it.

Table of Contents

Contributors   vii

Introduction Explorations of Forgiveness   ix
Court D. Lewis

Chapter 1   From Relationship Repair to Relationship Stewardship: Forgiveness and Friendship   17
Alexis Elder

Chapter 2   Restorative Justice and Care Ethics: An Integrated Approach to Forgiveness and Reconciliation   39
William C. Gay

Chapter 3   Injustice as Injury, Forgiveness as Healing   67
Raja Bahlul

Chapter 4   Filling that Moral Space: Forgiveness, Suffering, and the Recognition of Human Identity   99
Rebecca Dew

Chapter 5   "Her loyalty survived his foolishness:" Hannah Arendt, Martin Heidegger, and Forgiveness   133
Margaret Betz

Chapter 6   Unforgivable Evil and Evildoers   151
Jennifer Mei Sze Ang

Chapter 7   Unconditional Forgiveness and Practical Necessity   181
Christopher Cowley

Chapter 8   The Double Intentionality of Forgiveness: A Non-reductive Account of Forgiveness in Ricoeur and Confucius   201
Man-to Tang

Chapter 9   Christian Love and Unconditional
Forgiveness: A Response to Glen Pettigrove   223
Gregory L. Bock

Chapter 10   Buddhism and the End to Forgiveness   243
Christopher Ketcham

Acknowledgements   *279*

Index   *281*

Contributors

Jennifer Mei Sze Ang is Senior Lecturer at the Singapore Institute of Management University (SIM University) and a member of the executive committee for the Asia-Pacific Chapter of the International Society for Military Ethics (APAC-ISME). She is the author of *Sartre and the Moral Limits of War and Terrorism*. Her recent book chapter publications include "Fighting the Humanitarian War: Justifications and Limitations," in *Routledge Handbook on Ethics and War: Just War in the 21st Century*, and "Evil by Nobodies," in *The Problem of Evil: New Philosophical Directions*. Her main focus is examining Sartre's philosophy, in relation to Kant, Hegel, and Arendt, on various issues regarding ethics, war, revolutions, humanitarian interventions, and history.

Raja Bahlul is currently Professor of Philosophy at the Doha Institute for Graduate Studies. He received his B.A. from the American University of Beirut, and completed his graduate studies in Philosophy at Indiana University-Bloomington (Indiana, USA). He has written on a variety of subjects, including Islamic Philosophy, Identity and Individuation, Emotion, Cognitivism about Ethics, and Political Islam and Modernity.

Margaret Betz teaches philosophy at West Chester University and Rutgers University. She is the author of various articles on feminist theory, environmental ethics, and animal ethics, and is the author of the book *The Hidden Philosophy of Hannah Arendt*.

Gregory L. Bock, Ph.D., is Senior Lecturer of Philosophy and Religion at the University of Texas at Tyler. His research areas include ethics and the philosophy of religion.

Christopher Cowley is Lecturer in philosophy at University College Dublin, Ireland. He is the author of *Moral Responsibility*, and has edited two recent volumes: *The Philosophy of Autobiography* and *Supererogation*.

Rebecca Dew lives in Brisbane, Australia and is a recent graduate of the University of Hawaii at Manoa, where she received her Bachelor of Arts in English and completed her Honors thesis in 2012. Rebecca is currently completing her PhD at the School of Political Science and International Studies at the University of Queensland. Her current thesis "Hannah Arendt, Utopia and the Ideology of Modernity" reflects her interest in the role of ideology as informative to an understanding of the history of political philosophy, with particular applications to epistemic engagement, meaning acquisition and cultural memory.

Alexis Elder is an Assistant Professor of Philosophy at the University of Minnesota Duluth. Her research focuses on friendships and other close-knit social groups, including practices and technologies that affect them.

William C. Gay is Emeritus Professor (Retired) at the University of North Carolina at Charlotte. He received his Ph.D. in Philosophy from Boston College in 1976. Gay specializes in war and peace studies (focusing on weapons of mass destruction and nonviolent strategies), social and political philosophy (focusing on Soviet and post-Soviet Russian political thought), and continental philosophy (focusing on linguistic alienation and linguistic violence). He has authored numerous books, including, with Michael Pearson, *The Nuclear Arms Race*; with T.A. Alekseeva, *Capitalism with a Human Face: The Quest for a Middle Road in Russian Politics*. With Alekseeva, he has also co-edited two volumes: 1) *On the Eve of the 21st Century: Perspectives of Russian and American Philosophers*—the first post-Soviet collection of essays by Russian and American philosophers—and *Democracy and the Quest for Justice*. Finally, he is the editor of the English edition of *Global Studies Encyclopedia*. Gay is a member of several philosophical societies, including the Concerned Philosophers for Peace, having served as President, Executive Director, and Newsletter Editor. He has also organized numerous Russian-American exchanges and collaborations, particularly with the Institute of Philosophy in Moscow and with the Russian Philosophical Society.

Christopher Ketcham earned his Doctorate from the University of Texas at Austin. He teaches business and ethics for the University of Houston Downtown. His research interests are applied ethics, social justice, and east-west comparative philosophy. He has chapters in *Reconsidering the Meaning in Life* and *Commercial Space Exploration: Ethics, Policy and Governance*. He has published articles in *Philosophical Inquires, Per la filosofia, Leadership and the Humanities*, and the *Journal of the Philosophy of Life*.

Man-to Tang is a PhD Candidate at the Chinese University of Hong Kong, which excels at contemporary Confucianism and phenomenological research in Asia. He was been a teacher at the Community College at Lingnan University, HKSAR for many years. His main research areas are phenomenology and hermeneutics, the philosophy of psychological phenomena, and east-west comparative studies. He has published articles in *Meta: Research in Phenomenology, Hermeneutics, and Practical Philosophy, Sofia Philosophical Review, Existentia*, and *Phenomenological Review*.He can be contacted via email at mttang@link.cuhk.edu.hk

Introduction
Explorations of Forgiveness

Court D. Lewis

To explore is to seek out and to discover the yet unknown. Even though exploration is challenging and tiring, it is one of the most rewarding aspects of human engagement; for it is through exploration that we learn, grow as individuals, and mature as moral beings. The French use the term 'flâneur' to describe a visitor, who purposely gets "lost" in order to engage and gain a more direct and interpersonal understanding of the symbolic meanings and beliefs of a society. The flâneur immerses herself in the culture of society, ignoring advice featured in guidebooks, so as to intimately participate with and learn from the actual members of the society. In this way, the flâneur gains a more accurate understanding of the people and community being explored, while at the same time gaining a better understanding of her own values and assumptions.

Vernon Press's series on the Philosophy of Forgiveness is designed as a type of philosophical flâneur, engaging past and contemporary issues of forgiveness, in order to develop and arrive at a clearer, more dynamic understanding of forgiveness and its related concepts. The Philosophy of Forgiveness is multi-dimensional and complex. As recent scholarly philosophical works on forgiveness illustrate, incorporating personal, relational, political, ethical, psychological, and religious dimensions into one consistent conception of "forgiveness" is difficult. *Explorations of Forgiveness: Personal, Relational, and Religious* begins the task of creating a consistent multi-dimensional account of forgiveness by bringing together multiple voices from around the globe to analyze, discuss, and draw conclusions about how best to understand forgiveness.

It is my hope that by the end of the book readers' previously held conceptions of forgiveness will have been engaged, challenged, and clarified. The readings are diverse, and they contain a wide variety of philosophical schools of thought and interests. Each author has her or his own cultural, philosophical, and theological assumptions, and I have worked hard to ensure that their unique voices were not lost during the editing, and in some cases translation, process. I hope, like me, you will find this volume, and future volumes, rewarding and insightful.

As Series Editor, my goal is to provide contributing authors a platform on which to offer insightful analysis of the myriad of issues relating to forgiveness. The authors contained in this volume span the globe, and even though their interests and concerns vary greatly, there is considerable overlap in many areas. In order to gain a general understanding of the authors' divergent and convergent themes, I will provide a short summary of each chapter.

The volume is divided into three sections. Section 1, "Relational Aspects of Forgiveness," contains three chapters offering insights into the role of forgiveness in repairing, sustaining, stewarding, and healing relationships damaged by wrongdoing. Alexis Elder's "From Relationship Repair to Relationship Stewardship: Forgiveness and Friendship" begins the volume by questioning the common argument that forgiveness is solely a tool for relationship repair. According to Elder, recent work on belief norms in friendship suggests that forgiveness (at least partly) consists in the setting aside of the resentment of wrongdoing, in order for the friendship to be repaired. On such an account, forgiveness is the recognition and coming to terms with the fact that all people have shortcomings, including ourselves, and that by forgiving we commit to overlooking our friend's shortcomings, which then leads to a restored friendship. Elder, on the other hand, argues that forgiveness is consistent with the process of "cutting ties," especially if one is committed to maintaining (only) high-quality friendships. If true, then forgiveness can also be a tool for ending as well as repairing relationships. To support this conclusion, Elder suggests we view friendship in terms of stewardship, and that we replace the relationship-repair model of forgiveness with one of *relationship stewardship*.

William C. Gay's "Restorative Justice and Care Ethics: An Integrated Approach to Forgiveness and Reconciliation" continues the relational theme by arguing that restorative justice, when coupled with care ethics, grounds a robust and integrated approach to forgiveness and reconciliation. Gay develops an account of restorative justice, the aim of which is to repair the harm generated by criminal behavior by seeking cooperative resolutions for victims, offenders, and the community. According to Gay, such an approach has clear advantages for fostering forgiveness and achieving reconciliation, and generally works more effectively than the punitive approach suggested by retributive accounts of justice. When coupled with care ethics, which provides a useful philosophical justification that stresses particularity and connection, we come to understand that persons are entangled in a web of dynamic relationships, which they may wish to maintain or repair. Forgiveness, then, provides a means for this maintenance and repair. Gay concludes that punitive orientations of retribution found in corporal punishment, capital punishment, and international war can be replaced by focusing on preservative love, complementing strategies of nonviolence during conflict, and practices of forgiveness and reconciliation following conflict.

Raja Bahlul's "Injustice as Injury, Forgiveness as Healing" closes the opening section by exploring the nature of injustice and forgiveness, and how they relate to injury and healing. To understand their relations, Bahlul suggests an analogy between forgiveness and healing, based on two other analogies, one between injustice and injury, the other between resentment and pain. For Bahlul, injustice should be viewed as a species of harm, whereas pain and resentment viewed as aversive states with protective functions connected to motivating powers. After examining the nature of each proposed analogy, he argues: just as healing follows upon injury under certain conditions, so too does forgiveness follow upon injustice when conditions are right—in both cases, aversive states are superseded, and the organism is restored to a previous condition of wholeness and integrity. Realizing the nature of such an argument, Bahlul concludes with a discussion of some objections and possible replies.

Continuing with the relational theme, Section 2, "Relational Accounts Influenced by Hannah Arendt," contains three chapters that incorporate lessons from Hannah Arendt's philosophical teachings (both her writings and personal life). Chapter 4 features Rebecca Dew's "Filling that Moral Space: Forgiveness, Suffering and the Recognition of Human Identity." That is, Dew combines an analysis of Fyodor Dostoevsky's identification of the human experience with suffering, and Arendt's view of Jesus of Nazareth as the most powerful representative of human compassion, to show that forgiveness creates an experiential bond between individuals as humans susceptible to shared pain. She argues that Arendt is best understood as viewing human suffering as of social significance as an identifier of private personhood, by way of the forgiveness-act.

In "Her loyalty survived his foolishness": Hannah Arendt, Martin Heidegger, and Forgiveness," Margaret Betz explores Arendt's personal friendship with Martin Heidegger. For those unfamiliar with the controversy, Arendt's Jewishness and Heidegger's unapologetic affiliation with the Nazi party are at odds. Yet, in the face of such odds, Arendt forgave Heidegger after the war, and continued their friendship. Betz attempts to answer the question: How could Arendt continue to be friends with Heidegger, especially considering he never publicly expressed contrition for the role he played in the Third Reich? Betz suggests that by carefully examining Arendt's life and philosophical writings, we come to understand her forgiveness, which some have labelled "inexcusable" and "blind devotion," as a representation of the political act *par excellence*.

Continuing the theme of the "unforgivable," and closing Section 2, Jennifer Ang's "Unforgivable Evil and Evildoers" argues that there are times in which forgiveness is morally inappropriate. Ang develops a conception of "moral bankruptcy," as a class of wrongdoing that does not deserve forgiveness. To ground this class or wrongdoing, Ang explores the relationship between legal/political forgiveness and interpersonal forgiveness, within the context of Hannah Arendt's conceptualization of the crimes of the Holocaust—of wrongs that defy the limits of law, and are, hence, unpunishable. Moral bankruptcy occurs when an evildoer is unreflective and unrepentant, and when such evildoers commit wrongs against the community as a whole (and not only particular victims). According to Ang, forgiving in such cases compromises our moral integrity in two ways: 1) when we fail to mete out proper moral punishment, we concede our category of what is morally reprehensible (not just offensive) by accepting moral bankruptcy into our community; and 2) we fail to aid in the moral development of such individuals by not holding them responsible.

Section 3 shifts the discussion of forgiveness from matters of a strictly relational nature to four "Religious Perspectives" of forgiveness. Chapter 7 features Christopher Cowley's "Unconditional Forgiveness and Practical Necessity." In the chapter, Cowley defends unconditional forgiveness (such as that suggested by Christianity) against several prominent conditionalist accounts. According to conditionalists, victims must either have reasons for forgiving, or forgiveness is merely arbitrary. To show that such a disjunctive is incorrect, Cowley develops and explores the concept of "arbitrariness," and argues that if properly understood, unconditional forgiveness is a morally admirable type of forgiveness.

Man-to Tang's "The Double Intentionality of Forgiveness: A Non-reductive Account of Forgiveness in Confucius" attempts to develop a new sphere of forgiveness exploration by using Paul Ricoeur's hermeneutic account of intentionality and the Confucian doctrine of *shu* to create a conceptual bridge between Western and Eastern accounts of forgiveness. For Tang, traditional Western accounts of forgiveness tend to be reductive, dividing forgiveness into either purely personal or interpersonal accounts. Tang argues that instead of seeing forgiveness as an either/or between personal and interpersonal accounts, it should be reframed in terms of Ricoeur's hermeneutic account of "double intentionalities." Once this reframing is complete, parallels between Western forgiveness and the Confucian's doctrine of *shu* (translated as forgive, pardon, or excuse) can be developed, and such parallels promise to offer new approaches to addressing difficulties found in contemporary forgiveness literature.

Chapter 9 features Gregory Bock's "Unconditional Forgiveness and Christian Love," which provides a thoughtful and thorough examination of Glen Pettigrove's recent book *Forgiveness and Love*. According to Bock, Pettigrove stops short of endorsing unconditional forgiveness. To address this shortcoming, Bock explores the possibility of replacing Pettigrove's use of 'love' with the concept of *agape* love developed in the Christian New Testament, in order to ground a strong principle of unconditional forgiveness. He concludes by showing that unconditional forgiveness is not merely morally permissible, but also morally required.

Section 3 concludes with Christopher Ketcham's "Buddhism and the End to Forgiveness." Ketcham explores Theravada Buddhism, which is aligned to the Buddha's *suttas* (or lessons) as recorded in the Pali Canon, to argue that within its teachings the Buddha suggests an "end" to forgiveness, to be replaced with an unconditional compassion toward others. With disagreement in Buddhist literature about whether Buddhism contains the idea of forgiveness, Ketcham suggests that the Buddha would have told his followers to think beyond forgiveness. Since forgiveness requires an ill (i.e. wrongdoing), plus an attachment to that ill, and the path to enlightenment (*nibbāna*) requires aspirants to release attachments to all ills, a truly enlightened one will no longer be attached to any ill that could be forgiven. In other words, when one becomes enlightened, there is nothing left to forgive. So, according to Ketcham, Buddhism offers a different perspective of how to think of wrongdoing, forgiveness, and the goal of moral enlightenment.

As witnessed in these summaries, there is a lot of philosophical ground to cover. So with the task ahead in mind, I will bring my portion to an end and let the reader begin her or his own exploration of the chapters contained within.

Chapter 1

From Relationship Repair to Relationship Stewardship: Forgiveness and Friendship

Alexis Elder

Introduction

In this chapter, I argue that the relationship-repair model of interpersonal forgiveness ought to be replaced by the broader concept of relationship-stewardship.

Briefly, it is common to think of the work interpersonal forgiveness does as that of repairing relationships in the wake of wrongdoing. This seems to make forgiveness inappropriate or even immoral in circumstances where repairing the relationship is a bad idea. But it seems that forgiveness can also be an important part of the process of *ending* an interpersonal relationship. It can be a way to cut ties and distance oneself from a formerly close companion. One could say that the "forgiveness" involved here is like the other in name only, or only bears a superficial resemblance and is a distinct phenomenon. But it seems to have quite a lot in common with other instances of interpersonal forgiveness. Explanatory unity can be achieved by conceiving of interpersonal forgiveness on a relationship-stewardship rather than relationship-repair model. Forgiveness both for purposes of relationship repair and relationship termination, involves setting aside negative reactions to wrongdoing in the interest of fostering high-quality relationships, whether by sustaining good ones or terminating those that have run their course.

Some preliminary remarks here about terminology: by 're-lationship' I mean relatively close interpersonal relationships. Although 'relationship' is sometimes taken to be a shorthand for romantic relationships, I also include here friendships and familial relationships. I take a relatively inclusive conception of friendship to be a helpful model of interpersonal relationships. Aristotle's account of *philia*, which allows that our friends can overlap with our families, romantic partners, colleagues, and neighbors, also offers a normative ideal of friendship as a component of the best lives that can be more or less closely approximated by actual relationships. Although I am not committed to a faithful interpretation of his theory, I do find it a helpful starting place for reflecting on close personal relationships.

In Aristotle's account, friends (which can include siblings, spouses, children, co-workers, and neighbors) are those people whom we care about, who care about us in turn, toward whom we reciprocally wish well, and who both recognize and value being in this reciprocal arrangement. He distinguishes between friendships upon which the caring is founded on valuing a person's utility (friendships of utility), those where caring is based in valuing pleasure derived from the other person in some way (friendships of pleasure), and friendships grounded in mutual intrinsic valuing of the other, where each is valued for who they are—their character—and not merely for what they do (usually known as virtue or character friendships). Virtue friendships, he says, are the best, most stable, and most valuable friendships, but are also the rarest, and human beings as social animals aim to enjoy these friendships in particular as an important, perhaps even necessary, part of the good life (*Nicomachean Ethics*, Books VIII-IX).

Forgiveness is commonly construed as the setting aside of resentment (Hughes 2015), although alternative accounts, such as forgiveness as forbearing to punish (Zaibert 2009) or setting aside of contempt (Bell 2008) exist. Here, I start with a fairly inclusive definition of forgiveness as the setting aside of negative reactions, whether emotional or otherwise, because I am more interested in exploring the work it does than in entering debates on how to define precisely what constitutes it.

I. Forgiveness as a tool for relationship repair?

Forgiveness, especially interpersonal forgiveness, is commonly construed as a tool for relationship repair (Hughes 2014). For instance, Jeffrie Murphy says, "Forgiveness heals and restores; and, without it, resentment would remain as an obstacle to many human relationships we value. This can be seen most clearly in such intimate relationships as love and friendship" (1982, 504).

Philosophers sometimes distinguish forgiving a person (personal forgiveness) from forgiving a particular action (forgiveness of wrongdoing). One might wonder whether this conception of forgiveness as relationship repair is limited to forgiveness of wrongdoing. But even theorists who distinguish forgiving a specific action from forgiving a person seem to link personal forgiveness with repairing relationships. For instance, Christopher Bennett distinguishes redemptive forgiveness, which is the "acknowledgement that wrongdoing no longer constitutes a moral barrier to our relationship with the wrongdoer" (2003, 127) from what he terms "personal wrongdoing," characterized as an attitude toward the wrongdoer. He argues that even purely personal forgiveness counts as forgiveness because "it involves the resumption of relations between two individuals, where the forgiver recognizes the appropriateness of putting the wrong behind her" (Bennett 2003, 141). Macalaster Bell, who likewise distinguishes forgiving wrongdoing (which she associates with overcoming resentment) from forgiving persons (which she associates with overcoming contempt), says "overcoming our contempt for a person will *require* us, at least in many cases, to 'reengage' the offender" (2008, 656, emphasis added).

If forgiveness heals, restores, reengages, resumes relations, or otherwise repairs relationships disrupted by wrongdoing, then this suggests that the person who is faced with a friend's wrongdoing will have to choose between forgiving the wrong and thereby, to that extent, repairing the relationship, or refusing to forgive on the grounds that the relationship is not worth repairing. One could, in principle, forgive the wrong and then end the friendship for other reasons. A person might forgive her friend for spilling red wine on the white carpet, but end the friendship because she is moving across the country. But forgiveness would, even in such cases, constitute a repair, and undermine, to that extent, one's taking the forgiven wrongdoing as reason to end the relationship.

Although in an ideal world, best friends would never err and so never give each other reason to forgive, in our non-ideal one, forgiveness seems an integral part of friendship. As Murphy puts it:

> *The people with whom we are most intimate are those who can harm us the most... However, deep as these hurts of intimacy may be, what would be the consequences of never forgiving any of them? Surely it would be this: the impossibility of ever having the kind of intimate relationships that are one of the crowning delights of human existence. The person who cannot forgive is the person who cannot have friends or lovers. (504-5)*

Forgiveness' value, then, seems to be related to the value of friendship, in conjunction with the fact that we are prone to err. Relationships are important to us, as social creatures, and given our imperfections, they occasionally suffer damages that need repairing. Forgiveness is thus a useful tool for us to have around.

At first blush, the thought that forgiveness helps us move past our mistakes in relationships might seem to be connected to friends' natural tendency to overlook our flaws, or even to suggest that this tendency might constitute a norm of friendship. In a review of the literature on optimistic bias in social psychology, Lisa Bortolotti and Magdalena Antrobus discuss optimistic bias in romantic relationships, which they note is known as the "love-is-blind bias." People with this bias "are more likely to enjoy a satisfying and lasting relationship. ...a general disposition towards optimism leads to the adoption of more constructive approaches when difficulties in the relationship emerge..." (2015, 197). Forgiveness, then, might be part of a more widespread optimistic inclination that turns out to be good for relationships in our non-ideal world.

This would be consistent with two recent defenses of certain kinds of epistemic bias in friendship (Stroud 2006, Keller 2004). Both authors independently argue that norms of friendship require us, on at least some occasions, to downplay friends' flaws in the face of evidence that would have us, under other circumstances, negatively evaluate individuals' actions or character. For example, one might be more inclined to discount negative rumors about a friend's behavior than a mere acquaintance's, and norms of friendship might endorse this inclination even where epistemic norms do not.

But this is true neither to the phenomenon of forgiveness, which is distinct from forgetting or overlooking a wrongdoing, nor to friendship itself. Recent criticisms of Sarah Stroud's and Simon Keller's accounts have focused on the importance of valuing friends "warts and all," or of incorporating into norms of friendship attitudes and practices (including forgiveness itself) that take into account friends' shortcomings. Jason Kawall, for instance, argues against Stroud and Keller that:

> *...among the elements of friendship are such things as acceptance, hope, encouragement, and forgiveness. With our best friends we hope and expect that they accept us, flaws and all; they see enough value in our other traits, or enough potential to change that*

> *they stand by us. They will hope that we can typically improve, and will presumably encourage us to do so. They will also typically be more forgiving than others when we do fall short. But all of these important aspects of friendship only come into play as we recognize our friend's shortcomings, and they ours. Indeed, it is often taken as a mark of best friends that they are quite aware of our flaws yet they still find us worthy of love; they recognize our strengths and potentials. (2013, 356-7)*

In fact, one might think that these different elements are interrelated, in developing a robust account of forgiveness as a tool for relationship repair: one forgives a friend in order to repair a relationship when and because one because one accepts their flaws because one sees value in their other traits, or hopes they will improve, or sees potential to change, characteristically as part of encouraging them to do so. Friendship is an intimate relationship that requires vulnerability. Friends are people who exhibit mutual support and caring. In its highest form, friends are taken to engage in intrinsic valuing of each other as complete individuals and concern for each other's wellbeing (EN 1156b). These qualities of friendship, then naturally provide a framework for forgiveness as relationship repair. Because we are vulnerable to each other in friendship, we are especially likely to suffer harms when our friends err. But because friendship requires mutual support and caring, we want to support and care for our friends despite their slip-ups, and they desire the same for us. In valuing each other as complete individuals, friends seem committed to the idea that occasional errors are not grounds for dismissing whole persons, and especially when, as Jean Hampton (1990) suggests, forgiveness may help a person to seize the opportunity for self-improvement, forgiving cannot just help us set wrongdoing aside, but actively improve relationships, and each other.

So forgiveness between friends is not the result of mere blind optimism, nor is it reducible to condoning bad behavior by one's friends. Rather, it constitutes a rich process of dealing with friends as whole persons that is intimately related to other aspects of friendship, by having us consider our friends as creatures both prone to error and yet still valuable, and whose companionship we value intrinsically.

II. When repairing isn't right

But at this point, a concern arises. Even though forgiveness is often praised, if it repairs relationships, it may repair the wrong ones, and thus not always be praiseworthy. Despite the appropriateness of forgiveness in many friendships, some wrongdoings and character flaws can be major obstacles to a flourishing relationship, and perhaps ought to be grounds for terminating the relationship—that is, some ought not be repaired.

Some (such as Murphy and Hampton 1990) have connected morally inappropriate forgiveness with forgiveness that sustains bad relationships, like when an abused spouse forgives his/her abuser as part of their reconciliation. In such cases, forgiveness can seem bad for at least two reasons: because it is servile or lacking in self-respect to continue in such a relationship, and because the relationship being repaired is not a good one and so forgiveness is thereby not valuable as a means to supporting it. (These are not unrelated concerns, but emphasizing one angle versus the other may prove helpful in particular cases.) As Murphy puts it:

> *Forgiveness may restore relationships, but to seek restoration at all costs—even at the cost of one's self-respect—can hardly be a virtue. And, in intimate relationships, it can hardly be true love or friendship either (the kind of*

> *love and friendship that Aristotle claimed is an essential part of the virtuous life). When we are willing to be doormats for others, we have—not love or friendship—but rather what the psychiatrist Karen Horney called 'morbid dependency'.* (505)

It seems to me that restoring relationships may, in such cases, be distinct from *repairing* them: repair implies making better, while forgiveness, in some settings, may merely allow bad relationships to limp along without actually improving, even to the detriment of one or more participants. Sometimes it just isn't good for two people to be in a relationship with each other, whatever their personal qualities outside that context. Thus, constitutive features of friendship (promoting wellbeing, mutual caring, mutual respect) turn out to be themselves inimical to forgiveness in extreme circumstances, in that forgiveness may not promote friends' wellbeing or constitute caring or respect for people in the friendship—which, notably, includes oneself. This can help explain why forgiveness can look immoral where it constitutes servility or self-abnegation. Relationships where one partner is servile or self-abnegating are no healthier than organisms are healthy when organs are failing or damaged by the rest of the organism. (More about this in Section Three.)

In addition to these deeply personal reasons for rejecting forgiveness, one may think the more general concern that one not condone immorality may supersede considerations of friendship. As the singer in the band Gogol Bordello asks in their song "Troubled Friends," "What do you do/and what if it's true/When your best friend confesses to you/That he has become a serial killer?" It is not at all obvious that the answer should be, "continue the friendship." Elsewhere, I have argued that bad people cannot be good friends (Elder 2014). My reasoning was that friends characteristically are sensitive to each other's values and worldviews, and simultaneously concerned for each other's wellbeing. Given the eudaimonist premise that bad values will tend to negatively impact a person's wellbeing, being friends with a bad person will put sensitivity and concern for wellbeing at odds with each other, making it impossible for bad people to be consistently good friends—even when their wrongdoing is not specifically directed at the friend. Add in the qualifier that many people think that forgiveness is apt only (or at least mostly) in circumstances where the wrong done is to the person doing the forgiving, and forgiveness starts to look out of place in relationships with serious wrongdoers.

If the relationship-repair account of interpersonal forgiveness sketched in Section One is complete, then forgiveness is inappropriate when and where relationships are not worth repairing.

III. Forgiving as part of terminating relationships?

At this point, however, a problem arises. Forgiveness can seem to be an important part of the process of terminating a relationship, not just a tool for repairing a relationship damaged by wrongdoing.

Forgiving as Part of the Process of Terminating a Relationship

Suppose two academics, Kate and Lacey have a longstanding friendship, and have relied on each other in many ways over the years. Recently, Kate has listened to Lacey work out an exciting new idea for a paper. A few months later, Lacey opens up the latest issue of a journal, only to discover that Kate has utilized this idea in a paper of her own, without even giving her credit. Lacey's response is conflicted—on the one hand, she considers this betrayal so serious that she thinks she ought to terminate the friendship. On the other hand, the seriousness of the betrayal also makes her feel quite outraged, and her anger inclines her to confront Kate, to express her indignation, to demand recompense not just for the stolen idea but for the trust that has been violated. After several fruitless exchanges with Kate, Lacey realizes that her negative reactions are merely prolonging the relationship. Kate can explain her reasoning by describing the pressures of tenure expectations, emotional and financial stressors, and so on, and can even offer apparently sincere and heartfelt apologies, but Lacey comes to believe that the fact that Kate reacted to these stressors by taking advantage of a friend's trust makes her out to be someone with whom Lacey just should not be friends. Eventually, she settles on a course of action in which she forgives Kate for her weakness, but avoids resuming the relationship. Forgiveness is necessary in order to move past the anger and other negative reactions that keep drawing her into conversations in which she finds herself repeating things like, "How could you? I trusted you..." etc. Her reactions, she comes to believe, are inapt for the situation because their major effect is to cause her to express herself to or demand things of Kate. But the very thing that provokes these reactions is the thing that gives her justified reason to disengage from Kate altogether.

Lacey cannot, of course, just consciously forgive Kate and have it over with, like flipping a switch. But her experience of disengaging from her friendship may be that focusing on forgiving Kate is an important part of the process. She might find it helpful to find ways to move past her anger and resentment, forgoing opportunities to punish her. Rather, she can work on neutralizing her emotional reactions overall (perhaps by telling herself relatively dispassionate stories about her friendship with Kate: "We used to be friends, but we just aren't that close anymore"). Her efforts on this front may be tied to her increasing success at avoiding Kate at events, turning down her phone calls, not responding to emails or texts, and dwelling less on both their friendship and her sense of betrayal—to not getting drawn back into a relationship with someone with whom she does not wish to engage.

Something like Cheshire Calhoun's description of the role of biographical explanation in aspirational forgiveness may be useful for people in situations like Lacey's. (Although this is not meant to categorically associate her account with forgiveness for the purpose of terminating a relationship—it may also be useful in repairing some relationships, and other ways of conceiving of forgiveness may also help one to move past a friendship, depending on the circumstances.) According to Calhoun, in aspirational forgiveness one gives up on trying to make moral sense of an act but rather sees it as making biographical sense, where "the wrongdoing is less likely to be a blow directly aimed at us than simply shrapnel from something else more complicated and more interesting in the person's life," allowing one to "place respecting another's way of sense-making of her life before resentfully enforcing moral standards" (1993, 93 and 95). Lacey can accept that Kate's action makes biographical sense, given her character and circumstances, without taking it to give her reason to continue to be involved in that story. In fact, it can be part of the process of ending her involvement. (There may be other ways of disengaging through forgiveness as well… in fact, I suspect each circumstance may call for something slightly different.)

One might worry that what I have described here is a fairly cold and distancing account of a supposedly "warm" phenomenon. Kim Atkins, for instance, criticizes Calhoun's account of forgiveness, saying that "On the view Calhoun proposes, forgiveness could not be the resumption of trust, since one cannot expect a change for the better from the agent" (2002, 124). The inability to expect change or resume trust is a problem, says Atkins, because when it is invoked "we are prevented from expecting moral behavior from those close to us" (Ibid.). But whether or not a particular relationship is benefited from an expectation of moral behavior seems to be a fact rooted in the details of a given relationship. Some people may benefit from expectations and accountability on the part of their nearest and dearest, while others may require space and acceptance.

Those very distancing characteristics can also make forgiveness well-suited for ending relationships. It can serve as an important counter-balance to help us avoid resentment's tendency to have us reengage with those who have proved themselves incapable of reciprocal engagement. (In other circumstances, a more expectation-laden form of forgiveness might be necessary for a relationship to end cleanly—especially where those expectations of moral behavior allow one to set aside previous entanglements. Suppose James forgives his roommate John for leaving him in the lurch on rent money, but terminates their arrangement with an explicit expectation that the money will be repaid in installments.)

At this point, one might also worry that what Lacey is doing should not count as forgiveness in any interesting sense of the term, since her "forgiving" Kate is driven by pragmatic considerations such as her desire to avoid reengaging with a person she considers not worth engaging with. Murphy, for instance, presents the following case:

> ...You have wronged me deeply, and I deeply resent you for it. The resentment eats away at my peace of mind, e.g. I lose sleep, snap at my friends, become less effective at my work, and so on. In short, my resentment so dominates my mental life that I am being made miserable. In order to regain my peace of mind, I go to a behavior-modification therapist to have my resentment extinguished. (Let us suppose there are such techniques.) Have I forgiven you? Surely not—at least not in any sense where forgiveness is supposed to be a moral virtue. For my motivation here was not moral at all: it was purely selfish, i.e. the desire to promote my own mental health. (507)

One might, following Kathryn Norlock, be skeptical of Murphy's attempt to isolate "true" forgiveness (2008). But even if morally-virtuous-forgiveness is but one species of forgiveness, it is, or ought to be, an interesting one to moral theorists. If Murphy is right, the cases described here do not qualify as such. But it is not so clear to me that this is the correct response, either in Lacey's case or in the situation Murphy describes. Self-care can, I am persuaded, be a moral consideration. (See Jean Hampton's "Selflessness and Loss of the Self" for a persuasive defense of this view.) At least in cases like Lacey's, the desire to promote one's own mental health, as well as the desire to avoid getting bogged down in acrimonious and potentially toxic relationships, seem plausibly like important parts of self-care.

Theorists who argue that forgiveness in the service of maintaining a relationship is immoral when it compromises one's self-respect, as Murphy does, seem to think that maintaining self-respect can give moral reason to act one way rather than another. Furthermore, maintaining self-respect in interpersonal circumstances requires taking seriously the relationships in which one ought to engage. As Murphy puts it, "to seek restoration [of relationships] at all costs—even at the cost of one's self-respect—can hardly be a virtue... Morality... is not simply something to be believed; it is something to be *cared* about. This caring includes concern about those persons (including oneself) who are the proper objects of moral judgment" (505).

In fact, in at least one sense of the term, exiting a formerly close relationship with a minimum of "drama" may be an important part of protecting one's dignity, and may seem to be a component of comporting oneself in a way that is consistent with robust self-respect. "She isn't worth it" can be an important thing to tell oneself (or those one cares about) as part of showing self-respect.

In addition, making good decisions about which relationships to sustain, and which to avoid, are decisions I would take to be moral. In many cases, relationships which are bad for a person are relationships which ought to be avoided, thus giving one double disincentive to disentangle oneself, both from concerns of self-care and responsible stewardship of relationships. When and where forgiveness aids in this process, it thereby gains moral significance from this affiliation (in addition to any it may have for other reasons). Good relationships, in order to be good, need to be good for those in them. This comes out in Murphy's comment that relationships in which one person is servile are not instances of friendship but rather "morbid dependency." Close-knit relationships resemble organisms, with the people in them being analogous to interdependent, mutually responsive organs that constitute it. Their flourishing, like that of their biological analog, depends on both the individual wellbeing of their constituent parts as well as their interdependence and inter-responsiveness. Resentment can interfere with interdependence and inter-responsiveness, but when it does so at the expense of the wellbeing of a component part, the composite entity is not thereby benefited, on balance.

It is not my intention to argue here that every instance of overcoming resentment ought to count as forgiveness (that would be outside the scope of this project). But I think that it would be an overly restrictive account of morality that would place all cases involving forgiveness-as-self-care or forgiveness-in-the-service-of-self-respect (as when forgiveness enables one to leave a bad relationship in which one is at risk of being disrespected) in the purely-pragmatic category.

While those who are suspicious of forgiveness in cases where forgiving looks servile may be right to consider anger and resentment, on occasion, to have an appropriate role to play, it seems overhasty to assume that anger and resentment are always the right tool for the job of addressing unacceptable wrongdoing by loved ones. Standing up for oneself, refusing to be a doormat, etc., may be facilitated by hard emotions in the context of a relationship. But they also pose a risk when the relationship itself is not worth sustaining. It would be bad to rule out as amoral a kind of forgiveness that enables one to exit a bad relationship, in the service of protecting the moral importance of emotions that get their value from their connection to self-care and self-respect.

IV. Forgiveness as a tool for relationship stewardship

We thus seem to have ended up with what could look, on the surface, like a paradox: when your friends wrong you so badly that the relationship's continuation would be servile or self-abnegating, you both should and should not forgive them (because forgiveness both repairs and helps terminate the relationship). One obvious step toward resolving this would be to distinguish repair-forgiveness from disengagement-forgiveness. But I do not think our work here is done.

It would be unsatisfying to think that repair-forgiveness and disengagement-forgiveness have only a name in common. Adding on the commonality that both involve setting aside negative reactions to wrongdoing helps somewhat, but given the work both do for interpersonal relationships, an account that fleshes out their connections and distinctions would stand at an explanatory advantage, subsuming both into the category of interpersonal forgiveness in the service of promoting healthy and valuable relationships.

But the differences and similarities need to be explored, in order to better understand their relationship to each other. The functions of relationship-repair and relationship-ending seem obviously different. However, they have several constitutive features in common. I said at the start that I am not utilizing a particular restrictive constitutive theory of forgiveness (that is, one that reduces it to setting aside resentment, or anger, or revenge, or foreswearing punishment, etc.). This is because I think that what we call forgiveness can include any or all of these, and both relationship-repair and relationship-termination forgiveness seem as though they can involve one or more of these options. So I prefer an inclusive account of what constitutes forgiveness. People and relationships are complicated, and I am reluctant to give up conceptual tools without strong motivation to do so.

Importantly, it seems that each of the prominent options could be involved in various instances of either relationship-repair or relationship-termination. Setting aside anger could help a relationship heal, or keep one from getting drawn back into acrimonious exchanges. Forbearing to punish might be good for a friendship, or it might be an important part of distancing oneself from a person by refusing to continue to take responsibility for their actions. Setting aside resentment can help one keep up with a friend, or move on. Foreswearing revenge can help a relationship to resume, or allow people to go their separate ways. And so on.

What is key here is understanding that anger, resentment, desire to punish, interest in revenge, and so on, can do different things in different circumstances. They can harm people, or motivate us to harm people, in ways that are bad for our relationships with them. But because they implicate beliefs about how others ought to treat us, and are intimately involved in our response to wrongdoing to us, they can be used to correct injustices toward us. At the same time, because they are deeply personal, they motivate us to engage with those we feel have wronged us. When correcting a wrongdoing is undesirable, anger, desire for punishment, etc. will tend to get in the way, regardless of what makes it undesirable: that it will damage the relationship, or prolong it.[1] If you prefer a more restricted account of what constitutes forgiveness, I do not believe this will substantially change my account, as it should incorporate your restricted version in its more expansive conception, and the distinctions between constituents should not track the difference between relationship-repair and relationship-terminating forgiveness.

What makes anger/resentment/punishment-by-the-wronged/revenge/contempt right or wrong, then, is not what it does to relationships considered generically, but what it does to a particular relationship—whether it corrects an injustice so the relationship can be improved, or helps someone stand up for themselves in the face of oppressive treatment, or hurts someone who has the potential to self-correct if given the opportunity and the motivation (such as the hopeful attitude of a friend), or keeps people entangled with each other when they would be better apart. That is, whether interpersonal forgiveness is right or wrong, in a given situation, depends on what, if anything, could make the relationship good. But what makes a relationship good?

There is a temptation to think of the good of relationships in a fairly thin sense—the continued and frequent interaction of friends, for example. But this seems to under-describe good friendships and good personal relationships more gen-

---

[1] This is consistent with Leo Zaibert's (2009) account of forbearing to punish as deeply personalized: it involves thinking the world would be worse if YOU were to punish the person who wronged you, even if you think they should still be punished by someone else.

erally. Good relationships seem to be good for their members, and relationships that are not good for those involved do not seem to be very good (as Murphy notes with his diagnosis of "morbid dependency"). As I said in Section Three, we can think of relationships as being like organisms in that their flourishing depends on both the individual wellbeing of their constituent organs and their appropriate interdependence and inter-responsiveness. Friendships flourish when friends are doing well, and doing good things for each other, and each friend's doing well is a good for the other.

If this account is roughly correct, then when we take relationships to be reason-giving, as I contend that they do in giving us reason to forgive or not in the context of a relationship, we need to work with both an ideal of relationship, and what (if anything) it would take to make this particular relationship good. As was discussed in Section One, forgiveness can help friends to do well, and can be motivated by friends' recognition of potential, concern for each other, and recognition of the continued benefits of interaction (where 'benefits' include things like thinking that very person is a good in one's life, and not merely a tallying of instrumental perks of associating with someone). But at times, continuing to interact with someone can be bad for one or both parties—and at such points it would seem that the continued existence of the organism is itself bad for its parts. In these cases, it would be irrational to forgive for the sake of the relationship, because the relationship is already, in some sense, a nonstarter—its flourishing is simply not possible.

At this point, a strategy to unify relationship-repair forgiveness and relationship-terminating forgiveness suggests itself. Both can be thought of as instances of relationship-stewardship. People deciding whether to forgive find themselves in a position analogous to doctors deciding what is best for the health of the patient: in this case, the relationship. In some cases, forgiveness is appropriate because it removes an obstacle to healing. In others, it is inappropriate because it allows harmful patterns of wrongdoing, disrespect, or servility to persist within the relationship. In yet other circumstances, it is impossible for the relationship to continue in good health—amputation is the only solution, and in such cases forgiveness can help with separation rather than continuation of the relationship. But in all cases, the right decision is right because of its conceptual connection to the wellbeing of the relationship and negative reactions' interference with this wellbeing. If friendships, loves, and other personal relationships are important components of a good life, as Aristotle contended, then nurturing good relationships and avoiding bad ones are both important activities for the virtuous individual to engage in. Forgiveness is a tool, not just for relationship repair, but also for relationship stewardship more broadly.

This approach offers a richer account of relationship stewardship, which accounts for both commonalities and differences between kinds of interpersonal forgiveness, and in addition provides an organizing principle that explains how they are related, and when either would be appropriate or inappropriate.

And what of inappropriate forgiveness, of the sort described in Section Two? It turns out that forgiveness can be inappropriate in two ways. In one case, it is inappropriate when anger, resentment, or punishment would actually make the relationship better, by having one insist upon being treated better. But another, subtler way that it can be inappropriate is when one kind is used where the other would be better: forgiving-as-repair where the relationship would be better off terminated (better a short, healthy one than a long drawn-out one that limps along) or the reverse (alienating oneself from a friend rather than supporting them as they change for the better). The details of when and where each is appropriate will be provided by an account of what constitutes an ideal of good relationship, plus facts about how we can approach the ideal in our non-ideal actual lives. Forgiveness, in the non-ideal world, is an important tool, but must be used appropriately.

Conclusion

I have argued here that a relationship-repair model of forgiveness should be replaced by a relationship-stewardship model. The relationship-repair model gets something right, as a normative feature of friendships in which friends must occasionally overcome negative reactions to wrongdoing without losing their valuable relationships. But to tie friends' forgiveness too closely to continuing relationships misses an important phenomenon: that of forgiving as part of ending a relationship, especially one that is not worth keeping around. Both are instances of using interpersonal forgiveness as a tool for relationship stewardship. In both, one forbears negative attitudes or reactions in the service of promoting good relationship, even when that involves recognizing when a relationship is unsustainable or has run its course. This provides a unifying account of both kinds of forgiveness while implying norms about when each is appropriate, and under what circumstances.

References

Aristotle. 1999. *Nicomachean Ethics.* Translated by Terence Irwin. Indianapolis: Hackett Publishing.

Atkins, Kim. 2002. "Friendship, Trust and Forgiveness." *Philosophia: Philosophical Quarterly of Israel* 29.1: 111-32.

Bell, Macalester. 2008. "Forgiving Someone For Who They Are (and Not Just What They've Done)." *Philosophy and Phenomenological Research* 77.3: 625-58.

Bortolotti, Lisa, and Magdalena Antrobus. 2015. "Costs and Benefits of Realism and Optimism." *Current Opinion in Psychiatry* 28.2: 194.

Bennett, Christopher. 2003. "Personal and Redemptive Forgiveness." *European Journal of Philosophy* 11.2: 127-44.

Calhoun, Cheshire. 1992. "Changing One's Heart." *Ethics* 103.1: 76-96.

Elder, Alexis. 2014. "Why Bad People Can't Be Good Friends." *Ratio* 27.1: 84-99.

Gogol Bordello. 2004. "Troubled Friends." *Live At Maxwell's 04/25/2004.* New York: Re: Live.

Hampton, Jean. 1993. "Selflessness and the Loss of Self." *Social Philosophy and Policy* 10.1: 135-65.

Hughes, Paul M. 2015. "Forgiveness," *The Stanford Encyclopedia of Philosophy*. Edited by Edward N. Zalta. Accessed July 22, 2016. http://plato.stanford.edu/archives/spr2015/entries/forgiveness/.

Kawall, Jason. 2013. "Friendship and Epistemic Norms." *Philosophical Studies* 165.2: 349-70.

Keller, Simon. 2004. "Friendship and Belief." *Philosophical Papers* 33.3: 329-51.

Murphy, Jeffrie G. 1982. "Forgiveness and Resentment." *Midwest Studies in Philosophy* 7.1: 503-16.

Murphy, Jeffrie G., and Jean Hampton. 1990. *Forgiveness and Mercy*. Cambridge: Cambridge University Press.

Norlock, Kathryn. 2008. *Forgiveness from a Feminist Perspective*. Lexington: Lexington Press.

Stroud, Sarah. 2006. "Epistemic Partiality in Friendship." *Ethics* 116.3: 498-524.

Zaibert, Leo. 2009. "The Paradox of Forgiveness." *Journal of Moral Philosophy* 6.3: 365-9

Chapter 2

Restorative Justice and Care Ethics: An Integrated Approach to Forgiveness and Reconciliation

William C. Gay

Introduction: Philosophy and forgiveness

In recent years, the topic of forgiveness has received renewed philosophical interest (Griswold 2007; Hughes 2014). Nevertheless, when the topics of forgiveness and justice are addressed together, they are often seen as in conflict. This conflict arises most starkly when justice is understood in terms of retribution, namely, many view justice as requiring the punishment of the wrongdoer. Given the philosophical roots of retributive justice in Immanuel Kant, the tendency to view it as an absolute value, and one that excludes forgiveness is understandable. In this view, punishment is the public means by which the wrongdoer is made to "pay" for a purported crime; the punishment is what the wrongdoer "deserves" and aims to restore the public sphere to the way it was prior to the wrongdoing. When retributive justice is regarded as an absolute value, forgiveness does not have a place in the public arena; if forgiveness occurs at all, it is generally viewed as "exceptional" and is relegated to the private sphere. Within the retributive tradition, about the only alternative to a Kantian deontological approach is a pragmatic or consequentialist approach, yet even this alternative has difficulty finding an ethical foundation for forgiveness.

This view of the supposed philosophical conflict between forgiveness and justice is laid out especially clearly by Andrew Fiala, in an article in which he tries to resolve this conflict by taking a pragmatic approach that draws heavily from care ethics (Fiala 2010). Although Fiala cites the alternative non-retributive model of restorative justice in a footnote, he develops his argument by accepting retributive justice as the primary philosophical approach which functions in the public sphere and forgiveness as largely a religious approach that sometimes operates in the private sphere. While I will follow Fiala in turning to care ethics to include forgiveness in a discussion of justice, I also want to note that the view that forgiveness only functions in the private religious forum is not shared by all philosophers. Ari Kohen, for example, stresses that restorative justice does not necessarily rely on a religious foundation (Kohen 2009). Hence, since the forgiveness sought in restorative justice need not be relegated to the private sphere where religious practices typically occur, an argument can be made for its inclusion in a public criminal justice forum. Moreover, Bishop Desmond Tutu demonstrated that the inclusion of forgiveness and reconciliation in the public sphere could arise even from a religious perspective.

Tutu is one of the best-known and widely cited authors on forgiveness and reconciliation, and his view largely arises from his spirituality. Nevertheless, unlike most religious approaches to forgiveness, his treatment does not remain in the private sphere. His work on the Truth and Reconciliation Commission in South Africa was decidedly public and aimed for confession, forgiveness, and reconciliation and eschewed retribution and punishment (Tutu 2016). Though many critics were dissatisfied that so many perpetrators of Apartheid and its decades of injustice, violence, and murder were either given amnesty or altogether avoided public accountability, many others stress how the Truth and Reconciliation Commission avoided a bloodbath of revenge against these perpetrators and showcased for the global community a restorative approach to justice that avoided, as Tutu put it, "The endless and unyielding cycle of pain and retribution" (Ibid.). In a book on forgiveness, Tutu and his daughter Mpho Tutu present their approach as one that operates between the hopeless alternative of "Nuremburg or National Amnesia" (Tutu and Tutu 2015). In other words, the spiritually inspired restorative justice of Tutu is public and avoids both the retributive aim of the Nuremburg trials and the perhaps equal injustice of silence and avoidance of facing the truth about the violence done to victims. Hence, although I am not going to treat religious approaches to restorative justice, Tutu's practice of restorative justice provides a powerful example of a historically significant and largely successful instance of a public, religious approach to forgiveness and reconciliation.

In this essay, I am going to begin with how restorative justice has been introduced into the public sphere fairly recently within Criminal Justice and Social work. As used in Criminal Justice and Social Work, restorative justice emphasizes efforts to repair the harm of criminal behavior and to seek cooperative resolutions that include victims, offenders, and the community. As an alternative to punishment, particularly incarceration, restorative justice has clear advantages for advocates of nonviolence. Also, numerous studies show restorative justice in many cases works more effectively than punishment.

I will next examine within Philosophy justifications for restorative justice, beginning with the groundbreaking work of Rob Gildert. While I will also cite some views of John Rawls and John Dewey, I will make more extensive use of care ethics as developed by Carol Gilligan, Nel Noddings, Sara Ruddick, and Virginia Held. I will use their work to show how care ethics can supplement these other approaches to restorative justice in a manner that better facilitates aims of forgiveness and reconciliation. In my conclusion, I will suggest that, together, restorative justice and care ethics offer a very promising philosophical approach to a model of justice that fosters forgiveness and reconciliation.

I. Emergence of restorative justice in criminal justice and social work

a. Braithwaite

The modern restorative justice movement only began in the mid-1970s. Currently, John Braithwaite is widely regarded as the leading theoretician of restorative justice and has published dozens of scholarly works in this field. His approach has broad appeal in part because of the way he highlights connections with concerns that are also central to other perspectives. He states:

> *The appeal of restorative justice to liberals is a less punitive justice system. The appeal to conservatives is its strong emphasis on victim empowerment, on empowering families (as in "family group conference"), on [m]eeting home responsibilities, and on fiscal savings as a result of the parsimonious use of punishment. (2002, p. 10)*

He also stresses many of the themes that are now commonly associated with restorative justice, such as a focus on victim, offender, and community. Further, he notes two broad conceptions of restorative justice, namely, as process and as values. He and Heather Strang observe:

> *The process conception has been the more dominant one to this point. On this view, restorative justice is a process that brings together all stakeholders affected by some harm that has been done (e.g., offenders, their families, victims and their families, affected communities, state agencies such as the police). These stakeholders...discuss how they*

> have been affected by the harm and come to some agreement as to what should be done to right any wrongs suffered.
>
> On the second view, it is values that distinguish restorative justice from traditional punitive state justice. Restorative justice is about healing (restoration) rather than hurting. Responding to the hurt of crime with the hurt of punishment is rejected...The idea is that the value of healing is the key because the crucial dynamic to foster is healing that begets healing. The dynamic to avoid is hurt that begets hurt. (Strang and Braithwaite, 2002, 1-2)

The values view is the one that leads me to propose how care ethics offers a particularly attractive philosophical justification for restorative justice.

Braithwaite's perspective also affirms what he terms an "enforcement pyramid" that includes "the clear signaling of willingness to escalate international intervention" and rejects the "paradox of pacifism" because it would "lop the top off the enforcement pyramid" so that we have to "negotiate from a position of weakness" and be vulnerable to a "world exposed to the predations of twenty-first-century Hitlers" (2002, 195-6). This reticence to embrace pacifism is hardly unique to Braithwaite; basically, as Duane Cady has pointed out most people incorrectly assume that pacifists are passive and that they oppose any use of violence, when, in fact, most pacifists are activists and minimally only have to morally oppose war and so can support a role for police—even one that can resort to small-scale use of violence, including, in some cases, lethal violence (Cady 2010).

Even within Criminal Justice, restorative justice has been extended beyond an alternative to incarceration to an alternative to probation as well. While over two million persons were incarcerated in the United States at the turn of this century, David Karp and Todd Clear note that far more people are under conditions of probation—well over four million and rising (2002, ix). Currently, "casework" is the approach to managing so many parolees, but the typical caseload is now over 100 parolees for each officer (Ibid., x). For these reasons, "community justice," the approach to probation under restorative justice, offers a much more attractive option.

b. Social Work

Restorative justice quickly and almost naturally moved from Criminal Justice to Social Work. Elizabeth Beck, Nancy P. Kropf, and Pamela Blume Leonard edited a key text, *Social Work and Restorative Justice: Skills for Dialogue, Peacemaking, and Reconciliation*, which is based on the view that, like restorative justice, social work seeks to reduce violence and address the harms caused by violence of various kinds (2011). In their volume, Leonard offers a useful comparison.

Two Different Views

Criminal Justice	*Restorative Justice*
Crime is a violation of the law and the state.	Crime is a violation of people and relationships.
Violations create guilt.	Violations create obligations.
Justice requires the state to determine blame (guilt) and imposes pain (punishment).	Justice involves victims, offenders, and community in an effort to put things right.

Central focus: Offenders get what they deserve.	**Central focus:** Victim needs and offender responsibility for repairing them.

Three Different Questions	
Criminal Justice	*Restorative Justice*
What laws have been broken?	Who has been hurt?
Who did it?	What are their needs?
What do they deserve?	Whose obligations are these?

(2011, p. 32)

While earlier uses of restorative justice have occurred in courts, some efforts are now being made even in prisons, as Barb Toews and M. Kay Harris have noted (Beck, Kropf, and Leonard 2011). They state:

While social work finds its roots in social institutions such as prisons...its practitioners increasingly have distanced themselves from corrections...This exodus from the field of corrections is understandable, given the correctional trend away from rehabilitation and toward punishment and social work's reported shift from work with marginalized indi-

> *viduals and communities to psychotherapeutic practice ...*
>
> *Yet, the retreat from corrections by social workers is short sighted. It does not simply represent a turning away from an institution, but an abandonment of a vulnerable group of people—incarcerated men and women—and the personal, interpersonal, and social needs that result from their crimes, as well those that contributed to them. (Ibid., 118)*

This concern for even incarcerated individuals as a vulnerable population and one with needs that should be addressed, and not merely a population to be punished or hurt, squares well with the relational concerns that are central to care ethics, and I shall return to this point later.

II. Groundbreaking philosophical work of Rob Gildert

The work of Rob Gildert is central to philosophical treatments of restorative justice. In his efforts at a justification for restorative justice, he considers typical principles from utilitarianism. Because of limitations in these utilitarian approaches, he eventually turned to the concept of overlapping values that was developed by John Rawls in order to find a more satisfactory justification (Rawls 1971). Nevertheless, even this approach has limitations of which he was aware but did not resolve. For theorists who wish to seek a resolution that is broadly within this tradition, a promising extension of Gildert's efforts at justification can be developed on the basis of the pragmatism of John Dewey, especially in relation to his approach to the long-standing dichotomy of facts and values. However, Dewey's remarks on topics like punishment and criminal justice were made in passing and require interpretation and extension in order to provide a contemporary and robust foundation for restorative justice.

For this reason, in the next section, I will suggest that care ethics offers an even better basis for the philosophical justification of restorative justice.

In his essay "Toward the Globalization of Restorative Justice" Gildert suggests that restorative justice works by "instilling a sense of fairness and reciprocity among its participants" (2008, 169). Echoing much of the literature, Gildert contends that this approach and related ones offer a "non-adversarial form of justice that seeks to restore a harmony" among victims, offenders, and other communities (Ibid., 171). Further, he stresses that studies show that recidivism rates are 10% to even over 30% lower than under incarceration. Gildert observes that the retributivism of Kant has led some advocates of restorative justice to seek other philosophical justifications. After addressing limitations of shifts to utilitarianism, Gildert contends that Rawlsian overlapping consensus on morality already exists in pluralistic societies such as Canada and the United States (Ibid., 179).

Gildert's critique of utilitarianism and shift to Rawls continues in his essay "Pedagogy and Punishment" where he offers even more detailed criticism of utilitarianism, especially its advocacy of punishment as a pedagogical tool (2011). While he continues to emphasize how restorative justice works better than punishment, he does not completely abandon the penal system. Instead, he stresses that he is "arguing for the *increased* implementation of a system of restorative justice" (Ibid., 95). He concludes, "Restorative justice not merely reduced offender recidivism rates, but it has also aided in the construction of healthier communities to a greater degree than punishment" (Ibid., 96).

Since these essays by Gildert on restorative justice are readily available, I will not provide further summary. Instead, I will make an effort to take a few steps beyond what he says in relation to bringing restorative justice to the attention of the philosophical community and seeking to offer some reflections of my own on a more solid philosophical foundation. As I read his argument, even if he wanted a deontological foundation for justification of restorative justice, he would not pursue it because of the unacceptability of Kant's deontological ethics in which his theory of punishment has retributivism as its essence, a position antithetical to restorative justice.

Perhaps, Gildert might have found more acceptable deontological approaches elsewhere, but I leave that prospect for others to explore. Instead, I wish to point out what might further augment his turn to utilitarianism. While I find merit in his use of Rawlsian overlapping values, it has two shortcomings. First, as Gildert recognizes, it is not universal, especially in a pluralist society. Second, the basis for this broad consent is not consistent. This area is one where keeping silent may be a way to lessen only temporarily the possibility that it could collapse into partisan bickering or even hostile and possibly violent conflict. Nevertheless, I should note that Gildert is not alone in turning to Rawls. In his essay "Restorative Justice: The Role of Community" Paul McCold states:

> *The theory of justice, "justice as fairness", proposed by John Rawls...would not only be consistent with restorative justice, it would seem to lead to similar conclusions regarding the priority of the victims' interest in the process. Rawls claims that justice must be judged from the perspective of the person most disadvantaged in the circumstances. I believe, in the situation of crime, that would be the victim. (1995, n 7)*

McCold, however, only makes this claim without supporting it. As far as I can see, he leaves unresolved the problems posed by the inconsistencies at the foundations of the positions within the overlapping consensus.

I also wish to note a potentially more satisfactory option in John Dewey's pragmatism (Dewey 1945 and 1948). Dewey does not make lofty claims of universalism; instead, he gives empirical and rational grounding for the values he proposes—and ones he wants to arise from, rather than being imposed on, the moral community (Gay 2009, 47-9). A few writers on restorative justice have turned to Dewey, such as Ulf Olsson and Kenneth Petterson in their essay "Dewey as an Epistemic Figure..." (Popkewitz 2005). If one applies his views, some of the work by Robert Holmes is also relevant for turning to Dewy for a philosophical justification of restorative justice, particularly his essay "John Dewey's Moral Philosophy in Contemporary Perspective" (2013, pp. 11-31). While I could develop the positions of these writers on restorative justice, I leave to others these explorations. Instead, I am simply going to the perspectives that I have found to be the most robust and promising, namely, ones in care ethics.

III. Relevance of care ethics to restorative justice and forgiveness

An even more satisfactory approach for the philosophical justification of restorative justice and forgiveness can be found in the more recent moral theory of care ethics. First, care ethics provides an alternative to a deontological ethics. By giving primacy to the quest for justice, deontological ethics excludes pursuing forgiveness in the public sphere. By contrast, care ethics can include and affirm forgiveness in both the private and public spheres. Second, care ethics strengthens efforts to use a pragmatic or consequentialist ethics to provide a philosophical basis for forgiveness that does not have to rely on a religious practice within the private sphere. While some ethicists, like Andrew Fiala, have pointed to how care ethics can facilitate restorative justice and forgiveness, this prospect needs more development than the brief consideration that Fiala has given (Fiala 2010). So, since deontological ethics excludes and consequentialist ethics has given insufficient treatment to forgiveness, care ethics provides a robust alternative.

In this section, I will show how restorative justice and forgiveness can be advanced by using care ethics as developed by Carol Gilligan, Nel Noddings, Sara Ruddick, and Virginia Held. Through its stress on particularity and connection, care ethics avoids the problems that arise from seeking a universalized or generalized foundation. By beginning with the way in which persons are entangled in a web of dynamic relationships which they may wish to maintain or repair, care ethics replaces the punitive orientations of retribution found in corporal punishment, capital punishment, and international war. With its stress on the role of love, care ethics complements strategies of nonviolence during conflict and practices of forgiveness and reconciliation following conflict.

a. Gilligan

Care ethics can be traced back to Carol Gilligan's seminal work *In a Different Voice: Psychological Theory and Women's Development* (1982). During her doctoral studies in social psychology at Harvard, Gilligan was an assistant for Laurence Kohlberg who drew heavily from Kant. Gilligan came to realize that, like Kant, Kohlberg made moral recommendations that abstracted from personal differences and stressed retributive justice. Her book, *In A Different Voice,* challenged many of the Kantian assumptions in the dominant moral theories in the West. To distinguish a different moral voice from the capacities Kohlberg was measuring, Gilligan identified two categories: justice and care. "Justice Ethics" represents the abstract and retributive approach traditionally favored in philosophy. Alternatively, "Care Ethics" is a relational approach to morality that avoids generalization in favor of particularity and connection. So the major differences between Kohlberg and Gilligan center on concepts of connection, particularity, and emotion. Gilligan stresses connections among people and the relationships they established. Gilligan views the individual as entangled in a web of dynamic relationships, not all of which are freely chosen. Gilligan believes moral action requires knowledge of particular others and their circumstances, not a universalized case. Whereas Kant avoids the emotive and has no place for forgiveness, Gilligan's approach embraces feelings as a moral capacity that facilitates an ethical response that fosters forgiveness and reconciliation.

I give what I take to be one of Gilligan's key points:

For boys and men, separation and individuation are critically tied to gender identity since separation from the mother is essential for the development of masculinity. For girls and women, issues of femininity or feminine identity do not depend on the achievement of separation from the mother or on the progress of individuation. Since masculinity is defined through separation while femininity is defined through attachment, male gender identity is threatened by intimacy while female gender identity is threatened by separation. Thus males tend to have difficulty with relationships, while females tend to have problems with individuation. The quality of embeddedness in social interaction and personal relationships that characterizes women's lives in contrast to men's, however, becomes not only a descriptive difference but also a developmental liability when the milestones of childhood and adolescent development in the psychological literature are markers of increasing separation. Women's failure to separate then becomes by definition a failure to develop. (Ibid., 8-9)

She also notes, "While an ethic of justice proceeds from the premise of equality—that everyone should be treated the same—an ethic of care rests on the premise of nonviolence—that no one should be hurt" (Ibid., 174). Her association of care ethics with nonviolence and her emphasis on seeking to avoid hurt provide a clear link to a key feature of restorative justice.

b. Noddings, Ruddick, and Held

While Gilligan's work arose within and relies on the field of psychology, her perspective has been appropriated in many fields. I will examine how its use within feminism and philosophy impacted discussion of ethics and morality. One significant impact pertains to how care ethics provides a basis for consideration of forgiveness and restorative justice.

Within philosophy, Nel Noddings, in *Caring: A Feminine Approach To Ethics and Moral Education*, was one of the first and attracted a lot of early attention (1984). Although Gilligan's main task had been to separate Justice perspectives from Care perspectives, Nel Noddings tried to go further and interconnect these two notions by arguing for the idea that duty emerges out of care. Despite their differences, both these theorists helped crystallize the frustration of women with traditional ethics. In *Caring*, Noddings, like Gilligan, argues that women prefer to begin the analysis of a moral dilemma not from abstract principles but from concretized circumstances (Noddings 1984, 8). To Noddings, certain intimate situations of caring, such as the one between a mother and her child, are natural. So, caring and the moral imperative are related in the mother-child relationship. When an infant cries in the night, the mother wants to respond and remove the infant's pain (Noddings 1984, 82). For Kant the "I must" springs solely out of duty, whereas for Noddings it accompanies the "I want." This example implies that our inclination toward an interest in morality derives from caring, as does our capacity for forgiveness.

However, other feminists found her position to be too stark. A decade later, Sara Ruddick makes a fresh argument in *Maternal Thinking: Toward a Politics of Peace* (1995). She says:

> *Gilligan explicitly contrasts care with justice; where she speaks of justice, I prefer egalitarian fairness—an important but subsidiary virtue in domestic life and a sometimes dangerous, though not unworthy, public ideal. The question for different-voice theory, as I see it, is how to conceptualize, recognize, and focus on demands of 'justice' from the perspective of care. Gilligan's conception of justice, like Kohlberg's, is indebted to the work of John Rawls. Gilligan herself, however, speaks of justice as it is construed from the perspective of care. 'Justice in this [the care] context becomes understood as respect for people in their own terms.' (Ibid., 273-274)*

The quote at the end of this passage is from Gilligan, and Ruddick uses it to highlight how Gilligan's care ethics moves beyond Kant and Kohlberg.

Nevertheless, before I complete this survey of the use of care ethics in feminist philosophy, I need to note that Ruddick, in ways like Braithwaite, does not understand that pacifism can have non-lethal force and even lethal force forms and still stop short of embracing war or other large-scale military action. She states:

> *But—and here is the primary difference with pacifists—a...suspicion of violence does not betoken absolute renunciation. Although pacifists perform an essential service among*

> *peace activists by requiring every act of violence to be critically appraised, it is unnecessary and divisive to require of all peacemakers an absolute commitment not to kill.*
> *(Ibid., p. 138)*

I would respond to her as I would to Braithwaite by noting the very nuanced treatment of pacifism offered by Duane Cady (2014). Only absolute pacifism and nonlethal force pacifism reject categorically all intentional killing.

Before ending this discussion of philosophical treatments of care ethics, I want to jump next ahead one further decade and consider Virginia Held's *The Ethics of Care: Personal, Political, and Global* (2006). Held rejects the conclusion by Noddings that "care should replace justice as the central concept of morality" (Ibid., p. 63). She states:

> *care and justice are often seen as alternative values. "Care" and "justice" were taken to name different approaches to moral problems and characteristically different recommendations concerning them. Care valued relationships between persons and empathetic understanding; justice valued rational action in accord with abstract principles. Carol Gilligan saw these as alternative interpretations that could be applied to given moral problems, yielding different ways of construing what the moral problem was and how it should be handled...Gilligan saw both approaches as valid, but because interpretation from the perspective of care has been grossly neglected in the construction and study of dominant moral theories, it should now be*

> *seen as valid, and the deficiency corrected. Gilligan argued that if one sees a moral problem as an issue to be dealt with in terms of care, one cannot at the same time see i[t] as an issue to be dealt with in terms of justice because the two perspectives organize the problem differently. (Ibid., 62)*

As Held goes on to note "How to integrate the values of both justice and care have remained central concerns of feminist moral inquiry" (Ibid., 66). She adds, "I now think that caring relations should form the wider moral framework into which justice should be fitted" (Ibid., 71).

To be more specific in relation to Kantian, utilitarian, and virtue ethics approaches, Held makes the following observations:

> *The ethics of care differs with these theories in its assumptions, goals, and methods. It is closer to virtue ethics, which has enjoyed a recent revival, and it is sometimes thought to be a kind of virtue ethics. But the ethics of care is sufficiently different from virtue ethics as well as other theories to be counted, as I have argued, as a new and distinct kind of moral theory. (Ibid., 156)*

Her reason is as follows:

> *Among the characteristics of the ethics of care is its view of persons as relational and as interdependent. Kantian and utilitarian moral theories focus primarily on the rational decisions of agents taken as independent and au-*

> *tonomous individuals. Even virtue theory focuses on individuals and their dispositions. In contrast, the ethics of care sees persons as enmeshed in relations with others…the ethics of care is developed from the realities as well of unequal power and unchosen relations… (Ibid., 156)*

Her points about being enmeshed in relations that are not chosen but which also are unequal square well with restorative justice and give philosophical foundations for efforts at restoration.

Of course, while care ethics can lapse into gender essentialism (a dichotomy in which men pursue justice and women pursue care), it can go beyond such a reductive view. For example, Maurice Hamington in *Embodied Care* argues that feelings such as compassion, empathy, and care need not remain solely in the female realm (Hamington 2004, 16). He specifically contends that gender should not be a barrier to an empathetic response; otherwise, care becomes a concern for women alone. By stating how males and females are more similar biologically than many moralists seem to realize, Hamington aims to erase the gap between the genders and argue for an ethics of care that applies to all human beings. By making explicit this broad applicability, Hamington presents care ethics in a way that makes it quite suitable for addressing forgiveness and restorative justice in the public sphere.

c. Use of care ethics in criminal justice

Before concluding my reflections on care ethics, I need to make note of its use in Criminal Justice. Within the social sciences, particularly in Criminal Justice and Legal Theory, a few theorists who were dealing with restorative justice made use of care ethics in the late 1980s (Heidensohn 1986; Harris 1987). In her early essay on the use of care ethics in Criminal

Justice, Kathleen Daly reviewed this turn by some feminists (1989). Then, over a decade later, Daly returned to this theme in a critical essay on restorative justice, entitled "Restorative Justice: The Real Story" (2003). Given the importance of this essay, I will note some of the cautions it raises about the use of sharp binary oppositions between retributivist and restorative approaches.

In this 2003 essay, Daly analyses and challenges four myths (or, as she sees them, exaggerations):

(1) Restorative justice is the opposite of retributive justice.

(2) Restorative justice uses indigenous justice practices and was the dominant form of pre-modern justice.

(3) Restorative justice is a 'care' (or feminine) response to crime in comparison to a 'justice' (or masculine) response.

(4) Restorative justice can be expected to produce major changes in people. (Ibid., 195)

In presenting these contrasts as too stark, Daly uses the term "myth" to designate the way in which advocates of restorative justice weave a series of stories that present what philosophers would call a "false dichotomy." As noted above, the third of these myths concerns care ethics. She shows how theorists such as Heidensohn and Harris used Gillian's distinction to contrast the perspectives of "male dominance" and the "different voice" of women. In their work on responses to crime, (male) "justice" is depersonalized, universal, and abstract, while (feminine) "care" is personalized, particular, and concrete (Ibid., 202). Daly presents their contrasts as follows:

Restorative justice	*Retributive justice*
Pre-modern	*Modern*
Indigenous (informal)	*State (formal)*
Feminine (care)	*Masculine (justice)*
Eastern (Japan)	*Western (US)*
Superior justice	*Inferior justice*

Figure 1 Terms linked to restorative and retributive justice. (Ibid.)

Continuing her argument from 1989, Daly challenges the empirical accuracy of these contrasts. She contends that a call, based on care ethics, for women's voices as an alternative to "men's forms of criminal law and justice" is misleading in relation to the actual practices of criminal laws and criminal justice (Ibid., 202-203). She states, "In order to sell the idea of restorative justice to a wide audience, advocates have painted a dichotomous, oppositional picture of different justice forms, with restorative justice trumping retributive justice as the superior one" (Ibid., 208). Nevertheless, she concedes that for purpose of "selling justice ideas" this approach may be "telling mythical true stories" that are persuasive by avoiding the "murk and constraints" of the actual organization of justice (Ibid., 209).

I have sympathy for Daly's effort to expose the way advocates of restorative justice and care ethics may too easily fall into "arguing from the extremes." Such arguments, as philosophers term them, often commit the "straw person fallacy." So, I wish to concede to her the recommendation for proper qualification of claims.

In addition, I agree with some of the important critical concerns that other scholars in Criminal Justice have raised regarding all uses of the techniques of restorative justice. In this regard, Bruce Arrigo cautions that when restorative justice fails to address questions regarding the conditions, terms, and values operative in its conversations or mediations, it may unwittingly serve maintenance of the status quo (2004). In so doing, restorative justice might serve to endorse or embrace the system of order that is an integral component of the existing and related social conflicts. In more general terms, he is noting the need for theorists and practitioners of restorative justice to pay careful attention to the terminology used in order to avoid reducing actual differences to a presumed sameness or consensus that cloaks actual and persisting differences. Elsewhere, I have raised related concerns about the language used in discussions of issues of war and peace (Gay 2007). Language, even language used to resolve or reduce conflict, can function like a negative peace that fails to challenge and transform the underlying social and political conditions and, thus, may fall short of a practice of restorative justice that promotes positive peace.

Nevertheless, while mindful of these words of caution, I want to end this set of reflections by noting the expanded use of restorative justice over the last few decades from the resolution of interpersonal conflicts to even what appear to be the seemingly insurmountable challenges posed by the large-scale violence precipitated by atrocities, wars, and genocides. The use of restorative justice is now broadly international across multiple fields with applications from the interpersonal to the transnational (Galaway and Hudson 1996). Within primary and secondary education, restorative justice has been used to respond to the current verbal and physical abuse of LGBTQ youth, especially in U.S. schools (Wong 2010). At the level of higher education, restorative justice has been used as a means to promote student responsibility and campus community (Karp and Allena 2004). Some have even applied restorative justice to athletics (Janzen 2010). Whether this approach can be taken all the way professional sports, such as the currently beleaguered National Football League, remains to be seen. Perhaps such a prospect is not altogether unrealistic since restorative justice has been used in International Law for plea-bargaining in response to genocide and crimes against humanity (Combs 2007). Restorative justice has even been used in relation to armed conflict (Reddy 2012).

IV. Avoiding pitfalls in the pursuit of forgiveness

As I have tried to show in the previous section, reliance on care ethics can avoid some of the potential pitfalls in other approaches to forgiveness. Within the deontological approach, a call for forgiveness can mean almost nothing, since it is excluded from the public sphere. Within the pragmatic or consequentialist approach, efforts to reach a resolution of conflict—that can include premature claims that satisfactory forgiveness has been achieved—can mean almost everything. These positions at their extremes are a caricature of the end or goal of justice and the means or practice of forgiveness. Philosophers should be suspicious of the false dilemma of "nothing" or "everything" with respect to forgiveness. Most people do recognize both the obligation to pursue rights and duties in relation to justice and the reality of the need for concessions and forgiveness in relation to conflict resolution. By affirming both of these concerns, care ethics avoids the pitfalls of traditional ethical approaches.

Once we recognize that the concerns for justice and forgiveness lie along a continuum, we also may come to regard the differences between the two traditional approaches more as ones of degree than of kind. Nevertheless, given the difficulty of advocating and defending such a continuum within either of the traditional approaches, the value of care ethics as an alternative is clear. Care ethics can better facilitate a type of discourse and practice that respects both the aims of justice and the importance of maintaining or restoring community relations. Care ethics affirms the need to listen, dialogue, and compromise.

Family relations and community relations are not always neat or even fair; so, forgiveness does not eradicate injustice. Nevertheless, maintaining or improving relations is of equal, if not higher, importance; so, justice does not rule out forgiveness. Unless both of these concerns are given due consideration, forgiveness and punishment can both lapse into positions that are too narrow. We should not elevate victims to the status of special moral authorities. Likewise, we should not reduce offenders to a subhuman status. In fact, the distinction between victims and offenders is not so clear-cut, since each of us can be a victim in some circumstances and an offender in other circumstances. Perhaps, a more appropriate stance is the one forged by Albert Camus in *Neither*

Victims Nor Executioners (Camus 1986). In being neither victims nor executioners, we need not remain voiceless, powerless victims and we need not remain unforgiving, ruthless executioners. Care ethics allows us to be more holistic human beings who find a place for both the pursuit of justice and the practice of forgiveness and for doing so in the public sphere.

Conclusion: An integrated approach to forgiveness in the public sphere

In this essay I have presented restorative justice as an alternative to retributive justice and one that better facilitates forgiveness and reconciliation. To provide background on restorative ethics, I traced its emergence in Criminal Justice and in Social Work. Then, I examined more theoretical justifications. Philosophically, I took as my point of departure the groundbreaking work done in philosophy by Rob Gildert. I noted how his dissatisfaction with the deontological approach of Kantianism led him to utilitarianism; then, given problems in its classical expressions, he ended by embracing the concept of overlapping values in John Rawls—despite Gildert's own awareness of problems with it as well. I suggested that those who seek philosophical foundations in these more traditional approaches to ethics might find more satisfactory the work of John Dewey, especially given his own turn to pacifism following World War I (Gay 2009, 35).

Next, I offered a more extended consideration of care ethics in Carol Gilligan, Nel Noddings, Sara Ruddick, and Virginia Held as an alternative to deontological and consequentialist approaches. Care ethics stresses relations as the primary focus for ethics and provides a solid philosophical foundation for restorative justice as an alternative to retributive justice and as a basis for considerations of forgiveness in the public sphere. Still, following Kathleen Daly, I stressed the need for caution against exaggerations when appropriating care ethics as a philosophical foundation for restorative justice and forgiveness. I would extend this caution to the view that restorative justice can altogether dissolve the conflict with retributive justice. Issues of both punishment and forgiveness are involved. First, some forms of punishment may be required in order to make wrongdoers "pay" for their crimes and to give them what they deserve. Second, efforts at forgiveness and reconciliation likely will at best be only partial. Nevertheless, efforts to achieve justice likely need some form of apology, and restorative justice makes an explicit connection between apologies and forgiveness. Marilyn Peterson and Mark Umbreit begin with the fact that crime victims want an apology, and they cite evidence that apologies influence whether victims can reach forgiveness (2005). However, even if such apologies are necessary, they are not sufficient. Even if forgiveness can be pursued in a public forum, both a request by offenders for forgiveness and a granting of forgiveness by victims may not be sincere or may not be adequate. The limited positive outcomes of the Truth and Reconciliation Commission in South Africa make this point. Nevertheless, the Truth and Reconciliation Commission also provides evidence that attaining even limited forgiveness in the public sphere can make a significant contribution. Forgiveness attained in the public sphere can help thwart lapses into vigilantism and revenge and can help move a society and victims within it toward stability and at least satisfactory resolution of victim needs. Forgiveness in the public sphere is possible, and restorative justice and care ethics can help forge the forgiveness needed for a society to continue legally and peacefully toward justice.

References

Arrigo, Bruce. 2004. "Rethinking Restorative and Community Justice: A Postmodern Inquiry." *Contemporary Justice Review* 7.1: 91–100.

Beck, Elizabeth, Nancy P. Kropf, and Pamela Blume Leonard. 2011. *Social Work and Restorative Justice: Skills for Dialogue, Peacemaking, and Reconciliation*. Oxford: Oxford University Press.

Braithwaite, John. 2002. *Restorative Justice and Responsive Regulation*. Oxford: Oxford University Press.

Cady, Duane. 2010. *From Warism to Pacifism: A Moral Continuum*, 2nd ed. Philadelphia: Temple University Press.

Camus, Albert. 1986. *Neither Victims Nor Executioners*. Translated by Dwight MacDonald. Gabriola Istand, BC, Canada: New Society Publishers.

Combs, Nancy Amoury. 2007. *Guilty Pleas in International Criminal Law: Constructing a Restorative Approach*. Sanford, CA: Sanford University Press.

⎯⎯⎯⎯. 1989. "Criminal Justice Ideologies and Practices in Different Voices: Some Feminist Questions About Justice." *International Journal of the Sociology of Law* 17.1: 1-18.

Daly, Kathleen. 2003. "Restorative Justice: The Real Story." *Restorative Justice*. Edited by Eugene McLaughlin, Ross Fergusson, Gordon Hughes, and Louise Westmarland. Milton Keynes, UK: Open University Press.

Dewey, John. 1945. "Dualism and the Split Atom: Science and Morals in the Atomic Age." *The New Leader* 28: 1 and 4; Reprinted in *Concerned Philosophers For Peace Newsletter* 7, n1 (April 1987): 5-7. This text is now included in: John Dewey. 1989. *The Later Works, 1925-1953, Volume 15: 1942-1948*. Edited by Jo Ann Boydston. Carbondale: Southern Illinois University Press.

⎯⎯⎯⎯. 1948. *Reconstruction in Philosophy*, Enlarged Edition. Boston: Beacon Press.

Fiala, Andrew. 2010. "Forgiveness, Justice, and Care: A Pragmatic Balance." *Ethical Perspectives* 17.4: 580-602.

Galaway, Burt and Joe Hudson. 1996. *Restorative Justice: International Perspectives*. Monsey, NY: Criminal Justice Press. [Amsterdam: Kugler Publications, non-US distribution.]

Gay, William C. 2007. "Language, War, and Peace." *Handbook of Language and Communication: Diversity and Change*. Edited by Marlis Hellinger and Anne Pauwels. Berlin: Bouton de Gruyter.

⎯⎯⎯⎯. 2009. "Nuclear Weapons and Philosophy in the 21st Century: The Relevance of Initial Philosophical Responses to the Atomic Bomb." *After Hiroshima*. Edited by Edward Demenochonok. Newcastle upon Tyne, UK: Cambridge Scholars Publishing.

Gildert, Rob. 2008. "Toward the Globalization of Restorative Justice." *Parceling the Globe: Explorations in Globalization, Global Behavior, and Peace.* Edited by Danielle Poe and Eddy Souffrant. Amsterdam: Rodopi.

———. 2011. "Pedagogy and Punishment: A Utilitarian Argument for Restorative Justice." *Remembrance and Reconciliation.* Edited by Rob Gildert and Dennis Rothermel. Amsterdam: Rodopi.

Gildert, Rob and Dennis Rothermel. 2011. *Remembrance and Reconciliation.* Amsterdam: Rodopi.

Gilligan, Carol. 1982. *In a Different Voice: Psychological Theory and Women's Development.* Cambridge, MA and London: Harvard University Press.

Griswold, Charles L. 2007. *Forgiveness: A Philosophical Exploration.* Cambridge: Cambridge University Press.

Hamington, Michael. 2004. *Embodied Care.* Chicago: University of Illinois Press.

Harris, M. Kay. 1987. "Moving into the New Millennium: Toward a Feminist Vision of Justice." *The Prison Journal* 67.2: 27-38.

Heidensohn, B. 1986. "Models of Justice: Portia or Persephone? Some Thoughts on Equality, Fairness and Gender in the Field of Criminal Justice." *International Journal of Sociology of Law* 14.3-4: 287-98.

Held, Virginia. 2006. *The Ethics of Care: Personal, Political, and Global.* Oxford: Oxford University Press.

Holmes, Robert L. 2013. "John Dewey's Moral Philosophy in Contemporary Perspective." *The Ethics of Nonviolence.* New York: Bloomsbury.

———. 2013. *The Ethics of Nonviolence: Essays by Robert L. Holmes.* Edited by Predrag Cicovacki. New York: Bloomsbury.

Hughes, Paul M. 2014. "Forgiveness." *Stanford Encyclopedia of Philosophy.* Accessed February 2, 2016. http://plato.stanford.edu/entries/forgiveness/.

Janzen, Dennis. 2010. "Restorative Discipline in Athletics." *The Promise of Restorative Justice.* Edited by John Dussich and Jill Schellenberg. Boulder and London: Lynne Rienner Publishers.

Karp, David R. and Thom Allena. 2004. *Restorative Justice on the College Campus: Promoting Student Growth and Responsibility, and Reawakening the Spirit of Campus Community.* Springfield, IL: Charles C. Thomas, Publisher.

Karp, David R. and Todd R. Clear. 2002. *What is Community Justice? Case Studies of Restorative Justice and Community Supervision.* Thousand Oaks, CA/London/New Delhi: Sage Publications.

Kohen, Ari. 2009. "The Personal and the Political: Forgiveness and Reconciliation in Restorative Justice." *Critical Review of International Social and Political Philosophy* 12.3: 399-423.

Leonard, Pamela Blume. 2011. "An Introduction to Restorative Justice." *Social Work and Restorative Justice*. Edited by Elizabeth Beck, Nancy P. Kropf, and Pamela Blume Leonard. Oxford: Oxford University Press.

McCold, Paul. 1995. "Restorative Justice: The Role of the Community." International Institute for Restorative Practices, a Graduate School (Bethlehem, PA). Accessed February 11, 2016. http://www.iirp.edu/article_detail.php?article_id=NTA1.

Noddings, Nel. 1984. *Caring: A Feminine Approach To Ethics and Moral Education*. Berkeley, Los Angeles, London: University of California Press.

Olsson, Ulf and Kenneth Petersson. 2005. "Dewey as an Epistemic Figure in the Swedish Discourse on Governing the Self." *Inventing the Modern Self and John Dewey*. Edited by Thomas Popkewitz. New York, NY: Palgrave Macmillan.

Peterson, Marilyn and Mark S. Umbreit. 2005. "The Paradox of Forgiveness in Restorative Justice." *Handbook of Forgiveness*. Edited by Everett L. Worthington, Jr. New York: Routledge.

Popkewitz, Thomas S. 2005. *Inventing the Modern Self and John Dewey: Modernities and the Traveling of Pragmatism in Education*. New York, NY: Palgrave Macmillan.

Rawls, John. 1971. *A Theory of Justice*. Cambridge, MA: Belknap Press of Harvard University Press.

Reddy, Peter. 2012. *Peace Operations and Restorative Justice: Groundwork for Post-conflict Regeneration*. Farnham, Surrey, England/Burlington, VT, USA: Ashgate Publishing.

Ruddick, Sara. 1995. *Maternal Thinking: Toward a Politics of Peace*. Boston: Beacon Press.

Strang, Heather and John Braithwaite. 2002. *Restorative Justice and Civil Society*. Cambridge: Cambridge University Press.

Toews, Barb and M. Kay Harris. 2011. "Restorative Justice in Prisons." *Social Work and Restorative Justice*. Edited by Elizabeth Beck, Nancy P. Kropf, and Pamela Blume Leonard. Oxford: Oxford University Press.

Tutu, Desmond. 2016. "Truth and Reconciliation Commission, South Africa (TRC)." *Encyclopædia Britannica*. Accessed February 9, 2016. http://www.britannica.com/topic/Truth-and-Reconciliation-Commission-South-Africa.

Tutu, Desmond and Mpho Tutu. 2015. *The Book of Forgiving: The Fourfold Path for Healing Ourselves and Our World*. Edited by Douglas C. Abrams. New York: HarperCollins.

Wong, Dennis. 2010. "Adolescent Bullying: The Whole-School Approach." *The Promise of Restorative Justice.* Edited by John Dussich and Jill Schellenberg. Boulder and London: Lynne Rienner Publishers.

Chapter 3

Injustice as Injury, Forgiveness as Healing

Raja Bahlul

Introduction

My aim is to argue that forgiveness may be conceived by analogy to healing. The analogy is not self-evident. Nor will it be of much value unless an appropriate understanding of what healing amounts to is provided. For these reasons, we shall have to discuss a number of apparently unrelated concepts. The discussion, it is hoped, will reveal how forgiveness can be compared to healing in a significant and enlightening manner.

In Section Two I develop analogies between injustice[2] and injury, on the one hand, and pain and resentment on the other, along three distinct, but related dimensions. The first is a *causal dimension* where injury and injustice are viewed as *causes* that normally produce certain effects. The second dimension focuses on the *effects* which injury and injustice typically produce: *pain* in the case of injury, *resentment* (and other negative feelings) in the case of injustice. The third dimension has to do with *function* (role) played by the outcomes of injustice and injury (namely, resentment and pain) in individual and social lives, and the significance of failures in this regard.

---

[2] I use 'injustice' in a broad sense to mean being 'unjustly treated' or simply 'being wronged', with no specification of the kind of wrong undergone. More on this in Section Two.

In Section Three I present a proposal to view forgiveness of injustice by analogy to the healing of injuries. I present three reasons for thinking that forgiveness may be profitably compared to healing. The reasons I offer are grounded in, but also serve to extend the analogies between injury and injustice on the one hand, and pain and resentment on the other. Finally, in Section Four, I discuss some possible objections to the present proposal, and respond to them.

The present proposal presupposes that overcoming resentment is essential to forgiveness. However, I do not claim that forgiveness *reduces* to overcoming resentment. I shall discuss these matters in Section One, without pretending to offer conclusive arguments. Because my main contribution lies elsewhere, I shall take it more or less for granted that forgiveness is incompatible with harboring resentment, hatred, anger or indignation, and other negative feelings towards the wrongdoer.

I. Forgiveness and Emotion

Reflection on the many discussions of forgiveness reveals two major junctures at which emotion becomes relevant to forgiveness. The first has to do with the *necessary conditions* for acquiring a standing to forgive or to be forgiven. This can be seen by considering the conditions which need to obtain in order that forgiveness may be *contemplated* or *asked for*. (1) It is typically the case that a culpable act of wrongdoing, an injustice, has been committed. The victim is led to make moral judgments such as "You have wronged me," "I have endured evil on your hands," or "You have betrayed me." (2) The wronged party (a) *resents*, is *indignant, angry,* or has other (typically enduring) negative *feelings* in connection with the injustice. In addition to (a), perhaps as a consequence, it may be assumed that (b) the wronged party may (be motivated to) seek retribution of some kind or other against the wrongdoer.[3]

It is fairly obvious that conditions (1) and (2) do not purport to say *what it is* that one does when one forgives. But it is not hard to appreciate the extent of emotionality which they bring with them. Condition (1) involves making moral (value) judgments such as "I have been treated unjustly," or "I have been wronged." According to some writers, such judgments stand in a causal relation to what we subsequently feel. "When these judgments [of having been wronged] are warranted, our first response is… anger and resentment" (Hieronymi 2001, 530). Other writers make stronger claims about the relation between value judgments and emotions. According to traditional Emotivism, which continues to thrive and prosper in a variety of guises collectively known as "Expressivism," "moral judgments function to express desires, emotions, or pro/con attitudes" (Joyce 2002, 336-7).[4] This is by no means a universally held view, for many philosophers continue to insist that moral judgments do manage to *describe* something or other, be it Moral Reality, social norms, or the workings of the human mind. Nevertheless, as one writer says, "virtually no one in the debate over moral semantics thinks that moral content just *is* descriptive con-

---

[3] It must be kept in mind that only typical cases are being considered. Cases where one is wronged but does not judge that one has been wronged, or where one feels nothing but pleasure at the thought of what has been done, are not clearly cases where the wronged person can contemplate forgiveness.

[4] According to Jeff Wisdom, "moral judgments express propositional attitudes that do not represent or describe the external world" (2009, 285). Cf. Simon Blackburn: "an ethic is the propositional reflection of the dispositions and attitudes, policies and stances, of people" (1984, 310). A particularly good discussion of these matters can be found in Goldie (2009, 94-109).

tent" (Wisdom 2009, 295).[5] The idea of an emotional dimension in moral judgments cannot be lightly dismissed.

Sub-condition (a) is obviously emotional, because it is about how people typically feel when they perceive themselves as having been wronged, or unjustly treated. Condition (b) may not seem to involve reference to emotions. But the appearance is deceptive. For emotions *motivate* actions. One who is in a state of fear is inclined to flee; one who is in a state of anger is inclined to strike; one who is indignant or resentful is inclined to punish, retaliate, or take revenge. The action-motivating role of emotion is rightly emphasized in many contemporary discussions. It has led some to propose an account of emotion in terms of "action readiness."[6]

Emotion is thus relevant to forgiveness on account of the *conditions* which must obtain in order for one to be in a position to forgive or to be forgiven. But there is another major point where emotion enters into the discussion of forgiveness. On many accounts of *what it is for one to forgive*, emotion is constitutively involved in the very nature of forgiveness. The view is widely held. According to Murphy, "forgiveness is a matter of how I *feel* about you (not how I treat you)" (Murphy and Hampton 1988, 21). Of all the current

---

[5] See Bernard Williams (1973, 207-229). Williams argues that description, value, and feeling are irrevocably entangled in "thick" moral concepts.

[6] For an explanation of emotion in terms of action readiness see Julien Deonna and Fabrice Teroni (2012, 79-80). Action is not foreign to emotion. But this is not behaviorism. It is merely to say that the relation between actions and inner states such as anger, resentment or fear, etc., is not an external, contingent relation. Inner states are expressed through behaviour, which can on occasion constitute conclusive evidence of their reality. Inner states that cannot be manifested in behaviour have as much reality as physical objects which in principle cannot be observed. For a discussion of the relation between inner states and outer actions, see John MacDowell (2009, 75-90).

definitions of forgiveness, says one writer, "...the one that enjoys anything close to a kind of consensus is that forgiveness is the overcoming of resentment" (Newberry 2001, 233). According to another:

> *Most contributors to the discussion agree... that forgiveness entails the forgoing of resentment. In fact, all too often philosophers see forgiveness primarily as a matter of manipulating oneself out of this unpleasant and potentially destructive emotion. (Hieronymi 2001, 529-30)*

In opposition to this widely held idea about what forgiveness entails, some have suggested that forgiveness should be defined in terms of how one should be able to act, rather than in terms of how one should feel. This is substantially the position which Paul Newberry attributes to Bishop Butler, a position that is nicely summed in the words of Mrs. Dale, of Anthony Trollope's *The Last Chronicle of Barset*: "I forgive him as far as humanity can forgive. I would do him no injury" (Quoted in Newberry 2001, 233). Leo Zaibert has also suggested a view according to which A forgives B when "she deliberately refuses to try to offset B's wrongdoing" (2009, 387). This makes it possible for one to forgive but to continue to resent.

Zaibert acknowledges that "it sounds odd to say things to the tenor of 'I forgive you', but I still resent you and blame you for what you have done" (Ibid., 392). But it is actually more than just odd. Continued resentment and ill-feeling cannot be so neatly separated and boxed off from action. They can, and will, motivate actions ranging from merely giving cold shoulder to the wrongdoer, or speaking to him in a certain tone of voice, to outright punishment or retaliation. The rule is for feelings to be expressed in behaviour, not to remain hidden in one's bosom.

But even if we were to reject a close connection between feeling and acting, the oddness of the combination of forgiving and resenting still remains considerable. Try replacing the above statement, with its thin, sanitized 'resent' and 'blame', by a statement which says "I forgive you, but I still hate you on a daily basis for the despicable deed which you have done. I forgive you, but, still, the mere thought of you makes me sick." Most of us intuitively feel that such an attitude is incompatible with forgiveness. It strains credulity to think that one can truly forgive, but at the same time continue to seethe with resentment, hate, and anger. If having too *much* of these feelings is incompatible with forgiveness, then what forgiveness *ideally* requires is the overcoming of these feelings, either completely, or to a considerable degree at least. One cannot forgive and continue to resent.

If what we have said so far is a fairly accurate description of the relevance of emotion to forgiveness, then it will be true to say that forgiveness is an emotional affair from beginning to end. Resentment, anger, indignation and similar feelings play a major role, both in the conditions which make forgiveness possible to contemplate or ask for, and in what is needed to achieve forgiveness, when this is possible at all.

In order to gain a deeper understanding of the meaning and role of resentment at both junctures we shall compare resentment to pain. We begin with the situations that give rise to pain and resentment in the first place. In the case of pain, these are (typically) situations of injury. In the case of resentment, these are (again, typically) situations where one is subjected to an injustice or wrongdoing.

II. Two Analogies

In this section a case will be made for the claim that injustice is analogous to injury, whereas resentment is analogous to pain. The analogies will be developed along three distinct, but related dimensions. The first is a causal dimension where injury and injustice are viewed as *causes* that normally produce certain effects. Viewed as causes, injury and injustice may be conceptualized as species of 'harm', subject to the understanding that this conception subsumes many basic kinds of injury and injustice, but perhaps not all.

The second dimension focuses on the *effect* or impact which injury and injustice have on us: typically, pain in the case of injury, and resentment (and other negative feelings such as indignation) in the case of injustice. As we shall see in due course, it is by no means implausible to conceptualize these effects in terms of the more general notion of "motivating negative attitudes," provided we keep in mind that no understatement is intended by use of the general term 'negative attitude'.

The third dimension has to do with function (or role) which pain and resentment play in our lives, and the significance of failures in this regard.

a. Injustice and injury

Injustice and injury are different notions. This is good news for someone seeking to draw an analogy between them. For if injury and injustice were one and the same, or very similar notions, one could hardly expect to learn much by comparing them.

There is indeed an ordinary usage which allows one to call an act *both* unjust and injurious in one and the same breath, and in a sense which could be either literal or somewhat metaphorical. If somebody succeeds in pushing someone off a cliff with an intention to kill, such an act could be called both unjust (for it is a violation of right) and injurious at the same time. So could an act of burning down somebody's property. It can be called unjust and injurious, albeit the latter in a somewhat extended, but quite important sense.

These are ordinary, acceptable uses of words. But this is not something that we want to start from. We need to build on a more solid basis, one that does not help itself to metaphors and extended usages. Therefore we choose to begin with the idea of an injury as a *physically definable occurrence*, something which happens when someone stabs someone with a knife, or when someone falls and breaks a hand or a leg. In other words, we begin with a notion of injury in the sense of *tissue damage*, which includes not only injuries caused by "unjust acts" (such as attempted murder), but also injuries caused by accidents or natural processes (such as childbirth).

What about the other part of the analogy? The notion of injustice is considerably more problematic. Fortunately, the discussion of the nature and possibility of forgiveness (which is our main goal here) does not require a deeper, or more exact understanding of injustice than what is readily available to commonsense. Thus we should not find much disagreement if we were to say that we are talking about a moral notion, one that has to do with rights and allotments of goods, and violations which may be committed in regard to them. Suffice it to say, then, unjust acts are those that violate one's rights, or what one is entitled to. It does not matter to us whether the rights in question have to do with distribution of goods (distributive justice), or retribution (assuming that a person who is unjustly treated has a right of redress in the form of compensation or infliction of punishment on the wrongdoer).

Unlike the notion of injury, the notion of injustice necessarily involves humans affecting other humans wilfully and consciously, directly or indirectly. Unjust acts or arrangements for which human beings are responsible stand to have an impact on us which could be physical (such as when someone pushes us off a cliff) or more or less intangible (such as when someone spreads false rumours about us, or when social arrangements leave us with no opportunity to take care of ourselves). Thus an injury which is the result of a human *act* of injuring can be a subject of justice and injustice, whereas injuries which we suffer through nature or through accident are never a subject of justice and injustice.

In view of this, one may wonder whether it is possible at all to draw an analogy between injustice and injury, seeing that the two notions belong to different domains of discourse. But I think this is possible if we can find a feature which is common to both unjust and injurious acts or occurrences. Both types of occurrence, I want to suggest, change the state of the human being (who is at the receiving end) to the worse: in both cases (subject to a certain qualification to be explained presently) it is appropriate to speak of *harm*, or *being harmed*.

The move towards subsuming the notions of injury and injustice under the notion of harm, which is what we need to get the analogy going, raises at least two objections, one on behalf of the notion of injury, the other on behalf of the notion of injustice. Let us begin with the one which is more obvious and, apparently, more effective. It could be said that injury cannot always be viewed as a kind of harm, at least when we define injury the way we have chosen to define it—namely, as *tissue damage*. Medical surgery almost invariably requires injury in this sense. So do many kinds of ritual in certain cultures. The same could be said of childbirth, natural or not. All such cases involve tissue damage, and thus could be called 'injurious' in the present sense of the term. But it could hardly be said that medical surgery and childbirth involve *harming* the person who undergoes them.

None of this, I believe, need entail that we have to reject the idea that injury is a kind of harm. For it could be insisted that the cases mentioned above, and many others like them, *do* involve harm, but one that is either relatively minor, temporary, well-controlled, or (more importantly) done and endured for the sake of a greater good. In fact, our willingness to think of *greater* goods (and/or greater *evils*) when we submit to such injuries is an admission that leaving the person in a non-injured condition would have been *better*, had other things been equal. But it is precisely because other things are not equal, because greater goods are to be had, and greater evils are to be avoided, that we are not inclined to think of such injuries as cases of harm. But considered *in and of itself*, that is, in abstraction form everything external to it, a C-section, an open chest, or an amputation of a limb *is* a case of harm. It is not something that we welcome for its own sake. Not only are such cases of tissue damage painful, but they also expose the body to all kinds of dangers. This is why protective measures (such as sedation and antibiotics) are taken when somebody undergoes such kinds of injury for the sake of a greater good.

The case against subsuming injustice under the concept of harm faces other kinds of difficulties, more ill-defined and rather inconclusive. It may be doubted that the notion of a "harm of injustice" (the harm which injustice *constitutes*) is a serviceable notion, given that the notion of harm itself is relative, both in time and place, with different cultures having different ideas about what constitutes harm.

This is indeed true, but then the same could be said about injustice. We have chosen to understand the latter notion in the broad sense of "violation of right," but the notion of "right" is as much subject to the relativity of time, place, and culture. The question which we have to ask here is whether giving an account of forgiveness requires a full account of such notions as justice, wrong, and harm. It is not obvious that this is the case. We know that a discussion of forgiveness will inevitably bring in notions of wrongs, harms, resentment, violence, and damage done to relations between people. We also know of paradigmatic examples of wrong, injustice, harm, and injury. Such knowledge goes some way towards justifying belief in cross-cultural meanings, even if there is much indeterminacy around the edges. For example, it would be perverse to wonder whether an act of imprisoning someone against their will, or forcing them to work under inhumane conditions, does or does not involve injustice or harm. Our pre-theoretical understandings of such notions should be sufficient to get the discussion of the nature and possibility of forgiveness off the ground.

Thus we propose to say that injustice resembles injury in that both can be viewed as species of harm, however precisely we may end up defining these notions. The question which we must now deal with is the *impact* which injustice and injury have on us, and our reactions to them. As we shall see presently, the discussion stands to shed further light on (and strengthen) the analogy between injustice and injury viewed as species of harm.

b. Pain and Resentment

The analogy between injury and injustice has a companion analogy, one that holds between pain and resentment. As before, an analogy between pain and resentment will hold in virtue of some features which they have in common, features under which they can be subsumed. Before we look for such features, we make two brief remarks about how pain and resentment are related to injury and injustice, and the consequences which an analogy between pain and resentment might have for the analogy between injustice and injury.

Injury is typically associated with pain in the sense that, other things being equal, injury causes us to feel pain. Injustice (being wronged), on the other hand, typically arouses feelings of anger and resentment. The association between injustice and resentment is not unexceptionable (nor, for that matter, is the one between injury and pain), but we can in general say that suffering an injustice will be accompanied by feelings or resentment, anger, and a desire to retaliate.

Now for the consequences of establishing an analogy between pain and resentment: suppose we find a feature which pain and resentment have in common. Call this feature "F." Resentment will then be F, and so will pain. But because injury is experienced as painful, and painfulness is a kind of F, it follows that injury can also be experienced in terms of F. Similarly, because injustice is experienced as something-to-be-resented, and resentment is a kind of F, it follows that injustice, too, can be experienced in terms of F. By simple logic, it follows that both injury and injustice will involve experiences of F. Which is to say that injury and injustice will have in common, not only being species of harm, as we explained in the previous sub-section, but they will also have F in common. This means that the analogy between injustice and injury becomes stronger, with the addition of one more feature.

Let us see then how the analogy between pain and resentment can be developed. (It will become presently clear that we have in mind a free-standing analogy, one that makes sense apart from any considerations that have to do with injustice and injury) The analogy has two legs to stand on: *motivational role* and *function* in the life of the organism.

Pain, it is commonly accepted, is a motivating state. This means that being in pain *moves* one to do something in order to make it cease, or to shield oneself from further pain. This remains true even when we decide to *tolerate* pain because it is necessary for the sake of a greater good, such as when one submits to the extraction of a life-threatening foreign object from one's body in the absence of anaesthesia, or when the would-be mother tolerates labor pains because it means the birth of a child. Of course, pain (as it is universally acknowledged), is cognitively mediated, in the sense that it can be felt as tolerable or not depending on a variety of cognitive factors (Hardcastle 1997, 381-409; Clark 2006, 177-197; Radden 2008). But none of this gainsays the fact that pain, in and of itself, is (to use the homely but expressive description employed by Pitcher) "awful," something that we'd rather not have (Pitcher 1970, 481-492). Wincing, withdrawal, nursing, or just plain help-seeking are all proof of the fact that pain is a motivating state. Being in pain puts us in a state of mind which is "negative," or more precisely, aversive—we have a "con" attitude towards being in that state, and towards whatever we conceive to have been the cause of it.

What can be said about resentment? I think it can be viewed as a natural reaction to perceived injustice, as pain is a natural reaction to injury. The correlation between injustice and resentment has instinctive beginnings in our animal nature. Perception of danger arouses fear in the case of humans as well as animals. Similarly, threats to, and violations of vital sphere (and interests) typically arouse anger, as we commonly observe in animals and small children. Long before children develop a sense of justice and injustice, they are able to react with anger, aggravation, as well as aggression and physical resistance, to actions which violate their physical integrity (such as provocation or physical irritation), or deprive them of something that they have gotten hold of (a toy, or a chocolate bar).[7]

In saying that resentment may be viewed as a natural reaction to perceived injustice I do not mean to imply that it is a purely natural response, which nurture has nothing to do with. A raw emotion such as anger is transformed to indignation, or moral wrath, once normative considerations of right and wrong enter the picture (Zinck and Newton 2008, 18). Similarly, one may venture to aver that a realization of one's inability to change the situation which gives rise to justified anger can subdue the feeling of indignation and turn it into resentment.

It is true that we do not understand the *physical basis* which underlies our feelings of anger and (much later in our lives) resentment, to the degree that we understand the physical basis which underlies the feeling of pain. But for purposes of developing an analogy between pain and resentment, it is sufficient for us to note that there are regular, naturally-cum-socially explainable patterns which relate our emotional states to the way we are faring in the world.

It may thus be plausible to claim that our sense of justice and injustice develops from such simple beginnings; that emotions which eventually develop into what we call feelings of resentment, or indignation are there from the start, in our first encounters with situations which we experience as involving violation, or as being attractive or repellent (Johnston

---

[7] According to empirical research cited in Alexandra Zinck and Alber Newton (2006,17), infants begin to exhibit anger at the early age of 4 to 7 months.

2001, 183), comfortable or distressing (Zinck and Newton 2008, 11).

More can be said about resentment, in addition to its being a development of natural (emotional) responses to invasions and violations. Resentment, of course, is not exactly like pain. It does not have the urgency characteristic of pain. But like pain, it can be more or less intense, and it is certainly cognitively mediated, perhaps to a greater degree than pain is. Its intensity corresponds to our perception of the extent of injustice, and it can increase or diminish, depending on many cognitive factors, such as apology or knowledge of extenuating circumstances. And, like pain, there are times when it is so intense as to be unbearable.

When we consider resentment in and of itself, however, it is not hard to see the motivational aspect which it embodies. It is common knowledge that resentment can, and often will, lead to doing things—revenge, retaliation, or other types of behavior aiming at modifying the circumstances that led to it in the first place. This is not to mention expressions which fall short of being actions—expressive actions, so-called, such as tone of voice, facial expression, or picture-burning. Like pain, resentment is experienced as an unpleasant state, one that we would rather be free from. Like pain, resentment *clamors* for changing the world. It is associated with desires that have a world-to-mind "direction of fit," meaning, they aim at the changing the world so that it "fits" what we want. It can be characterized by the negativity, the very same "con" attitude which we find in the case of pain. For these reasons, we may conclude that resenting is similar to being in pain: both are negative states of mind that motivate us to act. (See Greenspan 1992, [293] on the aversive character of certain emotions). This is point at which the present analogy is driving.

The other leg on which the analogy between pain and resentment stands has to do with the function which both play in the life of the organism. Broadly speaking, the function is one of protection. Pain is protective in a fairly obvious and straightforward sense: it motivates us to pull back from harmful, or potentially harmful stimuli, and to seek help when the damage is done. Pain is also good at teaching lessons of what to avoid, which is why it works so well in the form of negative reinforcement.

Similar things can be attributed to resentment. Injustice, as we suggested above, can be viewed as a species of harm. Therefore, it makes a lot of sense for a creature to react to injustice with an attitude of anger or resentment, because this prepares the creature for taking measures in order to protect its interests, or whatever it sees as part of its well-being. As I suggested above, instinctive reactions to "encroachments" by outside agents on a creature's sphere of interest include anger, aggravation, and what (in the case of humans) later develops into a full-fledged emotion of resentment. And while resentment is not as volatile as anger and some other "hot" emotions, there can be no doubt that it plays an important protective function is the life of the human organism that is capable of feeling it.[8]

The analogy between pain and resentment can also be seen indirectly in cases where there is a marked failure of function. In the case of pain, many of the fairly well understood failures are classified as pathological. The incapacity to feel pain the way normal people do is found in such cases as asymbolia, congenital pain insensitivity, as well as cases where people undergo pre-frontal lobotomy in order to relieve chronic pains. As can be expected, radical failures of the pain system lead to shortened life span, due to lack (or

---

[8] The "protective" function of resentment is clearly recognized by Bishop Butler. In his Sermon "Upon Resentment and Forgiveness of Injuries," Butler says, "The natural object or occasion of settled resentment, then, being injury..., it is easy to see, that to prevent and to remedy such injury, and the miseries arising from it, is the end for which this passion was implanted in man. It is to be considered as a weapon put into our hands by nature, against injury, injustice and cruelty" (Butler 2006, 93).

weakness) of the motivation to withdraw from, or avoid harmful stimuli which normal people feel as obnoxious. Far from being a curse, pain is in fact a blessing without which we would not be able to lead a normal life.[9]

We may not be able to say the same thing with the same degree of certainty about resentment. The notion of a pathological *psychic* condition may not sound as scientific as that of a pathological *physical* condition. It is conceivable that people who are incapable of resentment are able to lead what looks like normal lives. Spock seemed to lead a normal life—normal for a Vulcan, at least—most of the time on *Star Trek*, despite reputedly being unable to experience emotions. But the case of a person who is systematically subjected to abuse but nevertheless never shows a sign of anger and resentment is not a sight that many of us would like to see. It indicates that something had radically gone wrong with the individual in question. The individual may not have a shortened life span as an individual who suffers from congenital pain insensitivity, but there can be no doubt that his or her fortunes in the world will decline, that he or she will not fulfil whatever potential they might have otherwise had.

---

[9] See the lengthy and touching narrative which Austen Clark quotes about Tanya, a child born with congenital pain insensitivity (Clark 2006, 93): "Tanya, now eleven, was living a pathetic existence in an institution. She had lost both legs to amputation: she had refused to wear proper shoes and that, coupled with her failure to limp or shift weight when standing (because she felt no discomfort), had eventually put intolerable pressure on her joints. Tanya had also lost most of her fingers. Her elbows were constantly dislocated. She suffered the effects of chronic sepsis on her hands and amputation stumps. Her tongue was lacerated and badly scarred from her nervous habit of chewing it."

III. Forgiveness and healing

If injustice is analogous to injury, and resentment is analogous to pain, questions will naturally arise about what happens after one is injured and experiences pain, and what happens after one suffers an injustice and experiences resentment. Are there ways in which such states do, or can, come to an end somehow, instead of continuing indefinitely?

Before we attempt to answer this question, we should note that there is a sense in which neither injury nor injustice can be undone. There is a certain kind of irreversibility that is characteristic of things that happen and become part of history, an irreversibility which we colloquially describe as "not being able to turn back the clock." This applies to injury and injustice in a simple way. Injuries often leave scars. It is also often the case that the injured body, or part of it, never goes back to what it was before the injury—it aches, or is more fragile. Beyond this, injuries leave painful memories, which remain alive in the mind for a long time, or are simply never forgotten. Similarly, an unjust act may leave a bodily scar, if it is literally an act of injuring, but it will anyway register in consciousness and memory as a wrongful act which we suffered. Some people may find the notion of "psychological scars" too metaphorical, but surely we must be allowed to speak of long-lasting psychological effects of many unjust acts. Think of the psychological consequences of rape, incest, violent robbery, and betrayal. Such acts are not just done and finished, but often leave the victim psychologically changed for an indefinite period of time. There will be the painful memory, the occasional nightmare, and the uncomfortable sense of déjà vu in certain situations, or just the sheer inability to function as well as before.

I do not introduce these similarities between injury and injustice in order to add to the analogies which we have already pointed out. I mention these as part of laying the ground for discussing what may be the more important and hopeful aftermaths of injury and injustice.

In the case of injury, this is, as might be expected, none other than *healing*. The body recovers. The pain ceases. One is able to walk, to work, or otherwise function as before. In some cases as good as before, in some cases not as good. But there is no question that in most cases of injury, healing can, and does take place. Integrity of the body is restored, and, with it, the ability to function more or less normally in relation to other bodies.

Forgiveness, too, I want to suggest, may be viewed as a kind of healing. There are a number of considerations that suggest this. They are related to each other without being equally important, or equally telling. I shall begin by discussing the most conspicuous consideration, one which is easiest to understand. It is based on the analogy between pain and resentment.

Forgiveness, we have been assuming, entails the overcoming of resentment and other retributive emotions, such as anger, hate, and the desire for retaliation. Taken in and of itself, cessation of resentment *is* a good thing. For it is well known, and stands in no need of argument, that feelings of resentment and anger, and the constant nursing of a desire to get even, are *disordering* kinds of emotions (not withstanding their defensive and protective functions which we have sufficiently acknowledged). To harbor them for a long time at a certain degree of intensity can damage one's psychic health as well as one's physical well-being, not to mention harm relationships to other people, and the prospect for happiness after injustice. In a way, such affective states are not much healthier than physical pain, which is well-known for disrupting one's whole being, physical as well as psychological.

Cessation of pain, in and of itself, is also a good thing, and for reasons which we have already considered. But more importantly for the purpose of establishing an analogy between forgiveness and healing, *cessation of pain is also involved in the healing of injuries*. Typically, when an injury heals, it ceases to hurt. This is not to say that whenever pain ceases, an injury heals. Ceasing to hurt is not a sufficient condition for healing. But this does not gainsay the fact that, normally, an injury that has healed ceases to hurt. Ceasing to hurt is part of healing in that we would not consider an injury healed (at least on a considered view of what healing is) if the subject continues to experience pain in connection with it.

Because resentment is analogous to pain, it is plausible to think that ceasing to resent is *like* ceasing to hurt. But since ceasing to hurt is part of healing, it becomes tempting to think that *forgiveness is analogous to healing*, because it involves the cessation of something which is analogous to pain, namely, resentment.

This does not yet lay a firm foundation for an analogy between forgiveness and healing, because (it could be said) ceasing to resent, or ceasing hurt, may be part of being (or becoming) completely *oblivious* to whatever it is that caused one to resent or to hurt. After all, we do not want to say that amnesia is analogous to forgiveness, or that general anaesthesia is analogous to healing. But this does not undermine the proposed analogy. Everything is similar to, and different from, an indefinite number of things in an indefinite number ways. Before we abandon the analogy, we should see if it can be strengthened.

The very shortcoming we have just alluded to shows us what we need to do in order to strengthen the analogy. Despite the importance to ceasing to hurt, healing involves *more* than ceasing to hurt, as we shall presently see. Forgiveness follows suit by requiring *more* than just ceasing to resent.

What does healing involve, in addition to ceasing to hurt? The most important thing that healing involves is restoring the body to a previous condition of wholeness and integrity. The broken bone is re-joined, and resumes its function of propping up the body in the usual way; the separated flesh closes up, and resumes its function of protecting the organs underneath it. True, the restoration may not be complete, for in the case of serious injuries, one may not be able to function as well as before. But for most practical purposes, we can say that after healing, the person (the body) goes about its business *as if* there had been no injury.

Something similar can be said about forgiveness. In fact, much of what contemporary writers say about the psychological significance of wrongdoing and forgiveness fits very well with what we have been saying. Consider, first, the kind of harm which wrongdoing is. It *has* been referred to as "injury." According to Murphy:

> *Intentional wrongdoing insults us and attempts (sometimes successfully) to degrade us—and thus it involves a kind of injury that is not merely tangible and sensible. It is moral injury, and we care about such injuries. (Murphy and Hampton 1988, 25)*

The use of the term 'injury' in connection with injustice and wrongdoing is well established. We find it in Lucy Allais (2008, 41), Murphy and Hampton (1988, 44ff), Jesse Couenhoven (2010, 150ff), William Young (1998, 108), Paul Newberry (2001, 235), Jerome Neu (2004, 173), and Alice Maclachlan (2010, 428), among others, including Butler, of course (2006, 93). The choice of words seems natural, not because moral injuries cause us to bleed, or because they break our bones (though sometimes they do precisely this), but because they interfere with normal functioning—they render us unable to go about as usual. They cause a kind of malfunction, a breakdown, big or small, in the way we deal with the world. Therefore calling them injuries, I think, is well-justified. It also facilitates drawing an analogy between forgiveness and healing.

Keeping in mind the analogy between injustice and injury, and the idea that the healing (of injuries) involves restoration to a previous condition of wholeness and integrity, the proposal to think about forgiveness in terms of healing begins to make sense. This is because forgiveness *also* involves repairing, mending, healing, or, as we shall say here, *restoring*. Some writers speak of "wiping the slate clean," which, to Allais, is "heart of forgiveness" (Allais 2008, 33). Others speak of "re-establishing" the sense of self-worth that one had prior to the offence (Verbin 2010, 617). According to Hampton, the resenter must conquer, in the sense of "transcend," the fear that that "the insulting message in the harmful action is correct" (Murphy and Hampton 1988, 148). All of this can be understood, and understood well, in term of the notion of *restoration*.

Restoration can take place at either one of two levels, the *personal* or the *interpersonal*. The first is that of the victim of wrongdoing. Writers who view forgiveness as an essentially *intra-psychic* event that need not involve the offender will treat forgiveness as something that restores, or (at least) involves restoring the *victim's* psyche to a previous condition of wholeness and integrity. Something of this kind is hinted at in Hampton's statement that "The first stage of the forgiving process…involves *regaining* one's confidence in one's own worth despite the immoral action challenging it" (Murphy and Hampton 1988, 83; emphasis add). The restorative dimension is evident here. The offence undermines our confidence in ourselves, but, as we move towards forgiveness, we *regain* that which we had lost; we are *restored* to the way we were.

Hampton wonders whether an act of faith in oneself might not be needed to accomplish this (1988, 148). Others offer a cognitive explanation of how this can happen. Following Roberts's view of emotion as "concernful construal of one's condition" (1995, 303), Verbin claims that the victim has a free choice to make between viewing herself in terms of the offence (in which case she will see her status as reduced), or in terms of her achievements, and how she is valued by people around her, etc. If she follows the second path, then she might well overcome the resentment, which was set off by belief in reduced status in the first place (2010, 608). The victim's psyche reverts to the condition it was in before the offence. It is *as if* she had not been wronged, or morally injured. (The same "as if" notion which we encountered in the case of physical healing is equally applicable here.)

According to Verbin, a victim who ceases to resent thereby bestows forgiveness (Ibid., 609). But she can continue to think that the offender is a morally rotten person with whom she does not want to associate (Ibid., 614). Many philosophers believe this does not qualify as forgiveness, because forgiveness involves an attitudinal change towards the offender. It is, I think, plausible to believe that forgiveness does involve such a change. For if forgiveness were a purely intra-psychic event, then there would be no reason why an end of resentment that is brought about by *any* means should not count as forgiveness. Verbin's type of cognitive therapy is not necessarily preferable to behaviour modification therapy, or the taking of an anti-resentment pill, should one be manufactured one day.

Viewing forgiveness as *inter*-psychic takes (or at least begins to take) forgiveness beyond the realm of the psychological to the social. It allows us as a first step to think in terms of the *attitude of the victim towards the offender*, and then (inevitably) how that attitude will be translated in terms of relations and other modes of behaviour. Here, the phrase 'wiping the slate clean' is very much at home. There is a restoration to a previous condition of wholeness and integrity. But it is not the psyche of the *victim* that we are primarily thinking of now, but the *relation* between the victim and the offender.

A relation between two individuals is in the mind before it is in the world. Here, according to Allais, the victim decides not to let her feelings towards the offender be affected by the wrongdoing. Feeling-wise, she is supposed to feel *as if* no offence had been committed. Viewing the offender in the light of how things were *before* the offence means readiness to resume relations.

A few paragraphs back we said that the restoration which forgiveness involves can take place at one of two levels, the personal or the interpersonal. The second level includes social relations in a general way, but one can also focus on the particular relation between the victim and the offender. Both aspects are worth considering on their own.

With reference to social relations in general, it is not far-fetched to say that every act of wrongdoing constitutes an attack on their wholeness and integrity. The social fabric of interpersonal relations undergoes damage whenever an act of injustice is committed. If it can happen to *her*, then it can happen to *you*: this is how a wrongdoing appears from the perspective of social relations. Conceived in broad terms, wrongdoing constitutes an attack on how people relate to each other. (It is hard to conceive how human association can take place if people are constantly being unjust to one another.)

Viewed from the perspective of social relations, forgiveness can be seen as a personal effort at repairing the damage. The victim, in wiping the slate clean, signifies her readiness to re-enter the scene of social interaction with good will, just *as if* she had not been victimized. For example, she will not let the wrong stand in way of her trusting people, or entering into new relationships. She will not let the memory of the wrong color her perceptions of what people are doing. In some cases, it could be hoped that the victim will resume normal relations with the offender.

This brings us to the second aspect of interpersonal restoration, where the focus is one particular social relation, the one between the victim and the offender. Initially, one might think that forgiveness involves no healing as far as the *wrongdoer* is concerned. But this is not true. It is often the case that an offender realizes the wrong he has committed. He is genuinely repentant. He blames himself. He feels guilty. He *holds it up against himself* that he did this or that. So now he needs forgiveness of two parties, it seems: himself and the victim. Self-forgiveness (which must be distinguished from mere self-indulgence) can be aided by the knowledge that one has been forgiven by the victim herself. As Hampton says:

> *...a victim's forgiveness of his wrongdoer can communicate the same message, so that the wrongdoer may reason, "If he can see enough in me to welcome me back, then maybe I am not such a hideous person after all. (1988, 87)*

This makes it possible for the wrongdoer to forgive himself. He wipes the slate clean on his own behalf, and is thus restored to a previous condition of wholeness and integrity. In a more subtle way, the quality forgiveness may be even more blessed than the quality of mercy has been said to be.

The question or restoring relations between victim and offender in the social setting which was witness to the offence compels one to think about conditions that may have to be met before this happens. The healing aspect that has to do with social relations in general and the relation between victim and offender in particular, depends not only on the forgiver, but on the offender as well. The offender may remain unrepentant, ever so ready to do wrong again. Or it may be that there is no good side to the offender no matter how hard we look. In that case I would say that forgiveness can still take place, but its healing effect will not extend far beyond the forgiver, and the example which he sets for all those who care to see. Still, what forgiveness intends, its *telos* as it were, remains unchanged: according to Roberts, it is "reconciliation—restoration and maintenance of a relationship of acceptance" (1995, 299). The forgiver is *ready* to resume relations with the offender. The damaged social fabric is *ready* to be repaired. But it is not unconditional. The offender has to meet certain conditions, which include genuine repentance and acknowledgment of responsibility, among other things perhaps.

Consideration of what the offender can do in order to facilitate resumption of relations, even the very event of forgiveness itself, finally brings us to the *third* (and last) consideration which speaks in favour of an analogy between forgiveness and healing.

Injuries, as we know, often require *nursing* before they heal. Broken bones need to be re-aligned, cuts need be bandaged, bleeding needs to be stopped, and so on.[10] If healing can be *aided* by nursing, we can ask if something similar applies to forgiveness. Of course, it is possible that sheer moral virtue may suffice to bring forgiveness about. In other words, it may be possible for a person, out of sheer goodness, to forgive a wrong however immense it is. (Perhaps this is what Jesus of Nazareth did on the Cross.) But it must be acknowledged that more is needed in the case ordinary human beings who suffer injustice. And indeed we can think of many things that facilitate forgiveness, at least in cases where the victim's psyche has not been irreparably damaged by the injustice. Here the offender seems to be the star of the show. Much depends on the offender. Sincere apology, repentance, restitution, and reparation help bring about forgiveness. Apology and repentance have special significance. In Murphy's analysis of forgiveness, the repentant and apologetic wrongdoer takes back the statement, implicit in her wrongdoing, that "I am up here, and you are down there." This does not guarantee, but it can help the victim regain lost pride, and a sense of importance. It is like nursing a wound back to recovery.

We can also think of other kinds of nursing which the victim, and others, can engage in. Public affirmations of value, moral support, and special treatment, can help the victim reach a stage of rising above the offence, and the offender.

---

[10] I do not mean to take this to extremes. It will be acknowledged in the last section that healing is basically a natural process. Wounded animals often heal without receiving much by way of nursing, unless one takes wound-licking (cleaning) and resting as forms of self-nursing.

Certain kinds of therapy can also play a role in bringing resentment under control, or getting rid of it altogether. A cognitive type of therapy might enable the victim to see the wrong doer as a fellow human being who has done wrong; to see wrongdoing as an inevitable part of human life, where one is cast in the role of wrongdoer as frequently as one is cast in the role of victim. One thinks, "there, but for the grace of God, go I." Dwelling on such considerations in a true philosophical spirit may curb one's enthusiasm to cast the first stone.

IV. Objections and replies

We have now explored a number of systematic similarities between injury, injustice, pain and resentment, leading up to the proposal to understand forgiveness in terms of healing. The structural similarities observed at the different levels are too numerous to be lacking in significance.

But the objection will inevitably be raised: there *are* numerous differences between the concepts invoked in our discussion which may render the analogies weak. Unlike an act of injustice, an injury is something that happens in the *natural order.* It is up to the body, as a system of organic processes, how and when an injury heals. Nobody tells blood to coagulate, thereby closing a bleeding wound. Nobody tells the body to replace burnt-off skin, or to sprout a new fingernail in place of one that has been badly damaged. Healing processes have a natural, almost mechanical aspect about them. What *can* happen *will* happen, barring unusual circumstances, such as when the body is robbed of its ability to heal—for example, a wound is so severe that the organism bleeds to death.

Over and above *naturalness* of healing, but intimately connected to it, is the fact that healing fails to give rise to *normative* questions. It makes little or no sense to ask whether it is *right* for a broken bone to mend or not. But it makes a lot of sense to ask if one *ought* to forgive or not. It may be that there are wrongs that are ought not to be forgiven, and ones that ought to be.

In these ways, it will be said, forgiveness seems different. It is not a physical occurrence or a material process. It is an affective/cognitive affair which takes place in the realm of meanings, intentions, reasons and feelings. There is no air of inevitability about it. One who has been wronged may or may not forgive. One contemplates, agonizes, and engages in emotional struggle. But forgiveness is not an inevitable result. It seems be to a *voluntary* action which one may or may not choose to do.

Nor, it could also be claimed, does the pain-resentment analogy fair any better. Pain is a physiological process subserved in the Central Nervous System in fairly well-understood ways, in function as well as malfunction. Resentment, on the other hand is a psychic affair, one that cannot be understood in physiological terms. It tends to be much more cognitively mediated than pain, and it is under our control to a much greater degree than pain is. Like forgiveness, it gives rise to normative questions which pain cannot give rise to. The question "is it right for him to continue to resent?" makes sense, but there is little sense to be found in the question "is it right for him to continue to feel a toothache?"

But these considerations need not mean that forgiveness cannot be meaningfully compared to healing. To begin with, it is not completely true that normative questions are out of place in the cases of injury and pain. Turning from question of "right" to questions of "good," one can certainly ask "Would it be good for the injury to heal, and for the pain to cease?" These are meaningful normative questions which we tend to answer in the affirmative, because we consider well-being to be a human good. Nor is it true that healing is invariably a purely physiological process, at least in the case of human beings. In many cases, there *is* such a thing as having or losing the will to live, which can have an impact on healing. Psycho-somatic illness and wellness are well-attested phenomena

Besides, all analogies involve similarities and differences. One does not make an analogy between two perfectly similar things. The real question is whether the similarities are significant enough to render the analogy enlightening, and whether the differences are relevant in a way that weakens the analogy.

Let us consider what, if anything, the differences prove. Recall the similarities between healing and forgiveness: both involve cessation of essentially aversive states; both involve restoration to a previous condition of wholeness, and normal function; and lastly, there is an element of nursing or caring-for that plays a role in both cases.

With these similarities in mind, we can ask: what does it matter that, in the case of (physical) healing, but not forgiveness, the healing process can come about naturally—as a matter of what the laws of nature dictate? Surely, we can imagine that there are two kinds of cases: cases where the restoration is brought about by natural means in the natural realm, and cases where restoration is brought about by other means—ones that involve moral reasoning, emotional struggle, faith, or whatever. There may also be two ways of caring-for, or aiding: one involving bandaging wounds, and one involving giving assurance or moral support. And (finally) there may be two ways in which aversive states may come to an end: one takes a pill, or one comes to realize that one should not feeling that way.

One may continue to insist that the similarity we are trying to capture by talking about "aversive states" (for example) is superficial. It could be claimed that talk of "two ways" in which states could come to an end is uncalled for, because there isn't some one thing that can come to an end in one of two ways. This criticism can be extended to the other two aspects of the comparison: neither restoration, nor nursing, it could be said, is a substantive notion of something that is common to such different things as suffering a physical injury and suffering an injustice.

Perhaps there is an ultimate clash of intuitions when it comes to thinking about the pairs: injustice, injury; pain, resentment; forgiveness, healing. One can be too impressed by (or one can be of two minds about) the differences to be found between members of each pair. The differences are undeniable. But then so are the similarities which, as we saw, can be elaborated, rather intuitively and naturally, along many dimensions. Add to that the fact that ordinary modes of thinking and speech are on the side of the analogies. We speak of injuries that are physical, psychological or moral (Cf. Murphy and Hampton [1988, 25] and others mentioned above). Pain and resentment are uncomfortable, with some emotional states being every bit as "awful" as pains. Talk of "healing" is also not out of place, as when we speak of people who have been psychologically traumatized by acts of wrongdoing or injustice.

There is thus no call for us to invent new words so that we can call things by different names in the present case. That would only make it easy for us to overlook meaningful analogies and similarities between injury, injustice, pain, and resentment. It is enough for us to acknowledge the existence and importance of differences while insisting on relevant similarities. If we do this, analogy between forgiveness and healing will be sustained.

Acknowledgments

Thanks are due to the editor, Tomis Kapitan, Michael Pendlebury, and anonymous referees for their useful comments.

References

Allais, Lucy. 2008. "Wiping the Slate Clean: The Heart of Forgiveness." *Philosophy & Public Affairs* 36.1: 33-68.

Blackburn, Simon. 1984. *Spreading the Word*. New York: Oxford University Press.

Butler, Joseph. 2006. *The Works of Bishop Butler*. Edited by David E. White. Rochester: Rochester University Press.

Clark, Austen. 2006. "Painfulness is Not a Quale." *Pain: New Essays on Its Nature and the Methodology of Its Study*. Edited by Murat Aydede. Cambridge: The MIT Press.

Couenhoven, Jesse. 2010. "Forgiveness and Restoration." *The Journal of Religion* 90.2: 148-170.

Deonna, Julien and Fabrice Teroni. 2012. *The Emotions: A Philosophical Introduction*. New York: Routledge.

Goldie, Peter. 2009. "Thick Concepts and Emotion." *Reading Bernard Williams*. Edited by Daniel Callcut. London: Routledge.

Greenspan, Patricia S. 1992. "Subjective Guilt and Responsibility." *Mind* 101: 287-303.

Hardcastle, Valerie G. 1997. "When a Pain is Not." *The Journal of Philosophy* 94.8: 381-409.

Hieronymi, Pamela. 2001. "Articulating an Uncompromising Forgiveness." *Philosophy and Phenomenological Research* 62.3: 529-55.

Johnston, Mark. 2001. "The Authority of Affect." *Philosophy and Phenomenological Research* 63.1: 181-214.

Joyce, Richard. 2002. "Expressivism and Motivation Internalism." *Analysis* 62.4: 336-344.

MacDowell, John. 2009. "Knowledge, Criteria, and Defeasibility." *Disjunctivism: Contemporary Readings*. Edited by Alex Byrne and Heather Logue. Cambridge, MA: The MIT Press.

MacLachlan, Alice. 2010. "Unreasonable Resentments." *Journal of Social Philosophy* 41.4: 422-441.

Murphy, Jeffrie G., and Jean Hampton. 1988. *Forgiveness and mercy*. Cambridge: Cambridge University Press.

Neu, Jerome. 2004. "Emotion and Freedom." *Thinking About Feeling: Contemporary Philosophers on Emotions*. Edited by Robert C. Solomon. Oxford and New York: Oxford University Press.

Newberry, P. 2001. "Joseph Butler: A Presupposed Theory of Emotion." *Journal of the History of Ideas* 62: 233-244.

Pitcher, George. 1970. "The Awfulness of Pain." *The Journal of Philosophy* 67: 481-492.

Radden, Jennifer. 2008. "A Confusion of Pains? The Sensory and Affective Components of Pain, Suffering, and Hurt." *Fact and Value in Emotion.* Edited by C. Lious Charland. Amsterdam, NLD: John Benjamin's Publishing Company.

Roberts, Robert C. 1995. "Forgiveness." *American Philosophical Quarterly* 32.4: 289-306.

Verbin, N. 2010. "Forgiveness and Hatred." *Ethical Perspectives* 17.4: 603-25.

Williams, Bernard. 1973. *Problems of the Self.* Cambridge: Cambridge University Press.

Wisdom, Jeff. 2009. "A Defence of Descriptive Moral Content." *The Southern Journal of Philosophy* XVII: 285-300.

Young, William E. 1998. "Resentment and Impartiality." *Southern Journal of Philosophy* XXXVI: 103-130.

Zaibert, Leo. 2009. The Paradox of Forgiveness." *Journal of Moral Philosophy* 6: 365–393.

Zinck, Alexandara, and Albert Newton. 2008. "Classifying Emotion: A Developmental Account." *Synthese* 161.1: 1-25.

Chapter 4

Filling that Moral Space: Forgiveness, Suffering, and the Recognition of Human Identity

Rebecca Dew

Introduction

Suffering is a human reality, a reality that points to the need for human forgiveness even as it facilitates the apprehension of moral awareness. In this chapter I argue that it is the possibility of human forgiveness that fills the gaps generated by the reality of human suffering. In this sense forgiveness fills the spaces of moral recognition requisite for coming to terms with human identity. Although the most famous identification of the human experience with suffering is that made by Russian author Fyodor Dostoevsky, political theorist Hannah Arendt considers the experience of shared suffering in its performative function as a catalyst of political revolution.[11] In the context of the French Revolution, suffering generated a socio-political movement to the extent that it was viewed as a structure capable of social deposition. However, in this chapter I will argue that Arendt views human suffering as carrying political weight not primarily as a stimulus to politi-

---

[11] However, this is done with primary reference to the French Revolution, with which Arendt takes issue for a number of reasons. See for example: Hannah Arendt, "Society and Culture," *Daedalus* 89 (1960), 279; Hannah Arendt, *On Revolution* (New York: Penguin, 1977), 42, 49, 51-3, 64, 82, 123, 146-7.

cal action but as an identifier of private personhood by way of the forgiveness-act.

Arendt's explication of suffering as a modern experience is drawn out in her *Origins of Totalitarianism, On Revolution,* and her assessment of the Eichmann trials for *The New Yorker.* These, along with her more theoretical treatment in *The Human Condition,* explore the legitimacy of political action in response to the suffering of the modern age, sounding the call to what some like Seyla Benhabib have interpreted to be a moral response.[12] First, I will explicate Arendt's conception of spaces of appearance. I represent Arendt's claim that it is in these spaces of appearance that human freedom is realized, but, more specifically, I argue that it is the space between forgiveness and suffering within which human identity can be recognized. Viewed in terms of Arendt's *vita activa,* the worldly reality of suffering presents the locus of Arendt's overlap with the exploration of suffering made by Dostoevsky (whom Arendt considers to be among "the great psychologists of the nineteenth century") (1977, 86). I will then proceed to explicate the differentiation between forgiveness as an individual act (compassion) and forgiveness as a collective gift (promise). This will be followed by an expansion upon Arendt's engagement with the contributions made by Rousseau and, more particularly, Jesus of Nazareth on suffering and forgiveness. Next, I discuss Arendt's notion of promise-making and -keeping (in that she considers them to be virtually inseparable). Lastly, I will interpret Arendt's recommendations in light of a practical approach to human forgiveness in relation to the value of human memory and the need for the human promise.

---

[12] As Benhabib argues, Arendt's *Human Condition* is a form of "philosophical anthropology" upholding *Besinnung,* a sort of "coming to one's sense morally" (2003, 195). Along these lines, see also: Seyla Benhabib, "Judgment and the Moral Foundations of Politics in Arendt's Thought," *Political Theory* 16 (1988): 29-51.

Suffering is a phenomenon inseparable from human experience. However, a response to suffering is not one that can be applied *en masse*. Such would be the sentimental response of pity—but unspecified action is as pointless as undirected movement is endless. Neither has an end as neither has an object. In fact, it is the stereotypical reduction of suffering (as of the human experience in general) to an informational equivalent that serves to reduce the human experience—its sensibilities, ideas, opinions and actions—to a variable to be quantified rather than a human voice to be heard. Arendt is critical of all such stereotyping or reducing of the human experience, whether in terms of the ideological accounts of modern sociology,[13] scientism, or, most famously, the class- or race-fixated logic of the totalitarian phenomenon. However, it is the way in which forgiveness and promise-keeping correlate to Arendt's *vita activa* by way of human suffering which I will begin with here.[14]

I. Spaces of appearance and human identity: suffering as the realm of recognition

Three attributes, or modes, of human activity figure in Arendt's *vita activa:* 1) man as *animal laborans*; 2) man as *homo faber*; and 3) man as *zōon politikon*. The last of these—translated as political action—is the highest of the three expressions of human activity, but even labor and fabrication remain inextricable features of the reality of human being. Arendt distinguishes between *animal laborans* ("the labor of our bodies") and *homo faber* ("the work of our hands"). Arendt's distinction between the human capacities of work in terms of labor (that which is undertaken by *animal laborans*)

---

[13] Baehr's assessment is thorough in this regard (Baehr, 2010).

[14] Another theorist who touches upon the role of suffering in relation to Arendt's assessment of criminal guilt and the application of justice is Susan Neiman (2001).

and fabrication or artifice (that which is undertaken by *homo faber*) parallels her understanding of the necessity of natural processes and her recognition of the human capacity for new beginnings. Fabrication is thus, in its creativity and its capacity for creating enduring artisanal products, a mode of activity superior to labor and its inherent ties to biological necessity, although fabrication (*poiesis*) is to be distinguished from action (*praxis*) in that "it has a definite beginning and a predictable end" (Arendt 1953, 322; and 1958, 587). In contradistinction, political action exists to the degree that a distance can be created between it and the former two elements of the *vita activa*. In other words, the exercise of political action relies upon the availability of a public space in which it can be presented.

For Arendt the exercise of personal will in political terms relies upon not only the availability but the accessibility of public spaces.[15] Similarly, forgiveness is only politically viable where there are spaces of respect in which it can occur.[16] In the context of her assessment of totalitarianism (Arendt 1967), it is the elimination of spaces of legitimate human action which similarly relegates the expressed will of the people to the ever-decreasing zone of the private sphere. The will of the dictator, as facilitated by his party and its expansive and invasive bureaucratic apparatus, replaces the vocalized consent of the people. Neither political action proper nor cultural contribution of any lasting significance beyond the immediate party objectives is permitted. As a result, there is no space in which the reality of human suffering can be recognized, and the apprehension of human identity—

---

[15] Arendt considers freedom as only finding its expression in the public sphere, in that Arendt's conception of modernized freedom involves the creation of a "public space between [citizens] . . . where freedom could appear" (Arendt 1968, 4).

[16] "Closed within ourselves, we would never be able to forgive" (Arendt 1998, 243).

the crux of human motivation itself—is lost. For forgiveness, like promise-making and -keeping, constitutes an affirmation of both personal experience and identity.[17] Forgiveness elevates, even as it affirms. This is not to say that human suffering for that reason ceases to occur; to the contrary, it is the radical extravagance of human suffering as a structural effect of the totalitarian movement which prompts Arendt's outrage. This is particularly the case with reference to the horrors of the concentration camps: "The old spontaneous bestiality gave way to an absolutely cold and systematic destruction of human bodies, calculated to destroy human dignity... [and thereby generating] horror... For to destroy individuality is to destroy spontaneity, man's power to begin" (Arendt 1967, 454-5). The elements of totalitarian methods of domination, Arendt makes clear, "utilize, develop and crystallize on the basis of the nihilistic principle that 'everything is permitted'" (Ibid., 440), which finds its parallel in the words of the character Ivan in Dostoevsky's *The Brothers Karamazov*.[18]

---

[17] "Without being bound to the fulfilment of promises, we would never be able to keep our identities; we would be condemned to wander helplessly and without direction in the darkness of each man's lonely heart . . . the presence of others . . . [serves to] confirm the identity between the one who promises and the one who fulfils." Hannah Arendt, *The Human Condition* (Chicago: University of Chicago Press, 1998), 237. In her assessment of suffering, Spelman also agrees that identification, a recognition of humanity, precedes the arousal of deep emotion. Elizabeth V. Spelman, *Fruits of Sorrow: Framing our Attention to Suffering* (Boston: Beacon Press, 1997), 61.

[18] "[T]here is decidedly nothing in the whole world that would make men love their fellow men [. . .] were mankind's belief in its immortality to be destroyed, not only love but also any living power to continue the life of the world would at once dry up in it. Not only that, but then nothing would be immoral any longer, everything would be permitted" (Dostoevsky 2002, 69).

The oft-heralded prophet of modernity, Fyodor Dostoevsky,[19] assigns suffering a validatory role in the apprehension of this-worldly evil. Dostoevsky's eight-year experience at Omsk Labor Camp in western Siberia prompted disgust comparable to that of Arendt at the dehumanization characteristic of any ideological system that treats humans as cogs in a machine or parts in a process.[20] In *The Brothers Karamazov*, Dostoevsky associates suffering with the human need for forgiveness. He does this by portraying four responses to the suffering experienced in the world through the primary characters of the novel. The first of these is seen in the most intellectual and rationalistic of the Karamazov brothers, the atheist Ivan. Ivan protests what he perceives as the gross injustices in the world as God has ordered it (Dostoevsky 2002, 245). However, Ivan's denial of God in the face of what he considers to be the unjustified and unjustifiable sufferings of the innocent, of children, culminates in murderous evil beyond that against which he expresses such loathing. And it is here we find the overlap between Dostoevsky's considera-

---

[19] Joseph Frank, *Dostoevsky: The Mantle of the Prophet* (Princeton: Princeton University Press, 2002); Hans Kohn, *Prophets and Peoples* (New York: Collier Books, 1961), 125, 143; P. Travis Kroeker and Bruce K. Ward, *Remembering the End: Dostoevsky as Prophet to Modernity* (Oxford: Westview Press, 2001).

[20] A troubled childhood led Dostoevsky to become a member of the revolutionary Petrashevsky circle. Apprehended and sentenced to death, he was saved at the last moment and exiled to western Siberia. After years of suffering at Omsk Labor Camp, Dostoevsky emerged a deeply religious man. The atheistic socialism of his youth was replaced by the conviction that the only solution to Russia's problems was the religion of the Russian peasant: Russian Orthodox Christianity. It was this belief that permeated his novels for the rest of his life, beginning with his *Notes from Underground*. For informative biographical accounts of Dostoevsky's early life influences, see: Joseph Frank, *Dostoevsky: The Mantle of the Prophet* (Princeton: Princeton University Press, 2002); Konstantin Mochulsky, *Dostoevsky: His Life and Work*. Trans. by M. A. Minihan (Princeton: Princeton University Press, 1967).

tion of suffering and Arendt's. For it is Ivan's abnegation of individual responsibility which results in the murder of his own father at the hands of the idiot Smerdyakov. And it is Ivan's denial of a standard of justice—that is, of any inherent ordering framework by which the evil he abhors can in fact be oriented—which he finds needful as a means of freeing him from taking responsibility for his own words and deeds. This abrogation of personal responsibility for moral action is also developed by Arendt.

In her report on the Eichmann trials in 1961, Arendt like Dostoevsky links the role of moral awareness (in her case via individual thought and the practical application of judgment) to the personal acceptance of moral responsibility. This is particularly the case in the face of societal norms to the contrary. For Eichmann as for Ivan, it is nothing less than a moral turpitude, a reluctance to take responsibility, which spreads the suffering the thinking soul abhors. Eichmann remains immune to his own guilt, deceived through the hypocrisy of his own disavowal of moral responsibility. Similarly, Ivan's father dies—is murdered, rather, at the hands of Ivan's unsought disciple—and Ivan's soul is filled with self-hate even as his mind's eye cannot escape the knowing leer of Smerdyakov's smile. Eichmann escapes judgment for 18 years in his chosen country of exile, Argentina, whereas Ivan is haunted by apparitions of the devil. However, both are brought to justice: Ivan, before the court of his conscience, against which he struggles to complete the futile task of self-vindication in a godless world, a world which, in the absence of a Higher Judge, finds also absent a court of appeal; Eichmann, before the Jerusalem court, at which his abnegation of personal moral responsibility is likened by Arendt to the arrogant assumption of the moral prerogative to which God is entitled—that of determining punishment as well as guilt.[21] From Dostoevsky we learn that where justice is banished, so too is innocence. The devilish apparition speaks forth from empty rooms, and the memories of Ivan's inaction fill him with shame. From Arendt we see that where responsibility is denied, guilt is multiplied. The unrepentant sinner is not less likely to commit future crimes—he is more.

In the case of Eichmann, his identity is not to be legitimated through forgiveness for the very reason that he insists on denying the identity of first, his crime, then the numerous victims his bureaucratic office managed to transport to their deaths. Eichmann remains "a robotic bureaucrat... incapable of judging his own acts" and therefore self-removed "from the realm of forgiveness" (Kristeva 2001, 233). The example of Dmitri Karamazov could not be in greater contrast. A sensualist at heart as in action, Dmitri's humanity brooks no restraint. For him, the humble admission of guilt is an acknowledgement of humanity, part of the experience of being alive just as much as the experience of pleasure. Dmitri revels in the self-castigation of remorse as in the less distasteful affliction of lovesickness. He prefers, with typical Karamazovian passion, to embrace the cross of self-inflicted pain and to declare himself publicly (but in a way with which we can identify)[22] a scoundrel, rather than to accumulate the still greater dishonour of telling a lie.

For Arendt as for Dostoevsky, suffering is a call to a return to action in a reconciliation mediated by a return to thought—a recognition of moral identity and an awareness of moral space. An acknowledgement of human suffering—

---

[21] Arendt considered Eichmann as deserving of hanging primarily because he acted as though he and his superiors possessed the "right to determine who should and who should not inhabit the world" Arendt 2006, 279.

[22] Similarly, "[i]n Eichmann in Jerusalem, Arendt suggests that our ability to establish new relations with transgressors stems, in part, from our ability to see ourselves in them" (Pettigrove 2006, 488).

of the perversities of the individual soul when left to its own devices for Ivan, or the horrors which fill the gaps where moral responsibility is absent in the case of Eichmann—precedes the exercise of forgiveness, even as it cries out for the response of divine justice or human vengeance. The attribution of the forgiveness-act as an expression of private compassion and the proffering of the forgiveness-gift as a symbolic gesture of collective import each presents a human attempt to forge a bridge from the pain of suffering to the potential for a shared future. In this sense, Hannah Arendt is right: Forgiveness does indeed free us from the irreversibility of the actions of the past as that which otherwise "encloses both doer and sufferer in the relentless automatism of the action process" (Arendt 1998, 241). In essence, forgiveness redeems us from futility. Suffering remains a call to a return to action, political, moral and, yes, religious.[23] In contrast to the calm confidence of Eichmann in his own innocence and the nonimpairment of his rational faculties,[24] the debauchery and self-admitted sensualism of a Dmitri Karamazov seems harmless and inconsequential. Ivan's brother Dmitri is in fact, despite his self-acknowledged depravity, closer to acknowledging human suffering and finding the forgiveness that ameliorates it than either of the aforementioned atheistic alternatives. In the admission of his own proclivity towards the licentious and his aptitude for the excessive, Dmitri is in fact more human in his humility than either Ivan or Eichmann is in the self-reliance of immoral pride. In the

---

[23] "The activity of forgiving, which is central to the New Testament discussion of aphienai on which Arendt draws" may be "often overlooked in the contemporary philosophical literature on forgiveness" (Pettigrove 2006, 486), but it does not for that reason lose its relevance.

[24] Incredibly, Eichmann "declared with great emphasis that he had lived his whole life according to Kant's moral precepts" (Arendt 2006, 135). Moreover, Eichmann was, as he himself declared, "in full possession" of his "physical and psychological freedom."

face of such pride, only a humble, self-aware and other-referent forgiveness can even venture to redeem and restore. In order to venture into a further assessment, a further distinction of terms is first necessary.

II. The differential quotient on pity and compassion: Arendt, Rousseau, and Jesus

Arendt's understanding of forgiveness must be approached with her distinction between compassion and pity in mind.[25] Pity as a general feeling of humanity is expounded best by the Romantic sentimentalism of Jean-Jacques Rousseau. Compassion as an expression of active love from one individual to another is best depicted in the person and work of Jesus Christ. For Arendt, Rousseau is the classic example of this indiscrete "shamelessness" phenomenal to the Romantic Age, in which individual emotion "stood out against a background of indefinite anonymity" which abrogated restraint because it denied distinction (Arendt 1977, 76).[26] Pity

---

[25] Spelman acknowledges that Arendt does have a "high regard for real compassion, especially in comparison with its cruel sister, pity" (Spelman 1997, 66). Spelman furthers this philosophical distinction when she cites Aristotle's view of compassion in his *Nicomachean Ethics* as a matter of *ought* as opposed to an issue of sentiment (pity). For Aristotle, pity premised upon class sentiment is unfounded because "slavery is natural and necessary and hence not a misfortune" (Ibid., 43, 38). Nevertheless, Spelman considers compassion to exhibit a potential towards harm; she likens the energy which compassion finds in addressing suffering to that of a parasite "upon its suffering host" (Ibid., 159). This is partially because Arendt considers compassion to be apolitical in that it tends towards diminishing if not abolishing the distance between men in which action of a political content and significance can take place (Arendt 1977, 76).

[26] "Everything was equally important and nothing forbidden. . . . The importance of emotions existed independently of possible consequences . . . Rousseau related neither his life-story nor his experiences. He merely confessed what he had felt, desired, wished, sensed" (Ibid).

is then the "perversion" of the virtue of compassion (Ibid., 78-9), removing its personal orientation and thus the most genuine aspect of its goodness in favour of a categorical assignation of sentiment on the part of society. Pity, in contrast to the voluntary and individuated exercise of compassion, is a sentiment based on the compulsion of another's necessity (or perceived necessity, through greed or a faulty sense of social or class merits or understanding of identity). Compassion, as with forgiveness, is a purely volitional and individual exchange. It is powerful because it is personal, potent because it is specified.[27]

Arendt locates compassion outside of the political realm and other established hierarchies until the eighteenth century. The point of contention Arendt takes with French Revolution's "passion for compassion" hinges upon its reductionistic view of human existence to material experience. The peasant masses were pitied on account of their hunger. It was in that time that the "passion for compassion" affected European society to such a degree that Rousseau's "innate repugnance at seeing a fellow creature suffer" (Ibid., 61) contributed the theoretical premise which made possible the French Revolution. Indeed, the French Revolution, as distinct from the realism of its American counterpart, adopted a naïve view of human nature, along with a perceived "right to burst with resentment, greed, and envy" typical of modernity

---

[27] This approach to human suffering has been problematized by others such as Spelman, who proposes four definitive modes of engaging with suffering in the human condition: 1) as a means of engaging with humanity directly and seriously; 2) as "the willingness to consider their view of what that suffering means;" 3) as the means of articulating crucial differences among humans; and 4) as applying the experiences of suffering as received by some to an application for the good of others (Spelman 1997, 167-71). For Spelman, compassion can be problematic in that it relies upon suffering in order to find its expression in the confines of the human experience.

and to be contrasted with the more balanced view of envy, greed and the like as vices "no matter where we find them" (Ibid., 63). Where individuals were considered, they were acknowledged by way of emotional sensation rather than rational capacity. As such, the indiscriminate application of pity in response to the perceived sufferings of mass poverty lends itself more to disenfranchisement and destruction than to restoration and rebuilding. Envy is at odds with forgiveness in that it prompts violence and stands as an obstacle to reconciliation. Rousseau's definition of compassion was as erroneous as his utilization of suffering, which he "pitted against the selfishness of society" in the name of a "great effort of a general human solidarization" (Ibid., 71). Thus, Rousseau allocated suffering a catalytic power towards revolutionary change, and it was compassion rather than forgiveness that he upheld as the "natural" solution to the social ills of the period. Arendt would add that forgiveness is political not because it is natural—which she would in fact criticize as "pre-political"[28]—but because it is human. Forgiveness is not natural. Forgiveness requires the focused exercise of human will; it is a product of concentrated effort and voluntary attribution, not of momentary feeling or sentimental impulse.[29] In Arendt's view, it was this sensed "immediacy of suffering" (Ibid., 82) that motivated the so-called compassion of a select segment of the population to amelio-

---

[28] Any re-assertion of the "pre-political" is, for Arendt, rife with problems given the negative connotations of the term. One of these would be the early Greek practice of slavery on the grounds of *politeuein*, that is, as a "pre-political condition" premised upon necessity and thereby demanded by nature (Arendt 2002, 286; and 2007, 718).

[29] Compassion requires the thoughtful differentiation of individuality. This is in contrast to Robespierre's identification of feeling with *le people* in *On Revolution*, "whatever he feels cannot be compassion, because by its nature compassion is something one feels for a particular person" (Spelman 1997, 64).

Filling that Moral Space   111

rate the poverty of the masses, although the primary motivation of the impoverished themselves could more accurately be traced back to hunger, envy or greed.

But it is Jesus, not Rousseau, who stands as the most powerful representative of human compassion and, as Arendt puts it, the "discoverer" of the applicability of forgiveness to human affairs. When Rousseau considered action as the inspiration of empathy to be the most natural human reaction to the suffering of others, he adhered to a faulty definition of compassion as a human feeling. Compassion is only to be considered a feeling in part, for compassion is an act of love—that is, a considered and chosen response to individual suffering. Compassion is not compassion without thought, for without thought it cannot be effectively administered or personally situated. Further, compassion, like forgiveness, is not such without a recognition of the human as an individual capable of volitional action. In Arendt's understanding, Rousseau's utilization of compassion could not be more different from that of Jesus. Indeed, Arendt points to the person of Jesus as "the only completely valid, completely convincing experience Western mankind had ever had with active love of goodness as the inspiring principle of all actions" (Ibid., 72). A closer look at Arendt's view of love shows it to be in fact (and counter to her expressed views elsewhere)[30] political in

---

[30] Although Arendt considers love to be "unworldly" and for that reason "antipolitical," preferring instead respect, which she likens to Aristotle's philia politikē, a "regard for the person from the distance which the space of the world puts between us" as the more political consideration, love is not for that reason to be denied access into the political realm (1998, 242-3). As Pettigrove argues, "forgiveness is one of two faculties that are necessary for political life" in that it counterbalances the unpredictable (and less-than-conducive) effects of action, which, however, remains necessary because it "enables us to emerge as distinct individuals from the backdrop of the undifferentiated life of the species" (2006, 483). Kristeva notes that there may be an element of extremism definitive to forgiveness, in that it is premised upon a "radical exteriority" of

the following sense: as an inspiring example for meaningful personal action.[31]

I will now turn to a discussion of forgiveness in the words of Jesus, whom Arendt considers to be its "discoverer… in the realm of human affairs" (Ibid., 238). Not only does Arendt acknowledge that the highest human exemplar of goodness is found in the person of Jesus Christ (Ibid., 72 and 75), but Arendt refers to Dostoevsky's contrast between "the mute compassion of Jesus" and "the eloquent pity of the Inquisitor" in decided favor of the former. For Arendt, the way that Jesus formulates forgiveness is "even more radical" than that of the Old Testament in that the human capacity to forgive, as encapsulated in his example and teachings, corresponds to God's own (Ibid., 239).[32] Similarly, Arendt upholds compassion as conducive to forgiveness in its recognition of human individuality. For her, compassion is affixed to suffering to the degree that it remains "co-suffering" (Ibid., 75). Thus, in stereotyping the suffering of individuals in mass terms, both the Grand Inquisitor and Robespierre "depersonalized the sufferers, lumped them together into an aggregate" with whom they looked upon through the eyes of pity rather than

---

faith in transcendence. Others such as La Caze expand upon Arendt's differentiation between love and respect. La Caze considers forgiveness, as an act of love, to be apart from politics to the degree that it is an act of individual volition; she points to Ricoeur's assertion that "[t]here is no politics of forgiveness" (Ricoeur 2004, 488).

[31] Arendt holds "that only love has the power to forgive. For love, although it is one of the rarest occurrences in human lives, indeed possesses an unequalled power of self-revelation and an unequalled clarity of vision for the disclosure of *who*" (1998, 242). This would seem to indicate the moral applicability of a consideration which has been typically associated with the private sphere, although it is not to conflate the compassion and forgiveness of love (which is expressed as an individual exchange) with the unthinking bestowal of pity (which is predicated upon the urgency of necessity and is proffered *en masse*).

[32] With reference to: Matthew 18:25 and Mark 11:25.

co-suffered by way of compassion.[33] Dostoevsky interpreted Jesus' ability "to have compassion with all men in their singularity... without lumping them together into... one suffering mankind" to be evidence of His Divinity (Ibid.). In contrast, the sentimentality of pity is comprised of a stereotype, a stereotype which can only distort one's view of the suffering to which the individual is exposed and to whose particularity an effective response could be broached.

Both Arendt and Dostoevsky return to Jesus as the exemplar of compassion and forgiveness in the face of the reality of experiential suffering. It was Jesus who took compassion upon the suffering and the sick, even as they pressed upon him as an amorphous multitude (Matthew 14:14). It was Jesus who acted out of compassion even as he suffered the grief of the beheading of his friend and cousin John the Baptist. It was Jesus who stepped across the perceptible barriers of cultural customs, race and gender to give "living water" to the woman at the well in Samaria (John 4:10). Only through the exercise of his individual choice were the multitudes who came together before the Messiah for healing fed when they had no food themselves (Matthew 14:13-23; 15:32-39; Mark 6:30-44; 8:1-13; Luke 9:10-17; and John 6:1-15.). Christ's compassion was the origin of the miraculous, even as he granted a dying gift of grace to the criminal on the cross at his side (Luke 23:32-43). Christ thus depicted in his very human presence and the individuality of his every interaction the forgiveness which comprehends God the Father's justice, the mercy which extends as an expression, not of necessity, but of human choice.[34] The answer to the call for mercy is

---

[33] The person of Christ evinces "[t]he sign of compassion in contrast to the [unacting] loquacity of pity." Arendt shows a marked preference for the former, although moral awareness as such remains informed by both judgment and thought (1977, 76).

[34] For example, Jesus individually responded to the cries of two blind men in Matthew 20, who reached out from the crowd. Jesus

not dependent upon the will of the crowd but upon the will of the supplicant and the will of the benefactor. Mercy is personal, not collective. Forgiveness, as Christ expressed it, is a voluntary act of compassion on the part of the individual—a personal choice.

Similarly, if the portrait the so-called prophet of modernity (Frank 2002) Dostoevsky paints is gazed at unreservedly, then we see as in a mirror the face, if not of God, then of man. Either man becomes God, and thence is obligated to assume responsibility for the suffering of this present age, or God becomes man, and we see in the person of the God-man Christ the exemplar of forgiveness beyond compare in the transformation of suffering into the bridge for human connection with the Divine. This is the God willing to send His One and Only Son to be the condemned and adopt the stance of victim, descended incarnate to suffer and die. The cross becomes, then, not a symbol of suffering so much as of forgiveness—a bridge to relational restoration, to reconciliation through the bestowal and reception of a merciful forgiveness. Guilt is absolved, and the victim becomes the victor, as the Creator transforms the Created through the expression of ultimate concern for the human plight of suffering, a concern that is demonstrated in action.[35]

The solution to the problem of evil as experienced through suffering in the course of human life is not, for Dostoevsky, the cessation of suffering (as many might wish) but rather

---

was known as much for His personal touch as for His healing. Indeed, the response of Jesus to the suffering of individuals is a reflection of his own sorrow and sympathy (see also Matthew 9:36, 14:14; 18:27; 15:32; Luke 15:20; Psalm 78: 38; 86:25; 145:8; 130:7; 103:8-18). This mercy is contiguous with the compassion ascribed to Jehovah in the Old Testament (Psalm 107:8, 13, 19, 28; Jeremiah 12:15).

[35] Divine action, with reference to the Incarnation, is perhaps most famous in the words of John 3:16: "For God so loved the world that He gave . . ."

the eradication of its power by way of the forgiveness-gift: "Let me be sinful before everyone, but so that everyone will forgive me, and that is paradise" (Dostoevsky, 290). Human weakness supplies the need which those around us can meet, the opportunity for God and others to love us unconditionally. In a perfect world, affection would be guaranteed, but love would then lose the agential aspect definitive to it. Suffering points, then, to the freedom of individual will, and with it the potential for further suffering but also forgiveness and voluntary love. The tale of Christ's compassion, as recounted by Arendt (and the fifth chapter of the Gospel of Mark) personifies in a highly individuated manner the transformative power of such love. The exercise of forgiveness as an act of voluntary compassion on the part of the individual is the only way to reconcile personal pain of the past, to heal the wounds inflicted by others and to forgive others for the actions omitted or the sins committed in past practice but now capable of redemption through the generous elevation of victim to benefactor and offender to freedman that is the result of the forgiveness-act.[36]

An evaluation of those around us as distinct individuals is the primary prerequisite for a meaningful interaction with others in the public world of human affairs. It is only when we as individuals can differentiate by way of *who*-ness as opposed to *what*-ness, in addition to the differentiation between who we *are* and who we are *not*, that we can in fact come to terms with our own identities and interact with

---

[36] This view may transcend what La Caze considers to be Arendt's view of political forgiveness as premised upon respect, rather than love. However, I would reiterate that although the categorization of individual forgiveness as an outflow of love (the forgiveness-act) may draw attention to some of its differences from collective forgiveness (the forgiveness-gift) in phenomenal terms, this does not indicate that forgiveness as an act of love cannot be practiced in the public realm, but simply that it must remain voluntary—uncoerced by law and unenforced by society.

other as such as well.[37] The pity so characteristic of Rousseau and Robespierre is like terror—it lumps and stereotypes rather than specifies and interacts. The terror of totalitarianism, for its part, is nothing less than the denial of human personality (an individual consideration) by way of mass mechanization in favor of social system. Terror eliminates the individual, and to that extent it is anti-human.[38] It is when human thought, feeling, will and judgment are subjugated to a bureaucratic system, as evinced most dramatically in the Eichmann trials or the totalitarian movements of the twentieth century, along with the rapid rise in human suffering associated with the banality of evil and pervasive spread of radical evil in modern times[39] that terror comes into effect. Suffering is thus intimately interconnected with forgiveness, in that although suffering does not necessitate (or even promote) forgiveness, suffering does promote the coming to terms with the disparity of human sensations as individuals and thereby serves as a marker of individuation of perspec-

---

[37] As Arendt sees it forgiveness is to be considered successful as a step in the direction of relational rapprochement to the degree that it retains, promotes or shares a sense of identity. "Forgiving and the relationship it establishes is always an eminently personal (though not necessarily individual or private) affair in which *what* was done is forgiven for the sake of *who* did it" (1998, 241).

[38] "Terror as the execution of a law of movement whose ultimate goal is not the welfare of men or the interest of one man but the fabrication of mankind, eliminates individuals for the sake of the species" (Arendt 1967, 311).

[39] There remains some dispute as to the distinction between the two. La Caze, for example, considers Arendt's description of *radical* evil to be defined as "a successive process of stripping human persons of their legal identity ... treating them as superfluous." This is to be contrast to *banal* evil, "an extreme but thoughtless evil, such as that of Eichmann, and cannot be forgiven and must be punished, even though that punishment is incommensurable with the extremity and nature of the crime" (La Caze 2014, 213; Arendt 1998, 241).

tive, responsibility and action on the road to forgiveness and the prospect of relational restoration.

III. Bridges towards a shared future: promises as forgiveness-frames

Arendt's understanding of forgiveness and the making and keeping of promises can be seen as constituting a distinct moral code of politics (La Caze 2014, 209-10).[40] Not only does human morality depend upon the human capacity to forgive and make as well as keep promises, but so too does human freedom. This is so due to the nature of action, which establishes new relationships with a consistency that calls for the need for "forgiving, dismissing, in order to make it possible for life to go on." It is only in such "constant mutual release" that "men remain free agents" (Ibid., 240). The complementary relationship of forgiving and promising correlates to the capacity of action to impact beyond the field of the contemporaneous and beyond the range of the intended. Forgiving is like promising in its (literally) supernatural power to redeem from the futility associated with the inevitable.[41] But it is the unpredictability inherent to forgiveness as a human attribute that facilitates the freeing of "both the one who forgives and the one who is forgiven." The voluntary temper of forgiveness derives from, on the one hand, a Pauline and Augustinian influence and, on the other, the Greek conception of political action. In this context, Arendt cites Jesus' teaching of forgiveness as "the freedom from vengeance"

---

[40] Similarly, Kristeva intimates in her philosophical assessment of Arendt that only moral beings can be forgiven (2001, 232-3). I would also add that only moral beings can forgive.

[41] "Forgiveness offers no route 'backwards' beyond the actuality of action, but has the capacity to break up the process engendered by it, and to negate the will to vengeance" and thus contribute to the capacity for new beginnings made more certain by the giving of a promise (Walsh 2011, 130).

and its bondage to suffering and the "relentless automatism" with which the human condition would be otherwise afflicted.

Forgiveness and the making and keeping of promises are interconnected—dependent, as it were, upon the will to use (and the means of accessing) spaces in which thinking adults can inter-relate "directly out of the will to live together." As such, Arendt likens them to "control mechanisms" for the capacity to act and begin what is new (1998, 246).[42] Thus, the choice to forgive also involves the stepping out into a relational space. Forgiveness is an inter-human passageway; as such, forgiveness provides a public space for freedom, for the exercise of political action proper.[43] Forgiveness does not cover over the past; rather, it bridges across it in the direction of a shared future. Indeed, Arendt is quite clear as to the propositional power of promise-making and -keeping as conducive to human stability: "The remedy for… the chaotic uncertainty of the future, is contained in the faculty to make and keep promises" (1998, 237). But this faculty is tied to the forgiveness-act, which "serves to undo the deeds of the past" and thereby frees us from the inadvertent consequences of past actions. A world without forgiveness, then, is for Arendt

---

[42] As per Pettigrove's assessment of Arendt, forgiveness involves the three elements of: 1) release; 2) commitment; and 3) gradual change. Moreover, "[t]o ask forgiveness is to imply and sometimes even to express a promise: you can count on me not to do this sort of thing again" (Pettigrove 2006, 485-6).

[43] This is not to dismiss La Caze's conclusion that "[m]uch faith and hope in goodwill" would be needed to apply forgiveness as an all-sufficient category to political life (La Caze 2011, 151). I agree with this statement. What I would like to contest is La Caze's problematization of Arendt's distinction between pity and compassion "Arendt views compassion as something that affects us without leading to action, and pity as a violent force in public life" (Ibid., 160). I consider this to be a faulty conflation of Arendt's views with those of Rousseau, whose ideas she represents rather than shares.

"not unlike the sorcerer's apprentice who lacked the magic formula to break the spell" (Ibid.). The political portrait Arendt paints is what Kristeva calls a trans-Christian locus of new beginnings,[44] based as it is upon two notions—"the birth of individuals and the frailty of actions"—and upon two so-called "psychopolitical interventions—forgiveness and the promise" (2001, 204). Arendt considers "the power of stabilization inherent in the faculty of making promises" as tracing back to both Abram's travels from Ur in the Genesis account, his "passionate drive toward making covenants" that demonstrates "the power of mutual promise" (Ibid., 243), and, in more legal terms, the system of the Romans with their *pacta sunt servanda*.

Promises are forgiveness-framing gifts from one group of humans to another (in contrast to the individuation inherent to compassion as forgiveness-act). Further, promises are only viable in proportion to the truthfulness of those who make them.[45] In much the same way as deception is the hallmark of the totalitarian regime (Arendt 1967, 333, 375-82, 413-5, 430), it is upon truth-telling that the very basis of political legitimacy rests. In their humanness, forgiveness and the making and keeping of promises mark a departure from the cyclical processes of nature. However, the moral agency of the individual so characteristic of the forgiveness-act does not deny the physical reality of human suffering. Rather, the

---

[44] Others view Arendt's conception of forgiveness in terms more political and secular than personal and religious, with a view of morality and politics as occurring in "two distinct realms" (La Caze 2011, 153 and 158). For La Caze, Arendt's analysis of the role of forgiveness in a political sense is based more on the political consideration of respect than on the moral consideration of love.

[45] See: Hannah Arendt, *Crises of the Republic: Lying in Politics, Civil Disobedience on Violence, Thoughts on Politics, and Revolution* (New York: Harcourt Brace Jovanovich, 1972); Hannah Arendt and Liliane Weissberg, *Rahel Varnhagen: The Life of a Jewess* (Baltimore, MD: Johns Hopkins University Press, 1997), 91-3, 244.

giving of forgiveness marks the completion of love through the rendering of that which is most distinctly human: the choice to give, to love without demand for repayment. For Arendt, the intimacy of love may be "always an eminently personal" affair; it is not for that reason private (1998, 241).[46] Rather, forgiveness, as an attribute of love can and does serve an identifying function in the public sphere. As Kristeva notes from Nietzsche, it is only moral beings who can suffer, remember and again suffer in remembrance of that which was experienced (2001, 231-2), but it is also only moral beings who can forgive and in turn be forgiven. Love completes the verification of moral agency as it solidifies human identity; and forgiveness, as an act of love, reaches out to extend, through promises and the memory that is retained of them, that which is lost with the death of each individual if it is not shared across the spaces *inter esse homines*, between which we are. Thus, the gift which Arendt most upholds is that of the promise—the promise orients the promise-maker to the human condition as a whole, and the making of a promise establishes the inheritance of the generations to come, prompting them to make and fulfil promises on their part.

IV. The power of forgiveness in practice: memory, narration, and the promise

This assessment of the relationship between forgiveness and suffering would be incomplete without some mention of the capacity which distinguishes humanity from the cyclical renewal of other animal life: the capacity to remember and retell. Forgiveness can only be apprehended in the contextu-

---

[46] However, love in its fullest manifestation can only be understood in personal terms. Similarly, as Spelman argues, Arendt points to the difficulty of communicating private pain, which suggests that "suffering cannot become public ... without becoming dangerously distorted" (Spelman 1997, 63).

alization of a narrative, and the forgiveness-act is one initiated by individual authors within a broader human story. In this sense, forgiveness possesses the capacity to affect beyond the immediate situation which it serves to redress; forgiveness, when coupled with the capacity to remember and retell, can not only heal the wounds of the past and restore the relationships of the present, but inspire forgiveness-acts of the future. In this section, I will discuss how forgiveness not only elevates the victim but restores the focus back from an issue of debt to the identity of the persons between whom the debt is remitted, and, thence, to a reinstatement of meaningful relations and practical exchanges.

Thus far in this chapter I have argued that Arendt views human suffering as carrying political weight not primarily as a stimulus to political action but as an identifier of private personhood. However, forgiveness occurs only in response to action. Indeed, it *is* in fact a form of action. In this sense forgiveness is not an abrogation of personal responsibility but rather the voluntary assumption of it. The creditor who chooses to release from a debt does not do so out of pity; he does so out of a personal response to a sense of higher duty, or as a personal exception to a general rule in response to the appeal of an individual voice. Those are not released from their debts who reform with the most vigor but who call out with humble and diligent desperation.[47] Forgiveness is that which can only be fostered, not forced. The power of forgiveness, then, is in direct proportion to the absorption of personal responsibility that the forgiver—who was transgressed against—is willing to assume and who thereby becomes a part of that incredible transformation of the victim into the victor, the reversal of positions so definitive to the

---

[47] God Himself forgives those who humble themselves and call upon His Name. See for example: 2 Samuel 22:4; 2 Chronicles 7:14; Psalm18:3; Psalm 145: 18; Joel 2:32; Acts 2:21.

forgiveness-act. When the forgiver forgives, the forgiven is released—saved, so to speak, from the consequences of his or her actions to the degree that the forgiver is willing (and capable) to take on these consequences instead.[48]

For Arendt, the power of forgiveness is that it calls a halt to the unintended or unanticipated consequences of human actions. The power of forgiveness lies not in the abrogation of justice or the absolution of physical consequence but in *the willingness to absorb the consequences of the sins of the transgressor.* This is not to say that forgiveness can undo that which was done.[49] Along these lines, Arendt describes the horrors of the Holocaust in dramatic terms, as if they "transcend all moral categories" as "something men could neither punish *adequately* nor forgive" (2006, 125). Arendt does not consider forgiveness as fully apprehensible by modern man, in much the way as the disease of evil often seems beyond hope of a cure. Against such horrors, only Christ's identification with human suffering stands in history as the fulfilment of full and gratuitous forgiveness in this comprehensive sense.[50] Similarly, only God's love is truly perfect (holy) and only Divine forgiveness can be full and free; only He has the ability to back up the promises He makes, and to keep the covenants which He makes. In the Christian understanding, humans are allotted the strength to "forgive those who sin against them" to the extent that they acknowledge and rely

---

[48] The substitution of Christ's sinless life for fallen man's earthly sins remains the purest example of this.

[49] The *skandalon* or "stumbling stone" of evil cannot be removed by human powers, nor can the damages it inflicts be fully repaired by human effort (Arendt and Kohn 2003, 125).

[50] Hebrews 2:17-18 "Therefore, in all things He had to be made like [His] brethren, that He might be a merciful and faithful High Priest in things [pertaining] to God, to make propitiation for the sins of the people. For in that He Himself has suffered, being tempted, He is able to aid those who are tempted."

upon God's superhuman strength to do so.[51] Forgiveness demands an admission of human weakness, a coming to terms with the record of the past,[52] before it can exercise a superhuman grace, the only grace which remains capable of elevating the subhuman to the lofty status from which he (or she) has fallen: the quality of being human in a prelapsarian sense, immune to evil's contagion and spared from its effects.

Forgiveness, therefore, relates to judgment. Only an entity capable of judging is capable of choosing, and only an entity capable of choosing is capable of acting. The giving of forgiveness recognizes the humanity and the feelings of both entities involved in the exchange. Forgiveness recognizes the humanity of the offended and restores the humanity of the offender. The bestowal of the forgiveness-act shifts the focus from the moral error of the transgressor to the moral goodness of the giver. However, forgiveness does not necessarily indicate a return of full trust—forgiving is not the same as forgetting. Dependent upon the evidence of a demonstrable record of previous actions to validate the claim of trustworthiness, trust is thereby not as independent of reciprocity as is forgiveness in isolation. If forgiveness can occur wherever the victim is willing to believe that what is to be gained from the release of bitterness surpasses what can be retained with it, trust is then based upon two considerations: 1) a record of demonstrable action on the part of the offender, which legitimates the reclamation of a relational orientation; and 2) the

---

[51] A recent example of this would be the unexpected forgiveness of Dylan Roof on the part of the surviving relatives of those he murdered at the Emanuel African Methodist Episcopal Church on June 17, 2015 in Charleston, South Carolina.

[52] As Arendt writes: "For us, it is decisive that, as we mentioned before, the faculty of remembering is what prevents wrongdoing" (Arendt and Kohn 2003, 124).

capacity to remember the benefits which such reconciliation promises.[53]

Arendt applies these principles implicitly when she associates the aptitude for promise-making and -keeping with the continuance of human creativity, the guarantee of human meaning through memory, and the means of maintaining the order of a common world in which meaningful actions can be shared, communicated and transcribed for the inspiration of the generations of the future (1998, 237, 243-7; and 1977, 158, 162-3, 166-8, and 173-4). Thus, the generative and reconciliatory power of forgiveness as a response to human suffering is realized and appreciated and full in the long-term. This is because forgiveness does not deny the presence of human pain; forgiveness does not change the reality of living within the parameters of the human condition. Nor does forgiveness demand a response; "forgiveness is aimed at the person, and not the act" (Kristeva 2001, 232). Forgiveness does not deny the possibility of future injury, as it does not forget the experiences of past hurt, which loses its formative value and educative role to the degree that it is forgotten. Rather, forgiveness is a practical mechanism—perhaps the most effective of all inspired ideals of action—to cope with the human condition and to address the problems systemic to human being-in-the-world in a personable and life-giving way.

Not all philosophers view the human capacity to remember or forgive in a favorable light. The reason Friedrich Nietzsche denounced the human "beast" for the continued suffering brought about through remembrance (Ibid.),[54] is that suffering is linked to memory. However, so too is relational lon-

---

[53] Although she does not propose these two statements in direct terms, Arendt would support both of these propositions.

[54] With reference to Arendt's *The Life of the Mind,* Vol. I, "On Thinking."

Filling that Moral Space 125

gevity, cultural meaning and socio-political stability. Humans can only be reduced to an animal existence to the degree that they are willing to farewell the safety and beauty, the cleanliness and order, the comforts and relationships of human community, which are passed down to us from preceding generations and maintained for the generations to come on the basis of promises and the continued trust that is placed in them. Nietzsche's description of the promise as "'an active refusal' or a 'memory of the will'" (Ibid.)[55] in terms of "hardness, cruelty, and pain because it inherits the debts [*Schulden*] of an invariably guilty conscience [*Schuld*] in the same way a debtor inherits the debts of his creditor" (Ibid.)[56] does remain useful, however, in that it denotes two claims for our inference: 1) only moral beings can remember; and 2) only moral beings can forgive and in turn be forgiven. Thus, the reception of forgiveness equates to an assumption of moral worth and the recognition of a moral standard by means of which individuals can inter-relate.

Further, not all theorists hold that forgiveness is possible. Jacques Derrida argues that unconditional freedom—and, as a result, the exercise of the forgiveness-act—is beyond the realm of the human.[57] And not all theorists consider forgiveness to be necessary. Marguerite La Caze, for one, asserts that reconciliation can occur without recourse to the for-

---

[55] Citing Friedrich Nietzsche, *The Genealogy of Morals*, 63, 62.

[56] Citing Nietzsche, *The Genealogy of Morals*, 63, 72-3.

[57] In point of fact, Derrida is partially correct in his claim that forgiveness without apology is possible, along with its implication that the victim is thereby obligated to forgive: Yes, forgiveness without apology is possible, but no victim can ever be obligated to forgive. It may be for the benefit of the victim to forgive the offender, to the degree that forgiveness entails the positional reversal of victim to victor I described earlier; forgiveness is freeing, in much the same way as confession is cathartic (Derrida 2001, 30 and 47).

giveness-act.[58] As such, La Caze reiterates Derrida's disassociation of forgiveness and reconciliation[59] because, for her, political forgiveness is based not on respect but on love (La Caze 2006, 456). Arendt does not consider love to be political (Arendt 1998, 242) and therefore views political forgiveness to be premised upon respect (Ibid., 243). Love is personal and demonstrated as human to the degree that it is a product of human volition and thereby goes beyond any normative expectation or justifiable demand for conscripted practice. The unconditional forgiveness which Derrida describes may be beyond the capacity of the human unaided by the divine—that is, by the self-giving of Christ-like love—but it is not for that reason to be denied the possibility of exercise in the public sphere of politics. In its relation to it, forgiveness remains, as does love in the words of Reinhold Niebuhr, "the impossible possibility."[60] In other words, forgiveness is be-

---

[58] I would like to express my gratitude to Marguerite La Caze for her informative conversation on this topic, in addition to her comments on an earlier version of this essay.

[59] La Caze considers the giving of an apology to be "a responsibility more central than that of forgiveness" in contrast to Derrida's categorization of apologies as inferior by virtue of their practicality. But this is an incomplete representation of the subtlety of relational interactions premised upon trust. Trust—not merely a return to the rigidity of external forms of interpersonal exchange—is an indispensable ingredient to any lasting reconciliation, as it is to the fulfilment of any promise. Reconciliation must include trust, which is not to be reduced to the perfunctory fulfilment of a transactional exchange. Forgiveness can take place with or without full reconciliation. But full reconciliation cannot be achieved without forgiveness. Moreover, forgiveness does not require an apology, and true forgiveness neither demands nor expects it.

[60] This is the theme of Reinhold Niebuhr's second chapter in: *An Interpretation of Christian Ethics* (New York and London: Harper & Brothers, 1935). Later on in the book, Niebuhr also describes forgiveness as an expression of love, the "genius of prophetic Christianity." Arendt would agree: "Compassion and goodness may be related phenomena," although the topic of compassion is "goodness beyond virtue and evil beyond vice" (1977, 73). Both are sup-

yond that which can be easily achieved, yet it is possible, as demonstrated by the example of Christ. Indeed, it is love that is the motivation for any meaningful repetition in the world of human affairs. This notion is encapsulated in Arendt's statement of *amor mundi* (Arendt and Kohn 205, 203), through which both mortality and natality retain their relevance as inextricable features of the human condition. But the effects of *amor mundi*—love of the world—go beyond those actions spanned by the individual human life, as does, I would assert, forgiveness.

Conclusion

To conclude, in this chapter I have argued that it is the possibility of human forgiveness that fills the gaps generated by the reality of human suffering and thereby draws our attention to spaces of moral recognition requisite for identification of human individuals in experiential terms. Arendt applies what is often considered to be a moral understanding of forgiveness to the spaces she identifies as indispensable to the political. For her, it was Rousseau who identified the compelling thrust of human emotion in the political realm. However, Rousseau and his unintended disciple Robespierre lost their bearings when they combined an aggravated sensitivity to human feeling with a politics of coercion. Recent developments of forgiveness by Derrida generate a similar

---

ported by those such as Derrida and Jankélévitch, who hold that in situations of unquantifiable evil, forgiveness may feel or indeed be impossible in human terms. Derrida is probably the most famous representative of those who argue that forgiveness may not even be a desirable end or a moral imperative in some situations: Jacques Derrida, "On Forgiveness," in *On Cosmopolitanism and Forgiveness*, trans. Michael Hughes (New York: Routledge, 2002), 25-60. See also Derrida, "To Forgive: The Unforgivable and the Imprescriptible," trans. Elizabeth Rottenberg, in Questioning God, ed. John D. Caputo, Mark Dooley, and Michael J. Scanlon (Bloomington and Indianapolis: Indiana University Press, 2001).

confusion of conceptual categories: While Derrida is correct in stating that forgiveness is to an extent attributable to the divine, it is not therefore beyond human applicability. A return to the well-considered exercise of compassionate mercy seen in the example of Jesus, a response to the desperate cry of the individual—as opposed to the reactive sentimentalism characteristic of undifferentiated pity—exemplifies through the God-man Christ the possibility of a human action inspired by divine impulse. For Arendt, forgiveness is of political application not so much in its affinity to the Divine as in its applicability to and by that which is human. It is forgiveness, paired with action, which lends us the capacity to not only complete what is willed and enact what is thought, but redeem that which was wronged and repair that which was broken. Forgiveness frees us from the irreversibility of past action even as it bridges towards the possibility of a shared future, a future that could only be fractured without it.

Suffering, as I have argued, is the gap which forgiveness bridges. As such, forgiveness creates an experiential bond between individuals as fellow humans capable of shared pain. Forgiveness thereby highlights the public need for spaces of appearance in which the voluntary exercise of individual choice can take place—filling, so to speak, a moral space. In this chapter I have outlined the significance of Arendt's treatment of the forgiveness-act in relation to both the suffering from which it springs and the promise to which it leads. Forgiveness as an individual act (compassion) differs in scope to forgiveness as a collective gift (promise), but neither of these merciful expressions is to be confused with the sentimental push of a plea made with reference to the urgency of material necessity (pity). Be that as it may, the presence and perception of great evil in the form of experiential suffering—as seen in the resolution of the problem of suffering in Dostoevsky's great novel—predicates the existence of the human potential towards good. From Dostoevsky we learn that where justice is banished, so too is innocence.

More—we learn that the cries of suffering can only be responded by the divine gift of human love. For Arendt, human history derives its significance insofar as it is a record of human sufferings and provides us with the opportunity for fuller self-recognition and forgiveness.[61] The purpose derived from memory of meaningful suffering reveals that hope is connected to memory; vision for the future is inextricably bound to knowledge of the past. The sufferings of others is only rendered valuable in this world to the extent that it can be shared through story to alleviate the current sufferings of others, prevent the enactment of those conditions which engender suffering, or, in the most compelling and virtuous of these, to remove the price that is paid by others for the infliction of suffering. As we have seen, an understanding of forgiveness depends upon a coming to terms, of sorts, with the reality of human suffering. From the cries of the innocent to the disturbing culmination of atheistic disregard in the sin of patricide committed in Dostoevsky's *The Brothers Karamazov*, to the importance of the individual's ownership of moral responsibility in Arendt's assessment of the Eichmann trials, we see that the reality of human suffering is tied to an understanding of the all-too-human need for the gift of forgiveness. Forgiveness is an act which ties together the considerations of individuals even as it recognizes the feelings which separate them as such. Forgiveness is the connective tissue which strengthens the remedial scar even as it heals, the regenerating material to repair bridges between the past and the present, with expansions extending towards the hope of a shared future.

---

[61] "In the modern age history emerged as something it never had been before. It was no longer composed of the deeds and sufferings of men, and it no longer told the story of events affecting the lives of men; it became a man-made process, the only all-comprehending process which owes its existence exclusively to the human race" (Arendt 1958, 585).

In the end desolation is in fact a reminder of humanity, a call to action and an opportunity for inspiration, in that it lays bare the need for infilling. Love, whether experienced in the intimacy of privacy by Arendt, or canvassed with all the publicity of moral inspiration (and thus political motivation), makes its presence felt by way of forgiveness. We cannot be forced to forgive. It must remain, by definition, forever a choice—not a duty. What we can do, however, is foster an environment in which forgiveness can operate freely. Forgiveness is only made possible by reliance upon the strength of divine example. It is not a requirement but a moral choice, and for that reason it is to be admired all the more when it is rendered. Suffering is thus, in the final analysis, the validation for the human need for forgiveness. What makes forgiveness human is in fact its proclivity to recognize humanity in individual terms, for it is only in the voluntary extension of forgiveness—much like the granting of a favor—that the reality of human suffering can come full circle in a recognition not only of human identity but of the human need for forgiveness. Suffering allows us to understand to a fuller extent what a world without forgiveness would be.

References

Arendt, Hannah. 1953. "Ideology and Terror: A Novel Form of Government." *The Review of Politics* 15.3: 303-27.

_____. 1958. "The Modern Concept of History." *The Review of Politics* 20.4: 570-90.

_____. 1960. "Society and Culture." *Daedalus* 89.2: 278-87.

_____. 1967. *The Origins of Totalitarianism*. London: Allen & Unwin.

_____. 1968. Between Past and Future: Eight Exercises in Political Thought. New York: Viking Press.

_____. 1972. *Crises of the Republic: Lying in Politics, Civil Disobedience on Violence, Thoughts on Politics, and Revolution*. New York: Harcourt Brace Jovanovich.

_____. 1977. *On Revolution*. New York: Penguin.

_____. 1998. *The Human Condition*. Chicago: University of Chicago Press.

_____. 2002. "Karl Marx and the Tradition of Western Political Thought." *Social Research* 69.2: 273-319.

_____. 2006. *Eichmann in Jerusalem: A Report on the Banality of Evil*. New York: Penguin Books.

_____. 2007. "The Great Tradition: 1. Law ad Power." *Social Research* 74.3: n.p.

Arendt, Hannah and Liliane Weissberg. 1997. *Rahel Varnhagen: The Life of a Jewess*. Baltimore, MD: Johns Hopkins University Press.

Arendt, Hannah and Jerome Kohn. 2003. "Some Questions of Moral Philosophy." *Responsibility and Judgment*. New York: Schocken Books.

Baehr, Peter. 2010. *Hannah Arendt, Totalitarianism, and the Social Sciences*. Stanford, CA: Stanford University Press, 2010.

Benhabib, Seyla. 1988. "Judgment and the Moral Foundations of Politics in Arendt's Thought." *Political Theory* 16: 29-51.

_____. 2003. *The Reluctant Modernism of Hannah Arendt*. Lanham, MD: Rowman & Littlefield.

Caputo, John D., Mark Dooley, and Michael J. Scanlon. 2001. *Questioning God*. Bloomington IN: Indiana University Press.

Derrida, Jacques. 2001. "To Forgive: The Unforgivable and the Imprescriptible'." *Questioning God*. Edited by J.D. Caputo, M. Dooley and M.J. Scanlon. Bloomington: Indiana University Press, 2001.

_____. 2002. "On Forgiveness." *On Cosmopolitanism and Forgiveness*. Translated by Michael Hughes. New York: Routledge.

Dostoevsky, Fyodor. 2002. *The Brothers Karamazov*. New York: North Point Press.

Frank, Joseph. 2002. *Dostoevsky: The Mantle of the Prophet.* Princeton: Princeton University Press.

Kohn, Hans. 1961. *Prophets and Peoples.* New York: Collier Books.

Kristeva, Julia. 2001. *Hannah Arendt.* New York: Columbia University Press.

Kroeker, P. Travis and Bruce K. Ward. 2001. *Remembering the End: Dostoevsky as Prophet to Modernity.* Oxford: Westview Press.

La Caze, Marguerite. 2006. "The Asymmetry between Apology and Forgiveness." Theory and Practice, Contemporary Political Theory 5.4: 447-68.

_____. 2011. "The Miraculous Power of Forgiveness and the Promise." *Action and Appearance: Ethics and the Politics of Writing in Hannah Arendt.* Edited by Anna Yeatman et al. London: Continuum.

_____. 2014. "Promising and Forgiveness." *Hannah Arendt: Key Concepts.* Edited by Patrick Hayden. London: Routledge.

Mochulsky, Konstantin. 1967. *Dostoevsky: His Life and Work.* Translated by M. A. Minihan. Princeton: Princeton University Press.

Neiman, Susan. 2001. "Theodicy in Jerusalem." *Hannah Arendt in Jerusalem.* Edited by S. Aschheim. Berkeley, CA: University of California Press.

Niebuhr, Reinhold. 1935. *An Interpretation of Christian Ethics.* New York and London: Harper & Brothers.

Pettigrove, Glen. 2006. "Hannah Arendt and Collective Forgiving." *Journal of Social Philosophy* 37.4: 483-500

Ricoeur, Paul. 2004. *Memory, History, Forgetting.* Translated by Kathleen Blamey and David Pellauer. Chicago: Chicago University Press.

Spelman, Elizabeth V. 1997. *Fruits of Sorrow: Framing our Attention to Suffering.* Boston: Beacon Press, 1997.

Walsh, Philip. 2011. "*The Human Condition* as Social Ontology: Hannah Arendt on Society, Action and Knowledge." *History of the Human Sciences* 24.2: 120-37.

Chapter 5

"Her loyalty survived his foolishness:" Hannah Arendt, Martin Heidegger, and Forgiveness

Margaret Betz

The unfolding of history

The more than half a century-long friendship between the philosophers Hannah Arendt and Martin Heidegger remains one of the most dramatic chapters of twentieth century philosophy. The nature and history of their relationship was fascinating, complex, and still remains confounding to many. At 18, Arendt met Heidegger when she was his student at the University of Marburg in the 1920s. A romantic affair began, complete with poetry, secret notes and clandestine meetings.[62] Not only was Arendt substantially younger than the married Heidegger, but she was Jewish and he was Cath-

---

[62] Arendt's affair with Heidegger has been the lens through which some view her and her work. The impact on the perception of Arendt has not always been flattering. (Catherine Clément's 2001 controversial novel *Martin and Hannah* fictionalizes this affair, with the book jacket describing how they "sustained their passion for five decades.") Critics note the harm a sensationalistic approach has done to Arendt's reputation as a woman philosopher in a way it has not affected Heidegger's (the one who was not only in the position of power, but the married one of the two). In an article on *Slate.com* entitled, "The Evil of Banality," Ron Rosenbaum begins with the question, "Will we ever think of Hannah Arendt the same way again?" Rosenbaum refers to Arendt's "lifelong romantic infatuation" with Heidegger and disgustedly considers hers an apologist approach to his Nazism.

olic. Eventually the affair ended with Heidegger encouraging Arendt to study under Karl Jaspers at Heidelberg. The two parted ways and their relationship transformed into a lifelong friendship for Arendt.

By the 1930s, that friendship was tested by Heidegger's involvement in the Nazi party and the accolades and opportunities it brought him, sometimes at the expense of a number of Jews to whom he had been close. In May of 1933, Heidegger became Rector of Freiberg University, weeks after becoming a member of the Nazi party. He presented his inaugural address in military attire, and many of the important seats were reserved for Nazi officials; the historical address has become noteworthy for Heidegger's praise of Nazism.[63] Furthermore, Heidegger continued his public support of Nazism even after leaving his official position as Rector and was no longer under obligation to officially promote it.[64]

Arendt's experiences during this period were equally as dramatic. In 1933, Arendt was in Berlin cautiously watching the rise of the Third Reich. The same year that Heidegger became Rector of the university under Nazism, Arendt was in the Prussian State Library gathering documentation of Germany's anti-Semitic activities; her findings would later be disseminated around the world. As Heidegger donned a Nazi

---

[63] One of the most troubling aspects of Heidegger's appointment was his issuing the "Baden Decree" which removed all non-Aryans from university positions, with full knowledge that would include his mentor, Edmund Husserl. (Born a Jew, Husserl had converted to Christianity yet was nonetheless ethnically a Jew according to Nazism.) Learning of this, Arendt surmised in a letter to Jaspers that this sent Husserl to an early grave. Heidegger also agreed to have his dedication to Husserl removed from later printings of his most important work, *Being and Time*.

[64] See Yvonne Sherratt's *Hitler's Philosophers* for an examination of Heidegger's anti-Semitism. Sherratt cites, for example, Heidegger's use of the term *Verjudung* ("Jewificiation" 2013) in a letter, the term Hitler used in *Mien Kampf*.

uniform, Arendt was simultaneously using her Berlin apartment as a safe house for those attempting to escape Germany and its increasingly anti-Semitic policies. Arendt was arrested for her subversive activities but managed to escape and leave Germany. Fleeing to Paris, she ended up in a French internment camp. Arendt was eventually able to flee the camp, an event of sheer serendipity considering that many of her campmates were later transported to Germany for extermination. By 1941, Arendt finally made her way to the United States. Arendt and Heidegger had no contact and would not communicate again for seventeen years.

Heidegger was among other German scholars, academics, and professionals who had supported Nazism and personally benefitted from it. With the fall of Germany and the end of the war came many pitiful attempts by those same intellectuals searching for whatever means possible to distance themselves from the regime; Heidegger was no exception. His personal writings of the time reveal a man feeling persecuted, troubled that he should be "singled out for punishment and defamation" (Sherratt 2013, 244). Heidegger convinced officials of his minimal involvement and was granted Emeritus status, yet was also banned from teaching. He sunk into a deep depression as he surveyed his tattered reputation, although not noticeably troubled by who or what the Third Reich had destroyed. Heidegger never publicly apologized for his involvement in Nazism, nor publicly expressed any sympathy for its countless victims.[65]

---

[65] Heidegger did explain to his old friend Jaspers that the reason he stopped visiting was "not because a Jew lived there [Jaspers' wife Gertrude was Jewish] but simply because I was ashamed." Jaspers believed Heidegger, and said as much in a letter to Arendt in which he declared, "Never an anti-Semite himself, he sometimes behaved very well towards Jews…[A]nd sometimes he behaved badly…[H]is behavior towards Husserl was another case of obedience to the Nazis" (*Correspondence*, 630). It is noteworthy those who knew

Once the war ended and the full extent of the atrocities became public, Arendt and Heidegger reestablished contact when Arendt returned to Germany for the first time in 1949. By Arendt's account of their first meeting post-war, Heidegger was "shame faced, like a dog with his tail between his legs" (Young-Bruehl 1982, 246). She clearly struggled with being betrayed by such a dear old friend yet Arendt chose, nonetheless, to forgive Heidegger and resume their friendship. Her former student and biographer Elisabeth Young-Bruehl writes, "she could…not change the fact that he had spent a year in the Nazi party or the fact that many people were unwilling to forgive him" (Ibid., 305). Arendt likewise knew that some would question her forgiving him. As a window into this thought process, Arendt revealed a great deal about how she regarded Heidegger post-war by contrasting herself with mentor Karl Jaspers, an old friend of Heidegger's who had become estranged from him: "Jaspers only sees the *Unheil* (mischief)," Arendt explained, "and not the other side of the coin" (Ibid.).

Arendt's willingness to forgive Heidegger tarnished her reputation as many have struggled over the decades to understand why, including Jaspers himself. How is it possible to forgive what has been regarded as unforgiveable? How, indeed, considering Heidegger never publicly expressed contrition for the role he played in the promotion of Nazi ideology and anti-Semitic policies. The contrite wrongdoer provides a gift to the wronged by opening a door—but what possible paths towards forgiveness exist for the non-contrite? The question, then, becomes why would she forgive him? In her book, *Hitler's Philosophers*, Yvonne Sherratt argues that Arendt "bought [Heidegger's] excuses and celebrated his

---

Heidegger did not particularly view his involvement with Nazism as motivated by anti-Semitism (*1992*, ft.3, 791).

genius."[66] While it is understandable some are left with this impression, such a view does not adequately grasp the depth of both Arendt's disappointment as well as her affection for Heidegger. Arendt's writings periodically critiqued Heidegger, and her private correspondences regularly criticized his behavior.[67]

This chapter explores the concept of forgiveness for Hannah Arendt and the impact it had on her relationship with Martin Heidegger. Nine years after their reconciliation in her book, *The Human Condition,* Arendt included a section she entitled "Irreversibility and the Power to Forgive." Utilizing Arendt's philosophy of forgiveness allows us to critically examine a choice some have labelled "inexcusable." In her recent John Locke Lecture Series, Martha Nussbaum's analysis of anger and the related concept of forgiveness is critical of "backward-looking anger," advocating rather a forward-looking constructive attitude through a forgiveness rooted in generosity. Arendtian forgiveness, focused on constructively moving forward, embodies Nussbaum's model.[68]

---

[66] For a more nuanced, philosophical interpretation of Heidegger viewing National Socialism as a "national aestheticism," see Dana Villa's *Arendt and Heidegger.* Villa writes, "Heidegger's thundering silence on the question of the Extermination – his blindness to its implications for 'the destiny of the West'—is clearly a function of his earlier complicity with a regime whose racism he found vulgar, yet which he nevertheless tolerated" (1996, 259).

[67] For instance, Arendt wrote to Jaspers that she believed Heidegger suffered from a "lack of character" (*1992,* 142). Jacques Taminiaux has written extensively on Arendt's work as a rejection of Heidegger's perspective. See his *The Thracian Maid and the Professional Thinker.*

[68] Nussbaum argues anger is often normatively problematic, as are many resulting forms of forgiveness that are often just veiled forms of vengeance through humiliation. See Nussbaum: *Anger and Forgiveness: Resentment, Generosity and Justice,* based on these lectures.

In reference to an allegory she wrote in her private journals, we learn that Arendt was prepared to forgive "the fox." Arendt's willingness to forgive Heidegger is often portrayed as a schoolgirl's "blind devotion." Far from this reductive explanation, Arendt's philosophy, often critical of Heidegger, offers an opportunity to grasp her reasons for forgiving the unforgiveable. It involves addressing the professional blind spot Heidegger possessed as a "philosopher's philosopher," according to Arendt, and the near-guaranteed failures and missteps that creates in the political realm. In contrast to Heidegger, Arendt possessed an almost-reverent regard for the *vita activa*, the political life of action. She contends that fundamental to the fragile existence of political action and its survival is the possibility of forgiveness. This chapter examines the philosophical basis for why Arendt was willing to forgive (which is not identical to excuse) Heidegger's endorsement of Nazism. It is based in Arendt's belief that, common to most philosophers, Heidegger's "political judgments and his actions [can] be found in his philosophy" (1992, 629).

Arendt's Political Philosophy

Within the "Action" chapter of her book, *The Human Condition* (published after reconciling with Heidegger), Arendt included a section entitled "Irreversibility and the Power to Forgive."[69] Forgiveness becomes an indispensable component of political action, according to Arendt, because of action's fundamentally radical nature, especially when com-

---

[69] It's worth noting that in her *Denktagebuch* or "Book of Thoughts," Arendt addresses the concept of forgiveness but arrives at somewhat different descriptions than the ones that appear in *The Human Condition*. It is beyond the scope of this chapter to fully address this discrepancy other than to say Arendt published *The Human Condition* nine years later, suggesting she had amended her earlier private thoughts on forgiveness.

pared to the other basic human activities of labor and work that comprise our "human condition." Labor involves the repetitive bodily tasks a living being must carrying out to stay alive. The activity of work, on the other hand, creates a durable world of things and therefore an end conclusion or product; it is characterized by a certain level of control and manipulation of objects to bring about an end result. Arendt argues the distinctly human activity is political action through which meaning and identity are alone possible. The mode of political action is speech and deeds and therefore necessitates interaction with others, as witnesses and recipients of our words and deeds. Characteristically, then, political action is by its nature complex, fragile, and unpredictable due to the diverse number of political actors contributing their individual words and deeds.

This "predicament," as Arendt calls it, allows for words and acts to set into motion any possibility and therefore a certain level of "irreversibility" exists within political action, she argues. Arendt claims this irreversibility involves "being unable to undo what one has done though one did not, and could not, have known what he was doing" (1958, 237). Yet humanity need not suffer through the unpredictability of political action without any recourse; Arendt offers the human faculty of forgiving as a remedy. She suggests that forgiving "undoes the deeds of the past, whose 'sins' hang like Damocles' sword over every new generation'" (Ibid.). She adds, "only by constant willingness to change their minds and start again can they be trusted with so great a power as that to begin something new" (Ibid., 24).

Forgiveness releases us from the consequences of what we have done and grants political power its ability to continually refresh itself, to start anew; this is what Nussbaum advocates as an anger that is "transitional" and constructively anticipates a future, not vengefully stuck in the past. Without forgiveness, Arendt argues, our ability to act would be strangulated by past acts from which we could not recover and we would remain limited and defined by them forever. Therefore, in many ways, Arendt sees forgiveness as the cornerstone of political action, that is, the very means through which it is able to persist. Forgiveness, more fundamentally than any human action, characterizes political action because it involves beginning and acting anew. A unique opportunity for a distinctly human freedom is therefore present in forgiveness, to be free from one's prior action.

In addition, Arendt views forgiveness as tied to our ability to make and keep promises. This ability also answers to the unpredictability inherent in political action, "for the chaotic uncertainty of the future is contained in the faculty to make and keep promises" (Ibid., 237). Binding oneself through promises, Arendt states, serves to overcome the uncertainty of the future and to create "islands of security" that allow for continuity in our relationships with one another (Ibid.). Making and keeping promises let us keep our identities, she argues, as others witness me make and keep a promise and therefore confirm that identity. Arendt contends both faculties presuppose a plurality, or the presence of others, since no one can forgive oneself, and no one can feel bound to a promise made only to oneself. Both faculties acquire a tangible, worldly quality by involving others not possible in solitude. These characteristics confirm that political action is not controlled by any one actor. As stated above, by its nature, political action exists "among men," humanity in the plural acting among one another, "intersecting and interfering" with one another. Recognition and acceptance of the qualities inherent to political action is crucial to Arendt. As we will see, she argues political philosophy since Plato displayed a level of discomfort with the inherent unpredictability of a diverse plurality interacting, and instead attempted to replace political action with the manipulatable means-end dynamic characteristic of the activity work by promoting rule. Rule involves a leader who uniquely begins, and followers who are dependent. Gone, then, is the inherent unpredictability of many actors creating new beginnings with their words and deeds characteristic of political action, in favor of the introduction of control found in the activity of work.

Arendt credits the historical Jesus of Nazareth as the origin of the concept of forgiveness, challenging the belief that only God can forgive. The fact that forgiveness has a religious origin does not discount its political power, Arendt contends. She distinguishes forgiveness in a way similar to how Nussbaum describes transitional anger as the opposite of vengeance which, both agree, only invites automatic perpetuation and retaliation, whereas forgiveness disrupts a chain reaction. In contrast to the reflexive nature of revenge, Arendt praises the rather unique function of forgiveness as the only act that cannot be predicted because it singularly reacts in an "unexpected way." As stated earlier, it is the only reaction to act anew, unmoored from the action to which it is a response. Forgiveness therefore creates a freedom both for the one forgiven and the one who forgives. Young-Bruehl argues that Martin Luther King, Jr., for example, shared an Arendtian understanding of forgiveness when he said, "Forgiveness does not mean ignoring what was done or putting a false label on an evil act. It means, rather that the evil act no longer remains as a barrier to the relationship" (2006, 112).[70] Arendt cites Jesus as the origin of the insight that vengeance locks both receiver and actor in an endless cyclical chain of events. Forgiveness is literally *creat*-ive, that is, creates new possibilities, whereas vengeance is destructive.

She concludes by asserting that forgiveness is exceptionally personal because an act is forgiven for the sake of who did it. Arendt believes this reveals the important role of love in forgiveness since "only love has the power to forgive" (1958, 242).

---

[70] See *Why Arendt Matters* for an analysis of Arendtian forgiveness applied to contemporary political events.

She explains:

> *Love...indeed possess an unequal power of self-revelation and an unequaled clarity of vision for the disclosure of who, precisely because it is unconcerned to the point of total unworldliness with what the loved person may be, with his qualities and shortcomings no less than with his achievements, failings, and transgressions. (1958, 242)*

Forgiveness is tied to love because it is through love for another that we are able to look beyond his/her "shortcomings...failings and transgressions" with the desire to free the other with the chance to start anew. Therefore, what is forgiven is the person, not the act. As Julia Kristeva explains, for Arendt, forgiveness "aims at *someone* and not *something*," that is, because of a love for the individual, the act is forgiven (emphasis in the original).[71] It is a for-*giving*, Kristeva points out.

It's worth examining the root of the word "forgiveness" in German, a concept explored by Marie Luise Knott in her book, *Unlearning with Hannah Arendt* in which one chapter is entitled "Forgiveness." Knott notes that *Verzeihen* (to forgive) comes from the verb *vezichten*, to forgo, as in a legal claim against another. As Kristeva underscores, in German

---

[71] Kristeva continues:

Heidegger, it seems clear, more than anyone else deserved forgiveness in Arendt's judgment. This is so not only by reason of that *love*...but also by reason, with the help of loving revelation, of the *consideration* that is awakened in her by Heidegger's thought,...which she discusses and dismantles without ever abandoning, namely a 'regard for the person from the distance which the space of the world puts between us' (emphasis original).

the verb *vergeben* (to forgive) is associated with *geben*, to give, as in the gift of (Christian) love for one's fellow man. In German, these two words, *vergeben* and *Verzeihen*, overlap. Clearly, Arendt's description of the role of forgiveness and its connection to love are influenced by this German etymological origin. Forgiveness means releasing the wrongdoer from his/her harmful act through an act of generosity and love.

Déformation Professionelle

Arendt's above philosophical outlook is the basis for understanding her forgiveness of Heidegger. Her philosophy allows us to both gain an understanding of why Arendt believed Heidegger joined the Nazi party as well as how and why she chose to respond to it. We begin with Heidegger's "*déformation professionelle*" as Arendt sees it. How could a brilliant mind be so susceptible to the political message of a dictator? It became one of the themes of Arendt's life's work to identify the troubled existence of the political in the history of Western philosophy, with Heidegger as no exception. Arendt distinguishes Plato as the one responsible for challenging the ancient Greek understanding of political action as the pinnacle of human endeavors. She argues, "Plato clearly wrote *The Republic* to justify the notion that philosophers should become kings, not because they would enjoy politics, but because…this would mean that they would not be ruled by people worse than they were…" (1982, 21). By Arendt's estimation, the result within the history of political philosophy was a degradation that never authentically respected political action, but instead looked to control it through the introduction of rule. By the twentieth century, it allowed an intellectual environment to germinate in which philosophers were poorly equipped to assess or respect authenticity and meaningfulness in the political realm. As a "philosopher's philosopher," Heidegger exemplified this phenomenon according to Arendt. She used terms like 'co-ordination', 'apolitical', and 'obsequiousness' to describe many German intellectuals' naïve acceptance of Nazism. Young-Bruehl summarizes Arendt's perspective this way:

> *Arendt believed that Western philosophers, from the trial and death of Socrates through the nineteenth century, had been more concerned with how philosophy could be carried out with the least disturbance from the political realm. There is no great thinker in the tradition who did not concern himself with politics, of course, but this concern did not reflect a conviction where politics is a domain where genuine philosophical questions arise. The political domain was one that ought to be regulated according to precepts that arise elsewhere and are accessible to a "higher" sort of wisdom than practical wisdom. (1982, 322)*

Arendt argues Plato viewed the political realm as something to be controlled after witnessing the symbolic treatment of philosophy through Socrates' trial and execution. As we saw above, political action is, by its very nature, unpredictable and therefore uncontrollable. Where the ancient Greeks' remedy was forgiveness and promise-making, Plato began a philosophical tradition of control of the polis with his "utopian" reorganization of it in which the philosopher rules. This was in contrast to the fragile nature of political action the ancient Greeks revered, one in which individuals equally contribute their words and deeds, and power is possessed communally. Plato encouraged a new political paradigm of power as possessed by a few over the many. Heidegger, and other intellectuals like him, was the inheritor of a Platonic political perspective according to Arendt.

Heidegger's susceptibility was further enabled by a personal commitment he found mirrored in Nazi ideology. In 1946 Arendt publicly addressed her old friend for the first time in her article "What is Existenz Philosophy?" She explains Heidegger's involvement with Nazism through German Romanticism, commenting, "Heidegger is really (let us hope) the last romantic....whose complete lack of responsibility is attributable a spiritual playfulness that stems in part from delusions of genius and in part from despair" (1994, 187). She assessed that the reason Heidegger left his praise for Nazism in later publications of his *Introduction to Metaphysics* was "to explain in an underhand way what he thought National Socialism was, namely an encounter between global technology and modern man. The idea is grotesque but...he is not the only one" (Ibid.). Arendt referred to Heidegger's Nazism as "confused business" and a kind of "cultural conservatism" because he lacked sound "political judgment" like other inheritors of Plato's political perspective, that *déformation professionelle* (Young-Bruehl 1982, 443). In short, Heidegger glorified the simple German peasant so much that his nostalgia and lack of appreciation for political action made him receptive to those same expressions within Nazism.

In a 1953 essay entitled, "Ex-Communists," Arendt extends this offer:

> *We know this century is full of dangers and perplexities; we ourselves do not always, and never fully, know what we are doing. We know that the best of us ...have been driven into the totalitarian predicament. Those who have turned their backs on it are welcome; everyone is welcome who has not become a murderer or a professional spy in the process. We are anxious to establish friendship wher-*

ever we can, and this goes for former Fascists or Nazis... (Arendt 1994, 399)

Why would Arendt be willing to extend such an unbelievable offer? Because she was committed to what Aristotle identified as the foundation of political life—*philia*, or brotherly love/friendship. Through it, there is "*mutual* release" (emphasis added). Heidegger's private expression of shame to Arendt and Jaspers represented a willingness to "change his mind," that he had "failed" and had "gone astray," as Arendt says.[72] Forgiveness for Arendt is therefore a thoroughly political act, in the classic sense of the word. No act could express more clearly her deep respect for political action than to forgive.

Young-Bruehl concludes on the matter:

By the early 1930s Heidegger's fascination with National Socialism came decisively between them. That the Nazi's nationalism was a perversion of everything admirable in German culture, Heidegger did not seem able to recognize. He was so fearful of modernization and so committed to pastoral, preindustrial values...that he could find in the Nazi evocation of primitive Germanness a compatible tendency. Because she could understand Heidegger's allegiances, and later even see the comicalness of them, Arendt remained loyal

---

[72] Young-Bruehl notes Arendt didn't clarify what constitutes a satisfactory "change of mind" to warrant forgiveness. Because of his *déformation professionelle*, it was no more than a private expression of shame in Heidegger's case. See *Why Arendt Matters* (103).

to him...For seventeen years they had no communication. But when she did meet him again, after the war, she was able to forgive him for his poetry." (1982, 69)

Arendt agreed with Jaspers that Heidegger attempting to explain his choices and actions would not have been "genuine, because he really doesn't know and is hardly in a position to find out what devil drove him into what he did" (1992, 168).

Arendt expressed a commitment to the *vita activa*, the "active life," in contrast to the *vita contemplativa*, the "contemplative life," which she believed made her an oddity in the history of philosophy. Her commitment shows why Arendt would place such value on the crucial role of forgiveness with regards to political acts that cannot be undone. When met with the result of the unpredictability and disorderliness of the political in her own life, Arendt chose the path of the ancient Greeks, she chose to forgive.[73]

Forgiving the Fox

In 1953, Arendt wrote in her private (intellectual) journal, *Denktagebuch*, an entry entitled "Heidegger the Fox" where she recounts the fact Heidegger referred to himself in this way. Arendt offers a tale about the "fox" with the introduction that this fox was "so lacking in slyness" that he "couldn't even tell the difference between a trap and a non-trap" referring to this as "shocking ignorance" (1992, 361). The allegory takes some twists and turns, and Arendt again announces the fox's "great ignorance about traps." The fox "grows annoyed with others since, despite their slyness, all foxes occa-

---

[73] For a deeper analysis of the philosopher's "suspicion" of the political, see my book *The Hidden Philosophy of Hannah Arendt*.

sionally get caught in traps." By beautifying a trap, he lures other foxes into it, "for this trap was the fox's burrow, and if you wanted to visit him where he was at home, you had to step into his trap." The fox declares that he must be the best fox because he has lured so many into visiting his trap. Arendt concludes, "there is some truth to that: Nobody knows the nature of traps better than the one who sits in a trap his whole life long" (Ibid.). In a 1964 interview with Günter Gaus, Arendt utilized the same metaphor when talking about how average Germans behaved during Nazism: "…they were not all murderers. There were people who fell into their own trap…" (2013, 24).

I posed the question above, why did Arendt forgive Heidegger? The answer, we now see, is twofold: first, because Heidegger was typical of other professional philosophers in Arendt's opinion by being ill-equipped to recognize and therefore promote or protect an authentically human political realm. She was disappointed but not surprised Heidegger was naively duped into thinking ("so lacking in slyness") that a totalitarian regime offered a positive political opportunity for Germany.[74] And, second, in response to this, Arendt embodied her philosophical commitment to a reverence for political action and its built-in corrective feature of forgiving an act that cannot be undone. She forgave Heidegger, the man, not the allegiance to Nazism, because she extended love to him so as to allow him not to be defined by his shortcomings but to be given the gift of a chance to start anew. Arendt's forgiveness of Heidegger was the *par excellence* of political acts.

---

[74] What may have influenced Arendt's assessment of what the "typical" philosopher was capable of in the political realm is the fact Arendt routinely singled out Jaspers as uncharacteristically appreciative of the political. Jaspers also stood out among German intellectuals by refusing to collude with the Nazis, for which he was punished.

References

Arendt, Hannah. *Essays in Understanding: 1930-1954.* Edited by Jerome Kohn. New York: Harcourt Brace & Company. 1994.

_____. 1958. *The Human Condition.* Chicago: University of Chicago Press.

_____. 1982. *Lectures on Kant's Political Philosophy.* Edited by Ronald Beiner, Chicago: University of Chicago Press.

_____. 2013. *The Last Interview and Other Conversations.* Brooklyn: Melville House Publishing, 2013.

Arendt, Hannah and Karl Jaspers. 1992. *Correspondence*: 1926-1969. New York: Harcourt Brace & Company.

Clément, Catherine. 2001. *Martin and Hannah: A Novel.* New York: Prometheus Books, 2001.

Hull, Margaret Betz. 2002. *The Hidden Philosophy of Hannah Arendt.* New York: Routledge Curzon.

Knott, Mary Luise. 2011. *Unlearning with Hannah Arendt.* New York: Other Press, 2011.

Kristeva, Julia. 2001. *Hannah Arendt: Life is a Narrative.* Toronto: University of Toronto Press.

Nussbaum, Martha. 2016. University of Chicago Law School Lecture: "Anger and Forgiveness." Youtube.com. Accessed January, 8, 2016.

Rosenbaum, Ron. "The Evil of Banality." *Slate.com*. Accessed June 3, 2015.

Sherratt, Yvonne. 2013. *Hitler's Philosophers.* New Haven: Yale University Press.

Villa, Dana. 1996. *Arendt and Heidegger: The Fate of the Political.* Princeton: Princeton University Press.

Young-Bruehl, Elisabeth. 1982. *Hannah Arendt: For the Love of the World.* New Haven: Yale University Press.

_____. 2006. *Why Arendt Matters.* New Haven: Yale University Press.

Chapter 6

Unforgivable Evil and Evildoers

Jennifer Mei Sze Ang

In cases of genocide and mass atrocities, is forgiveness the morally appropriate response? This chapter looks at how interpersonal forgiveness between survivors and the perpetrators of mass atrocities may be a morally inappropriate and a harmful response, in spite of the psychological and political recovery they promise to promote. In the first section, I outline a category of wrongdoers who suffers from what I call "moral bankruptcy," using the case of Adolf Eichmann. I show how these wrongdoers can be radical, not because of their banality, but because of their lack of conscience. I proceed to discuss the tension between forgiving and not forgiving repentant and unrepentant wrongdoers of "unforgivable" wrongdoing in the second section, for which I will use the works of Hannah Arendt, Vladimir Jankélévitch and Jacques Derrida. Finally, I show that survivors of atrocities who are unforgiving are not resentful, irrational moral failures. Rather, their resentment is legitimate, and not forgiving unforgivable evil is a morally appropriate response when morally bankrupt wrongdoers do not show that they deserve (via repentance) to be forgiven by acknowledging their misdeeds and accepting punishment.

Moral Bankruptcy

To understand how forgiveness may be a morally inappropriate response to mass atrocities, we must first grasp the concept of moral bankruptcy, which will allow us to comprehend the evil nature of certain wrongdoers. We begin with Arendt who identified two types of evil in her work—the "absolute evil" found in the final stages of totalitarianism, and the notion of "thoughtlessness" used to describe the banal evil of Eichmann.

Arendt's conceptualization of absolute evil relates to an objective state; the final stages of totalitarianism where humans are made superfluous by having their individuality stripped, and their human freedom and spontaneity reduced to conditioned reflexes (Bernstein 1997, 208-13; and Arendt 1994, 458-9). What we see immediately is how the Nazi machinery served the sole purpose of total domination of all men by erecting "factories to produce corpses," and at a more fundamental level, how it served a more sinister ideology: to make all of humanity—prisoners as well as the perpetrators of the system—superfluous. In short, the essence of this new evil called totalitarianism lies in the making of human nature superfluous its absolute end.

Here we find the first sense of 'absolute'—where the doctrine of the *Volk* underlying the Nazi ideology is absolute in that all institutions, and apparatuses must serve to safeguard its total power, so as to achieve what was considered ontologically and historically necessary. As a matter of fact, the concentration camps themselves were anti-utility and militarily unnecessary, especially towards the later years of the war, as efforts at accomplishing the Final Solution were increased (Arendt 1950, 54). This shows that the destruction of human dignity is absolute in the Nazi totalitarian framework because *any* respect for human dignity implies the recognition of fellowmen as subjects, and this creates an unpredictability of explaining historical events and determining their future course that a totalitarian regime cannot tolerate (Arendt 1994, 458). Hence, far from seeing absolute evil as irrational, Arendt shows us that within the framework of the totalitarian ideology, "everything follows comprehensibly and even compulsory once the first premise is accepted" (Ibid., 457-8). What thus seems apparent is that Nazi ideology has its own rationality and logic, because its premise is considered absolute such that all social, political, moral principles and even human dignity are redefined to serve the achievement of the absolute end of the Third Reich.

The second sense in which the evil of totalitarianism is absolute is that "it can no longer be deduced from humanly comprehensive motives" and appears to be unintelligible (Ibid., viii).[75] For Arendt, the destruction of human nature is incomprehensible in that it breaks with the traditional philosophical accounts of evil, while at the same time being unable to explain its new proposed reality. For instance, from the Socratic view, one does not knowingly choose evil (Svendsen 2001, 206). But the links between ignorance and evil, and rationality with good, do not explain how perpetrators of the Holocaust knowingly chose evil for the sake of achieving what they believed to be a historical and metaphysical inevitability. As we turn to Augustine's account, we find that his notion of ontological evil is perhaps able to account for exterior evil, and his idea of human wickedness may be able to explain the perversion and corruption of the perpetrators.[76] Yet, Augustine left the idea of evil itself unintelligible because to him, it is God who judges good and evil.[77] As for Kant's conceptualization of moral evil, evil must be freely chosen—arising from the "perverted ill will" that is backed by com-

---

[75] Arendt argues, "If it is true that in the final stages of totalitarianism an absolute evil appears (absolute because it can no longer be deduced from humanly comprehensive motives), it is also true that without it we might never have known the truly radical nature of Evil."

[76] According to Charles Matthews, "the Augustinian tradition interprets evil's challenge in two distinct conceptual mechanisms, one ontological and the other anthropological" (2001, 6). He finds that Arendtian evil too, is objective and ontological.

[77] There are varied interpretations of Arendt's different concepts of evils that lies beyond the scope of this project. For instance, Jari Kauppinen tells us that while Charles Matthewes argues that Arendt's idea of the ontology of evil is situated in the Augustinian tradition, he finds that Arendt's thesis contains different modes of evil. See Kauppinen (2010, 49-51).

prehensible motives of the corrupted heart (Kant 1960, 32). But the absolute evil Arendt describes cannot be explained by Kant's notion of radical evil because absolute evil "could no longer be understood and explained by the evil motives of self-interest, greed, covetousness, resentment, lust for power, and cowardice" (Arendt 1994, 459). In fact, because all human freedom and spontaneity are destroyed by totalitarianism, there is no freewill to speak of. We can at this point conclude that for Arendt, the horror of the final stages of totalitarianism that confronts us is absolute evil in that "we actually have nothing to fall back on in order to understand [this] phenomenon" since it "breaks down all standards we know" (Ibid.).

Absolute evil is in short, making the impossible possible; and it is precisely this explosion of all limits of the law that Arendt claimed constituted the monstrosity of Nazi crimes (Ibid., 458). For her, the relationship between the punishability of a crime with forgiveness is clearly political, and also asymmetric. What this means is that punishment is the alternative to forgiveness, and in the case of Nazi crimes, because they lie outside existing laws, they also lie outside of forgiveness (Ibid.). In Arendt's words, the Nazi has discovered "crimes which men can neither punish nor forgive," where "anger could not revenge, love could not endure, and friendship cannot forgive" (Ibid., 459). Furthermore, prior to Eichmann's trial, Arendt corresponded with Karl Jaspers and shared his apprehension that the events of the Holocaust stood outside "of what is comprehensive in human and moral terms—and to address it in legal terms [was] a mistake" (Arendt and Jaspers 1992, 410). This is an unprecedented crime that Arendt was right to point out needed a coherent definition; one not left to a "court of victors," where historical, political, and educational objectives underscore the trial in which vengeance is favored over justice (2006, 251).[78]

The new criminal we are faced with also required a rethinking of the terms of justice. While Arendt agrees with the verdict, she tried to capture the nature of this new crime in her own judgment of Eichmann:

> *...just as you supported and carried out a policy of not wanting to share the earth with the Jewish people and the people of a number of other nations—as though you and your superiors had any right to determine who should and who should not inhabit the world—we find that no one, that is, no member of the human race, can be expected to want to share the earth with you. This is the reason, and the only reason, you must hang. (Ibid., 279)*[79]

In *Eichmann in Jerusalem*, Arendt paints a portrait of the new type of criminal who is terribly and terrifyingly "normal," without any diabolical or demonic profundity. She tells us that this "banal evil" can be found in the extraordinary

---

[78] Arendt spoke of her apprehension: "The purpose of the trial is to render justice, and nothing else; even the noblest ulterior purposes—'the making of a record of the Hitler regime ...' can only detract from the law's main business: to weigh the charges brought against the accused, to render judgment and to mete out due punishment."

[79] Judith Butler makes an interesting observation that "Arendt's principle of justifying the death penalty seems to group together those who deliver the death sentence with those who commit the crimes," since "state-sponsored death penalty is clearly one way of deciding with whom to cohabit the earth". See Judith Butler. 2011. "Arendt's Death Sentences." *Comparative Literature Studies* 48.3: 292.

shallowness of thoughtless individuals we observe in their behavior—they extinguished their private conscience and automatically applied fixed Nazi rules, while hiding behind Nazi clichés as justifications to their own actions. These behaviors, according to Arendt, describe the thoughtlessness of Eichmann, contrasted with the thinking individual who unfreezes what he thinks he knows by examining and questioning these ideas and rules so that he can judge anew and make up his own mind. Eichmann is thus a textbook case of an unrepentant criminal hiding behind self-fabricated stock phrases, who sees himself as a cog in the Nazi machinery and a victim of history, and as a result, denies his responsibility. Yet, even if we could not establish an evil intent, Arendt argues, insofar as what Eichmann did was criminal, "all the cogs in the machinery, no matter how insignificant, are in court forthwith transformed back into perpetrators, that is to say, into human beings" (Ibid., 289).

Arendt's account of banal evil, however, does not fully hold up to the facts about Eichmann. Eichmann was found to have embraced the logistical challenges of his post, creatively adapted to his situation, and took initiatives to overcome obstacles in order to accomplish his tasks. As such, even though he had no malevolent tendencies, took no pleasure in the suffering of others, and found the Final Solution to be "one of the greatest crimes in the history of Humanity" (Ibid., 22), he was not an automaton, nor was he "removed from reality, and shielded by self-deception, lies and stupidity," as Arendt suggested (2005, 54). There was thus little doubt that he made his choices freely and was not coerced, and that his actions were deliberate and not accidental. David Cesarani in *Becoming Eichmann* documented how with great effort, the lowly-educated Eichmann was able to rise quickly in the bureaucracy because of how he attended to the Final Solution creatively instead of blindly following orders. As Cesarani argues, there was nothing banal about him, his institutional setting, intentions, or actions (2007, 6).

More importantly, it is arguable that thoughtlessness can lead one into becoming an active supporter of administrative murders or becoming a génocidaire. In fact, Arendt in her later work, *Life of a Mind* also admits that "thinking inevitably has a destructive, undermining effect on all established criteria, values, measures of good and evil, in short, on those customs and rules of conduct we treat of in morals and ethics" but does not replace it with new ones (175). Thus, if all thinking does is to unfreeze and dissolve accepted rules of conduct, Richard Berstein aptly observed that Arendt has failed to show that thinking has moral consequences and also failed to account for why "some persons lose or show no signs of the ability to think and (a few) others still maintain their ability to judge" (1997, 317).[80]

If thoughtlessness cannot account for why the author of this previously unknown and unimagined evil lacks the ability to judge, will the absence of a private conscience provide an explanation? Our private conscience works as an inner judge that guides our beliefs and actions, making it necessarily an independent standard from which we judge public conscience and morality. The guilt and remorse we feel appear as afterthoughts when we fail to follow what our inner

---

[80] Larry Busk argues against Berstein's two criticism of Arendt in "Sleepwalk: Arendt, Thoughtlessness, and the Question of Little Eichmanns," *Social Philosophy Today*, 31: 60. First, Busk argues that "it is not Arendt's (or any moral theorist's) task to explain why some people behave morally while others fail to," for all Arendt wants to claim is that "thought is a moral imperative because thoughtlessness is an immanent moral calamity." Second, he replies to Berstein's objection to the Heidegger problem in the lack of connection between thinking and moral action by arguing that Arendt "explicitly denies that thinking could ever 'produce' a moral action on its own accord," but there is "the propensity for evil that thoughtlessness harbours within it." And this lack of relationship between thought and morality also leads us to question whether there is a moral difference between wrongdoers who are thoughtless and those who are thinking, and whether we should find Eichmann or Heidegger equally unforgivable.

judge instructs, due to the weakness of will or moral courage (that means, one knows the right thing to do but fails to do the right thing), or upon realization that we have made the wrong judgment when the harmful consequences of our decisions come to light. This explains how in a regular case, one who followed his private conscience would have been able to judge the wrongness of Nazi ideology and resisted. And for those who succumb to Nazi orders, they will regret their lack of moral courage and feel guilty when faced with the consequences of their decisions.

But the absence of a private conscience is another matter altogether. Eichmann felt free of guilt and lacked any sense of regret or remorse even when confronted with the consequences of his actions. This is a clear case of moral bankruptcy—where the absence of an independent basis to judge whether Nazi morality was right or wrong led him to not be able to feel any shame, regret, guilt, or remorse over the consequences of his obedience to Nazi orders. Instead, his notions of right and wrong were based on whether his own will followed the principles behind Nazi laws, which is, whatever that might please the Führer. We find that he only suffered from a bad conscience "if he had not done what he had been ordered to do—to ship millions of men, women, and children to their death with great zeal and meticulous care"— and thus took initiatives to ensure the completion of his tasks (Arendt 2006, 25). He was to organize foot marches when the transportation system was destroyed after Allied bombings to ensure that the Final Solution would not be compromised, and he also sabotaged Himmler's orders because they were running counter to the Führer's order (Ibid., 136-7). This shows that he did not momentarily suspend his judgment and replace his conscience with Nazi morality, but that he was unable to judge whether these orders were morally right or morally wrong because he was morally vacuous. He had a misplaced sense of guilt over his failure to follow Nazi morality which he saw was his Kantian duty. Moreover, his assessment of himself tells us that he was not in bad faith because he was clear that he did not want to be one of those who now pretended that "they had always been against it," whereas in fact they had been very eager to do what they were told to do (Ibid., 24).

Although Eichmann's conscience (or lack of) is not on trial, it is undeniable that it holds moral significance for any discussion of forgiveness, moral repair and reconciliation for crimes of such nature. Morally bankrupt individuals do not regard others nor themselves as moral agents who bear responsibility for their judgment and actions, because to them, every human being is superfluous, including themselves. And where the essence of such a worldview aims to rid the humanity of every human being and turn them into pure material for soap, wigs, lamp shades, and test subjects for diseases, it is not a matter of having a different moral worldview, but the complete lack of a moral worldview.

David Livingston Smith captured an aspect of this worldview where morality is absent in *Less than Human*. He explained that it is through methods of dehumanization that génocidaires take away the identity and individuality of their victims so as to reduce them to sub-human creatures (2011, 26). This explains dehumanization as bad faith—where perpetrators first see their victims as human beings that needed to be dehumanized in order to justify treating them as sub-humans.[81] Under a set of different circumstances, and at a

---

[81] The common use of 'sub-human' refer to a lower order of being than humans, and by inference, a racist does not consider 'sub-human' as a being that is not worthy of being treated as human beings. But it is exactly because sub-humans continue to share some characteristics of humankind (which differentiate them from other beings such as God, animals or machines) the racist finds that they must be dehumanized. This is similar to how Smith conceives of 'sub-humans' as species that are human-looking, but are not really people. Hence, to him, dehumanization made carnage possible. On the other hand, to differentiate the racist from Eichmann-like perpetrator, I have used the term "non-human" to refer to a

different time, we see that perpetrators become overwhelmed with guilt over what they have done to their victims when they no longer think of their victims as sub-humans. But can we say the same for those who do not feel guilt and remorse? Not only did Eichmann not find himself guilty of any crimes when he came face to face with the survivors, he was proud that "he had always acted against his 'inclinations', whether they were sentimental or inspired by interest, that he had always done his 'duty'," and in fact, as a Kantian, he "[did] more than obey the law, that he [went] beyond the mere call of obedience and identify his own will with the principle behind the law—the source from which the law sprang." Neither did he regret any of his actions, since "repentance [was] for little children" (Arendt 2006; 24 and 136-7).

At this juncture, we find that in identifying this new crime, Arendt was right that normality offers no protection against the commission of terrible crimes and this, to her, includes the Jewish leaders who cooperated with the Nazis. But the new criminals we are dealing with are morally bankrupt individuals who do not feel remorse, not thoughtless individuals in bad faith as Arendt suggested. Eichmann is in this way different from the Jewish leaders who were coerced. What then should we consider a morally appropriate response to this new type of wrongdoers who are without conscience, and who had committed crimes that we cannot adequately punish? Under what circumstances, if any, will it be morally legitimate to forgive, pardon, forget, and reconcile with unrepentant wrongdoers?

---

species that do not share any characteristic of humankind. This better explains why Eichmann does not need to dehumanize them to justify extermination.

Forgiving the Unforgivable

While Arendt thinks that the monstrosity of the Holocaust lies outside of human, moral, and legal comprehension, where capital punishment is simply an inadequate response to absolute evil, others argue that it is unforgiveable and impossible evil that requires forgiveness. True forgiveness for Jankélévitch and Derrida, for instance, operates outside of the jurisdiction of the legal code and retributive justice, and does not require the misdeed to be forgotten, understood or justified. Can their idea of forgiveness be a morally appropriate response to absolute evil and evildoers without conscience?

In *Forgiveness*, Jankélévitch introduced three defining features of true forgiveness by contrasting them with what he considered pseudo-forgiveness. The first relates to the temporal factor where he distinguished between an event and an interval. He argues that true forgiveness is an event for it is "initial, sudden, and spontaneous," a decisive moment where the victim grants a gracious gift to the wrongdoer (2005, 5). Forgiveness does not take place after a process of reasoning or deliberation of the will, which contrasts with "excusing" the wrongdoer, through which we aim to achieve an understanding in order to forgive. Jankélévitch called this process of coming to an understanding "intellection"—the taking of "a position on the wrongs of the culprit of whom a fault is reproached" in order to appreciate the wrongdoing it excuses (Ibid., 58). Intellection is not an event because to come to an understanding of the wrongs takes time and sustained attention. Furthermore, an excuse is also not a gift that happens in a relation to others because in intellection, there is no wrongdoer or victim given that the wrongdoing is already made nonexistent (Ibid., 61-3).

For Jankélévitch, understanding does not lead to forgiveness; it only leads to excuse. We see that in instances of reconciliation without forgiveness, the process of reconciliation requires the giving of reasons as to why the misdeed has occurred in exchange for understanding, or for establishing truth, such that the misdeed can be excused and the wrongdoer be granted a pardon or amnesty. It does not require the wrongdoers to repent, show remorse, or apologize because it deems that there is no offense to punish or forgive, and hence, there is no wrongdoer in this case that needs to be forgiven. This describes the case of the South African Truth and Reconciliation Commission (TRC) where all parties agree that there will be no punishment for wrongdoing in exchange for the full confession of crimes.

Second, true forgiveness takes place as a personal relation with another person. This feature distinguishes true forgiveness from acts of clemency where the person granting the clemency is indifferent to the wrongdoing and thereby, also indifferent to the wrongdoer. In this sense, clemency is not forgiveness because it "excludes every truly transitive or intentional relation with [the] other person," whereas to forgive is to "release the guilty one from his punishment or from a part of his punishment, or to liberate him before the completion of his punishment" (Ibid., 7-10). It is also questionable if public apologies and the accounting of crimes through TRCs can achieve interpersonal forgiveness, given that it is too psychologically distant. But more importantly, a third-party type of pardon cannot be considered forgiveness since it does not concern any personal relations between victims and wrongdoers.

Liquidating wrongdoing also means that the relation with the wrongdoer is not considered because the person who liquidates is one who "hardly dares to confront the wrongs of the Other courageously in order to forgive them" and instead, acts as if the past never happened, with no wrongdoer to forgive (Ibid., 99). But with an attitude of "getting rid" of the wrongdoing, the victim does not look into converting the guilty person, nor does he deal with his own legitimate resentments and sacred memories, and more importantly, disregards injustice by renouncing truth and giving up what is within his rights (Ibid., 103). His negligent and casual gestures towards the wrongdoer reveal his thoughtlessness and superficiality rather than seriousness and profundity that should be expressed through his resentments, which are needed for true forgiveness. In other cases, the victim swallows and stomachs the offense, and integrates this antithesis into a higher synthesis for reconciliation. This is also not true forgiveness by a generous person, but an egoist who wants to turn insults to his advantage, snubs and humiliations into profitable lessons, and continues to hold a grudge.

Finally, true forgiveness does not decay through time because it requires memories of a past offense to forgive. When we forget or overlook past misdeeds with an eye only on the future, it is considered forgetful forgiveness which is "more amnesia than amnesty, more asthenia or atrophy than generosity, for it results from anesthesia and increasing apathy" (Ibid., 29). Thus, what time can do is only to neutralize "the *effects* of the misdeed, but it cannot destroy the *fact of* the misdeed" (Ibid., 48). It seems then, for Jankélévitch, one cannot forget, but one can forgive. When Jankélévitch asks whether twenty years was sufficient for establishing statutory limitations and beginning the process of pardoning Nazi war criminals, he replies that not only does time not have "a diminishing effect on the unbearable horror of Auschwitz," but to "forget this gigantic crime against humanity would be a new crime against the human species" (1996, 553, 557).

As such, even though Jankélévitch recognized that the punishment of the Nazi criminal will never be proportional to his crime in this case, he warns us against the indifference, the moral amnesia, and the general superficiality of a pardon. However, Jankélévitch went on to assert that "pardoning died in the death camps," and yet, in *Forgiveness*, he maintains that it is the unforgivable that we forgive:

> *[w]hen a crime can neither be justified, nor explained, nor even understood, when, with everything that could be explained having been explained, the atrocity of this crime and the overwhelming evidence of this responsi-*

> *bility are obvious before everyone's eyes, when the atrocity of has neither mitigating circumstances, nor excuses of any sort, and when hope of regeneration has to be abandoned, then there is no longer anything else to do but to forgive. (Ibid., 566-7)*

Here, forgiveness becomes madness—as the "supreme recourse and the ultimate grace" for the inexcusable precisely because it is inexcusable (Jankélévitch 2005, 106). But even mad forgiveness is conditioned on one thing: repentance through the admission of guilt. In *Forgiveness*, Jankélévitch stresses that the basic condition that is required for forgiveness to make sense is "that the guilty person, instead of protesting, recognize himself as guilty without pleas or mitigating circumstances, and especially without accusing his own victims," for without which, "the entire problematic of forgiveness becomes a simple buffoonery" since "unrepentant criminals themselves are precisely the ones who have no need of forgiveness" (Ibid., 157-8). Thus, returning to the issue of imposing a statutory limitation on Nazi crimes, it is a "sinister joke" because "[t]o presume to be pardoned one must admit to being guilty, without conditions or alleging extenuating circumstances" (Jankélévitch 1996, 566-7). And in the case of Nazi crimes, we will not be able to excuse (since we cannot achieve an understanding), or forget because of its absoluteness, nor will we be able to forgive unrepentant wrongdoers like Eichmann because he has no need for forgiveness.

Derrida on the other hand, holds the view that pure forgiveness should be unconditional because if the perpetrator were to repent or mend his ways before being forgiven, then forgiveness is unnecessary since the perpetrator is "no longer exactly the same as the one who was found to be culpable" (Derrida 2001, 39). Furthermore, being skeptical of instrumentalist accounts of forgiveness in politics, Derrida finds conditional forgiveness to bear an element of exchange. He compared pure forgiveness with reconciliation; where the former is an exceptional moment to the law and occurs in spite of judicial or political decisions, whereas the latter serves the goal of reestablishing normality through mourning or setting up an ecology of memory. An example is the case of the South Africa TRC where a conceptual mistake was committed when it assumed that forgiveness had taken place when there was only reconciliation. Thus, just as forgiveness is impure when it serves the goal of reestablishing normality, Derrida argues that it is also impure if it seeks noble or spiritual ends of atonement, redemption, reconciliation or salvation. To him, unconditional forgiveness is one that is "gracious, infinite, uneconomic forgiveness granted to the guilty as guilty, without counterpart, even to those who do not repent or ask forgiveness" (2001, 31-4).

Finally, following from the fact that it is a gracious gift that is uncorrupted by instrumentality or conditionality, pure forgiveness can interrupt the natural course of history—that develops as violence and counter-violence in a Hegelian fashion—by starting anew rather than a conditioned reaction. Whereas for forgiveness that is conditional, it achieves reconciliation which affirms a Hegelian synthesis instead of remaining "exceptional and extraordinary, in the face of the impossible: as if it interrupted the ordinary course of historical temporality" (Ibid., 32). To break the dialectic, towards the end of *On Forgiveness*, Derrida briefly touches on unconditional forgiveness as unsettling the power of the subject by advocating unconditional forgiveness to come as a surprise to forestall reciprocal violence.

From Derrida's account, it seems that a wrongdoer like Eichmann is the object of impossible forgiveness by the very fact that he will always be unrepentant because he is morally bankrupt. But this is not the case for Jankélévitch because even mad forgiveness is conditioned minimally on repentance. Furthermore, absolute evil is no limit to forgiveness for Derrida because forgiveness transcends politics and law, since only the victim has the right to forgive; while for Arendt, "one only forgives where one can judge and punish, therefore evaluate, then the putting into place, the institution of an instance of judgement, supposes a power, a force a sovereignty" (Ibid., 59).[82] Thus, in the same way as Arendt, Derrida understood unforgivable evil as lying beyond the realm of "not only judicial concepts of responsibility and punishment but also the moral faculties of forgiveness and redemption," yet, unlike Arendt, he believed that this is precisely the point where forgiveness begins (Verdeja 2004, 25). Is unconditional forgiveness the only thing that remains for us to do when faced with the impossible—the morally bankrupt evildoer who is without conscience?

When forgiving is morally inappropriate and harmful

The debate between conditional and unconditional forgiveness brings to the fore two different approaches—those who defend the moral legitimacy of resentments, and those who focus on the psychological recovery and virtue of victims who forgive. Although these accounts do not directly deal with absolute evil and evildoers who lack conscience, they enable us to discuss the moral legitimacy of resentment and the moral significance of genuine repentance at the personal and political levels. A common starting point for both approaches is Joseph Butler's definition of forgiveness.

Butler first described anger and resentment as natural emotions reacting against personal injury and injustice, whereas indignation is felt when the injury does not affect oneself. And when he speaks of forgiveness, it relates to the

---

[82] Derrida seemed to have only read Jankélévitch's "Should we pardon them" to conclude that he takes the same position as Arendt in seeing forgiveness as asymmetrical to punishment. However, Derrida may have misread Jankélévitch's argument in "Should we pardon them?" Jankélévitch was referring to 'political pardon' rather than interpersonal forgiveness when he says that "pardon died in the death camps."

feeling of resentment raised by personal injury rather than a sense of indignation over injury experienced by to others. His key concern is that when these natural feelings are left uncontrolled, they become excessive and turn to malice and revenge. And when we pass sentence on our own cause out of malice and revenge, we often think of ourselves being injured when we are not, and have a tendency to represent an injury greater than it really is. As a result, if we were to allow ourselves to indulge in our desires for revenge, our revenge will produce effects that are not proportional to the offense. Furthermore, in the context of a society upon whom the revenge is taken for retributive or deterrent effects, revenge produces more harm than good because the end revenge seeks is to bring misery to perpetrators.

What we thus see here is that for Butler, resentment in and of itself "is not inconsistent with goodwill," but when "this resentment entirely destroys our natural benevolence towards [the wrongdoer], it is excessive, and becomes malice or revenge" and to prevent this, we have "to forgive injuries" "because that love is always supposed, unless destroyed by resentment" (Butler 1827).[83] He further argued that even in

---

[83] Joseph Butler, "Sermon VIII" in *Fifteen Sermons*. http://anglicanhistory.org/butler/rolls/08.html. Margaret Walker points out interestingly that the overcoming or letting go of resentment as an essential or constitutive part of forgiveness for many philosophical accounts have misunderstood Butler. See Margaret Urban Walker, *Moral Repair* (New York: Cambridge University Press, 2006), 154. One example is Jean Hampton who believed that resentment has to do with the doubts that arise in victims over their self-worth or humiliation and is hence directed at their wrongdoer. Taken in this sense, forgiveness is personal and necessarily involved the victim overcoming his resentment by seeing the wrongdoer in a new and more favorable light. This may involve a change of heart towards the wrongdoer, and also accompanied by an offer of reconciliation. And for the victim, by overcoming his resentment, he is also overcome the hurt and indignation he felt. It also helps him move forward in his life by letting go of claims for requital and restitution. See also Jean Hampton, "Forgiveness, Resentment and ha-

public executions, the guilt or injury does not dispense with or supersede our duty of love and good will, nor would the guilt or injury justify the severity of the punishment. What justifies public executions is a separate reason—that the wrongdoer's life is inconsistent with the quiet and happiness of the world. Thus, forgiveness as Butler seems to suggest, presents itself as a break from our natural feeling of resentment (when the injury is real) because when left unchecked and uncontrolled, resentment can turn to malice and revenge. But feelings of resentment itself is natural and not morally problematic, and in fact, serves as "a guard against the violent assault of others; and in our own defense; some, in behalf of others" (Ibid.).

In *Getting Even*, Jeffrie Murphy brings to light that resentment is not only morally legitimate, but also has an important role to play in defending three values: self-respect, self-defense, and respect for the moral order (19). Murphy argues that a person who never resents any injuries directed at him lacks "respect for himself and respect for his rights and status as a free and equal moral being" (Ibid.). Resentment is also a form of self-defense as it presents itself as a warning towards potential wrongdoers. Lastly, resentment stands as "testimony to our allegiance to the moral order itself" (Ibid., 19-20). In giving attention to the moral legitimacy of resentment, Murphy's account of forgiveness cautions against "hasty forgiveness" that could compromise these important values while following Butler's footsteps in defining forgiveness as the overcoming of "the vindictive passions—the passions of anger, resentment, and even hatred" (Ibid., 16). This is unlike unilateral accounts of forgiveness that are primarily focused only on the process of forgiveness on the part of the victim as an act of virtue and

---

tred," in *Forgiveness and Mercy*, edited by Jeffrie G. Murphy and Jean Hampton. (Cambridge University Press, 1988), 84-5.

the promotion of psychological healing, such as the overcoming of resentment either through a perceptual change of themselves or their assailants, and the change of heart or action of reconciliation that should follow.[84] By only emphasizing the virtue and psychological healing that forgiveness can bring to the victims, these accounts underplay the moral legitimacy of victims' resentment when the misdeed is real, and instead, paint the picture of unforgiving victims as resentful and irrational moral failures. In doing so, it tends to prompt one into forgiving hastily.

The question that Murphy's account thus presents us with is not whether we should forgive, but when we should forgive in order to avoid hasty forgiveness, or as Charles Griswold puts it, conditions that come attached to avoid the "moral blindness" of condoning misdeeds (2007, xv). In deciding when to forgive, we should focus on the quality of deserving forgiveness according to Griswold. He details six indispensable stages of action undertaken by the wrongdoer in order to be forgiven: acknowledge the misdeed; repudiate the misdeed; express regret; commit never to repeat the misdeed; express sympathy and understanding for the victim's suffering; and be able to provide an account of the misdeed as well

---

[84] Jean Hampton asserts that "the first stage of the forgiving process, namely, the psychological preparation for this change of heart, involves regaining one's confidence in one's worth despite the immoral action challenging it. This is accomplished by overcoming, in the sense of 'giving up' or 'repudiating', emotions such as spite or malice, and 'overcoming' in the sense of 'transcending' resentment ... when they are overthrown, enable the following change of heart to take place: 'the forgiver who previously saw the wrongdoer as someone bad ..." See Jean Hampton, "Forgiveness, Resentment and Hatred," 83. Garrard and McNaughton were to place their emphasis on loving the wrongdoer: "forgiveness requires something more positive – an attitude of good will (or even love) toward the wrongdoer. There must be some concern for the welfare of the wrongdoer for there to be forgiveness." See Eve Garrard and David McNaughton, "In Defense of Unconditional Forgiveness," *Proceedings of the Aristotelian Society*, 103.1 (2003): 44.

as the self in the context of the misdeed. As a norm-governed dyadic relationship, there are also conditions for victims when these conditions by the wrongdoer are met. These include the forswearing of revenge, moderation and eventual commitment to overcoming resentment, a reframing of the relation with the offender, and granting an expressed declaration of forgiveness. Griswold concludes that only when these conditions are met, and that the injury is humanly forgivable does "forgiveness come off at all" (Ibid., 115).

We need not agree with the full set of conditions Griswold describes or agree that forgiveness is tantamount to condoning the misdeed, to find it reasonable to see that the minimal condition of repentance is necessary for forgiveness to even begin. This is because there needs to be firstly, as Jankélévitch stressed, a guilty party that needs forgiving. Secondly, this condition tells us if there is indeed some wrongdoing to forgive since we have the tendency to perceive injury and take offense when there is none, or exaggerate our injury as Butler pointed out. But I believe that it takes more than an acknowledgement of the misdeed to establish genuine repentance. It entails also repudiation and the acceptance of punishment (in order to authenticate the expressed apology or regret) and the promise of not repeating the misdeed without any expectations of forgiveness or reconciliation. And although the restoration of a moral relationship between the wrongdoer and victim is not always necessary or possible in forgiveness, genuine repentance makes future reintegration of the wrongdoer into the community possible by first restoring the wrongdoer as a moral agent. Any genuine attempt at doing so ought to entail helping the wrongdoer change their perceptions of themselves and others so that they recognize their misdeeds in the context of a moral community. In acknowledging their misdeeds, they assume responsibility for their choices as moral agents, and in admitting guilt, they accept their punishment as part of what it takes to restore the rights of their victims. Lastly, by restoring wrongdoers as moral agents, trust in the community is reestablished and this will enable their future reintegration into the moral order.

Genuine repentance as I have outlined focuses on the relationship between the victim and the wrongdoer, and it is for this reason that makes a forgiving response appropriate. Eve Garrard and David McNaughton call such reasons an "object-focused" reason, contrasted with "attitude-focused" reasons which are "reasons for getting oneself into a particular psychological state, in this case the state of having a forgiving attitude" (2003, 51). Unilateral accounts of forgiveness for instance, give attitude-focused reasons for forgiving, such as recovering one's self-worth and rising above the humiliation inflicted by the wrongdoer in Jean Hampton's account, or to promote the good of the forgiver that is advocated by Margaret Holmgren. But because the reasons for forgiveness in these accounts are centered on the psychological recovery or the moral virtues of the victims, they do not consider whether forgiving is an appropriate response within the context of a relationship.

The problem with attitude-focused reasons is apparent in the TRCs in South Africa and Rwanda. In South Africa, given the country's limited political and economic resources, it is unwise and impossible to impose a "Nuremberg trial paradigm" because it will place undue burden on the system without sufficient attention on the restoration of victims and forward-looking political healing for the nation. Instead, Desmond Tutu advocates unconditional forgiveness as the way ahead for transitional justice and reconciliation by setting up the Truth Reconciliation Commission since it is "the only alternative to Nuremberg on the one hand and amnesia on the other" (Tutu 1996). In Rwanda too, President Paul Kagame encouraged forgiveness on a national level while also emphasizing that the perpetrators must "show courage and to confess, to repent, and to ask forgiveness" (Brudholm and Rosoux 2009, 42). To reduce their sentences, prisoners began to confess their crimes through statements that were prepared in identical ways with no expressions of regret or remorse, and took no personal responsibility by hiding behind group action, nor ask for forgiveness. In response to this "cheap" repentance, survivors denounced the "politics" or "ideology" of reconciliation and became resistant to forgiveness.

In reaction to this, Derrida was right to point out that there is a conceptual mistake to assume that forgiveness has taken place when there was only reconciliation. More fundamentally, it is a mistake to think that forgiveness can be normalized in the form of political reconciliation through national effort. Forgiveness is an exception, one which only persons and not states can grant. Thus, it may seem to governments that reconciliation is a more sensible option than retributive justice in their post-conflict societies, but they are mistaken to think that forgiveness is a matter that can be achieved through political will.[85] In these TRCs, the call for unconditional forgiveness for the purpose of political reconciliation has been met with resistance precisely because forgiveness is an inappropriate response in these contexts where genuine repentance is absent. Genuine repentance is what constitutes a real reason for forgiveness—a guilty party, a misdeed, and a victim—and does not focus only on reconciliation for the sake of the future of the country. As Jankélévitch rightly reminded us, recommending forgiveness based on the rea-

---

[85] There are also other convincing reasons to delink forgiveness from politics such as those given by Colleen Murphy in "Political Reconciliation, the Rule of Law, and Genocide", *The European Legacy*, Vol. 12, No. 7 (2007): 853-865. Murphy aptly pointed out that political reconciliation neither entails nor necessitates forgiveness in the first place because it is not negative emotions between persons that damaged political relationships. Moreover, political relationships are fundamentally different from personal relationships, thus giving no basis for modeling political reconciliation as forgiveness on the requirements for interpersonal reconciliation such as what we see in the cases of South Africa and Rwanda. The achievement of political reconciliation requires the re-establishment of the mutual respect for the rule of law, not the overcoming of resentment.

son that the sin is a past that we should forget is imprudent and is a means for making us disgusted with it.

Moreover, when we unconditionally forgive the guilty as guilty on Derrida's terms, or forgive only by changing our perceptions of ourselves because we want to move on with our lives, it is pseudo-forgiveness because it is not based on a relationship between equals. Victims continue to view wrongdoers as beings different from themselves, resulting in the unequal relationship of power that Derrida is concerned with. Derrida's suggestion is to grant forgiveness as a surprise or keeping it in secret to avoid forming an unequal power relation, but this is too abstract, and can only serve as an ideal for which to strive. Unconditional forgiveness that is only attitude-focused is also a form of hasty forgiveness because victims do not confront their resentments and sacred memories seriously, but instead, repress or forget them so as to recover from the injury. And in Jankélévitch's terms, liquidation is not forgiveness. Furthermore, it does not promote the moral restoration of the wrongdoer that is necessary for the moral repair in the relationship within a community because there is no genuine repentance that makes forgiveness concrete and meaningful for victims, and does not restore the wrongdoer as a moral agent that can be reintegrate into the moral order in the future.

An object-focused reason on the other hand, can help us look at forgiveness within a context that is morally appropriate, avoids hasty forgiveness, and focus on restoring wrongdoers as moral agents so as to make it possible for their future reintegration into a moral order. Garrard and McNaughton for instance, argue for unconditional forgiveness with an object-based reason—a sense of shared human solidarity with wrongdoers founded on "a sense of ourselves as less than morally impressive, as closer to the moral condition of the wrongdoer than we would like to be" (2003, 58). Forgiveness for them does not focus on whether the wrongdoer deserves forgiveness because "it involves a kind of humility, a readiness to see the forgiven one as not so markedly inferior to oneself" (Ibid.).

Although their account of unconditional forgiveness is object-focused, we may find that it fails to be a morally sufficient reason because first, it isn't convincing that we share similar moral conditions with wrongdoers such as the Nazis. By assuming this is the case, they run into two issues. First, I found it difficult to see that the Nazis are "failures at practical reasoning" but not failures at "being human, in any other than a metaphorical sense" because some Nazis (like Eichmann, as I have described) are failures as moral beings because of their lack of conscience (Garrard 2002, 161).[86] For another, for Eve Garrard and David McNaughton to argue that "we are closer to the moral condition of the wrongdoer," they would need to defend the problem of collective guilt that Arendt reminds us: that if everyone is guilty, nobody is, and therefore nobody can be judged. Because of these issues, our shared human solidarity is better built on the humanness or conscience we have as moral agents, rather than to build it on what is "weak, pitiful and degraded" for the sake of keeping "firmly in center-stage the undeniable fact that we are a pretty bad lot" (Garrard and McNaughton 2003, 59). Second, not all relationships between victims and wrongdoers embody this power structure, especially within the framework of unconditional forgiveness, because there is no need for wrongdoers to seek forgiveness which puts them in an inferior position. The feeling of superiority on the part of the forgiver is hence a mistaken perception since there is no guilty party that seeks forgiveness. Third, to not see the object of forgiveness as inferior does not need to stem from a

---

[86] I have elsewhere shown that this category of evildoers is significantly different from those who failed at practical reasoning. See Jennifer Ang, (2016), "Evil by Nobodies," *The Problem of Evil: New Philosophical Directions*, edited by Benjamin McGraw and Robert Arp, 51-68 (Lanham: Lexington Books).

sense of humility. In conditional forgiveness, the wrongdoer is restored as a moral agent because he repents and takes responsibility for his choices and actions.

Yet, we find that even an object-focused conditional account of forgiveness can be an insufficient moral reason when it does not have a full account of what moral agency entails. Trudy Govier for instance, proposes that we ought to forgive when wrongdoers repent based on respect for their moral agency and their capacity for rational change, since there is another sense in which they are not only wrongdoers but also human beings with new choices in the future to make (1999, 59-75). As such, "no one is absolutely unforgivable," even for atrocious acts of evils so long as they repent. As for those who do not repent, the wrongdoer is identified with the evil deed and we are thus justified in not forgiving them. This separation of the person from his act is also echoed by Desmond Tutu who gives a theological framework that understands the deed as evil, and not the doer, and also puts forth that "it is possible for people to change, insofar as perpetrators can come to realize the evil of their actions and even be able to plead for the forgiveness of those they have wronged" (Ibid.., 110). Garrard and McNaughton however, rightly question why we should respect "the presence of moral agency in those who have put that capacity to so distorted a use," and why the mere capacity for moral change should be reason enough for forgiveness (Ibid., 52-3).

What I found missing in Govier's account, as the encounter with evildoer without conscience shows us, is the fact that moral agents must assume personal responsibility for their choices, decisions and actions, and not just have a capacity for changes in the future. This more holistic view of moral agency will help us firstly, to distinguish between genuine repentance from cheap repentance, so that forgiveness is a morally appropriate response, and secondly, makes forgiveness a matter between moral agents of equal status. Thus, we will find a case of genuine repentance of morally vacuous evildoers when they understand what ethics means:

they must regard others and themselves as human beings with dignity and equal status (as not less-than-humans), with freely chosen principles and alternative courses of action from which personal responsibility follows, so that they can be considered as moral agents. It will also require their full realization that their misdeed arises from a lack of an independent moral standard from which they should judge from, so that they may become personal judges of their own misdeeds and the orders they choose to follow. This is necessary, if we want them to judge their decisions and actions as moral agents and not just cogs in the system. Furthermore, with genuine repentance expressed through apology and remorse, and the acceptance of their punishment, they present themselves to the community as a moral agent—one with a common agreement of what constitutes ethics and what it means to be a being-in-the-world-with-other-moral beings—that has the ability to reintegrate into the moral order, possibly through subsequent processes of rehabilitation and restoration.

This notion of genuine repentance—acknowledgement and repudiation of misdeed, and assuming personal responsibility by accepting their punishment—as a definition of moral agency reveals a limit to accounts of conditional forgiveness when we are confronted with evildoers without conscience. Evildoers with no conscience are non-moral agents because they lack the ability to differentiate and judge what is morally reprehensible and what is morally good, and as a result, are unable to experience feelings of regret or remorse and unable to offer apology and repent. They regard ethics in abstract terms rather than concrete situations which require moral judgments regarding people's lives, and also believe that the moral principle of the day is responsible for its outcome rather than individual choices. They thus have no basis for establishing ethical relationships between free individuals that requires them to assume responsibility for their free choices, decisions and actions towards others that are fundamental in all moral orders.

It also reveals a limit to accounts of unconditional forgiveness. To forgive evildoers without conscience unconditionally, we have to accept them the way they are as non-moral agents. But being non-moral agents undermines the very idea of morality itself. It also defeats the moral order we want to achieve—that one cannot escape from personal responsibility for their evil misdeeds. Furthermore, given that ethics is only possible if others are also ethical, if we were to integrate non-moral agents into the community, any efforts aimed at upholding collective morality will be hampered. More fundamentally, because there are no guilty parties and no evil misdeeds, it is questionable if forgiveness is required at all. In fact, our hasty response to the call for unconditional forgiveness will mean that we are thoughtless in not making any distinctions between morally bankrupt wrongdoers and wrongdoers who express genuine repentance, and instead, grant forgiveness too lightly.

Concluding remarks

When we come face to face with absolute evil and evildoers without conscience, we are burdened with the task to rethink our terms of justice, because firstly, these crimes challenge our legal limits when they involve crimes where no punishment is adequate; secondly, the nature of evil lies beyond our comprehension and imagination; and lastly, the evildoers' lack of conscience challenges what we can humanly expect from victims. What I have shown is that our resentment is not only a morally legitimate response, but it may in the end be the only way we can refuse being made superfluous. It helps us guard against being transformed into something less-than-human in the future, with injury to our dignity, rights and status as free and equal beings, and it helps us uphold the idea of morality in the face of absolute evil, to ensure that the promise of "never again" is taken seriously. Without genuine repentance from these evildoers, granting forgiveness is only a psychological tool for the victim, and does not restore the morally vacuous evildoer to his moral agency, nor promote moral repair in the community. Unconditionally forgiving morally bankrupt evildoers when there is no need for forgiveness is thus morally inappropriate. We must hence ensure that we forgive only when evildoers show genuine repentance, which involves an acknowledgement and repudiation of his misdeed, the acceptance of punishment, and a promise to not repeat the misdeed, without any expectations of forgiveness or reconciliation.

References

Arendt, Hannah. 1981. *Life of Mind*. San Diego: Harcourt.

_____. 1950. "Social Science Techniques and the Study of Concentration Camps." *Jewish Social Studies* 12.1: 49-64.

_____. 2006. *Eichmann in Jerusalem*. New York: Penguin Classics.

_____. 1994. *The Origins of Totalitarianism*. San Diego: Harcourt.

_____. 2005. *Responsibility and Judgement*. New York: Shocken Books.

Ang, Jennifer. 2016. "Evil by Nobodies." The Problem of Evil: New Philosophical Directions. Edited by Benjamin McGraw and Robert Arp. Lanham: Lexington Books.

Arendt, Hannah and Karl Jaspers. 1992. *Correspondence: 1926-1969*. Edited by Lotte Kohler and Hans Saner. Orlando: Harcourt Brace International.

Berstein, J. Richard. 1997. "The 'Banality of Evil' Reconsidered." *Hannah Arendt and the Meaning of Politics*. Edited by Graig Calhoun and John McGowan. Minneapolis: University of Minnesota Press.

Brudholm, Thomas and Valérie Rosoux. 2009. "The Unforgiving: Reflections on the Resistance to Forgiveness After Atrocity." *Law and Contemporary Problems* 72: 33-50.

Busk, Larry. 2015. "Sleepwalk: Arendt, Thoughtlessness, and the Question of Little Eichmanns." *Social Philosophy Today* 31: 53-69.

Butler, Joseph. 1827. *Fifteen Sermons*. http://anglicanhistory.org/butler/rolls/.

Cambridge: Hilliard and Brown. Accessed February 16, 2016.

Butler, Judith. 2011. "Arendt's Death Sentences." *Comparative Literature* Studies 48.3: 280-295.

Cesarani, David. 2007. *Becoming Eichmann*. Cambridge: The Perseus Book Group.

Derrida, Jacques. 2001. *On Cosmopolitanism and Forgiveness*. London and New York: Routledge.

Garrard, Eve. 2002. "Forgiveness and the Holocaust." *Ethical theory and Moral Practice* 5.2: 147-165.

Garrard, Eve and David McNaughton. 2003. "In Defense of Unconditional Forgiveness." *Proceedings of the Aristotelian Society* 103.1: 39-60.

Govier, Trudy. 1999. "Forgiveness and the Unforgiveable." *American Philosophical Quarterly* 36.1: 59-75.

Griswold, Charles. 2007. *Forgiveness: A Philosophical Exploration*. Cambridge: Cambridge University Press.

Jankélévitch, Vladimir. 2005. *Forgiveness*. Chicago and London: The University of Chicago Press.

_____. 1996. "Should We Pardon Them?" *Critical Inquiry* 22.3: 552-572.

Kagame, Paul. 2009. Address at Urugwiro Village in Kigali (June 18 2002). http://scholarship.law.duke.edu/cgi/viewcontent.cgi?article=1514&context=lcp. In Thomas Brudholm and Velerie Rosoux. "The Unforgiving: Reflections on the Resistance to Forgiveness after Atrocity." *Law and Contemporary Problems* 72.2: 33-49. Accessed on 16 February 2016.

Kant, Immanuel. 1960. *Religion within the Limits of Reason Alone*. Translated by Theodore M. Greene and Hoyt H. Hudson. Las Salle, IL: Open Court Publishing.

Kauppinen, Jari. 2010. "Hannah Arendt's Thesis on Different Modes of Evil." *Collegium* 8: 48-66.

Matthews, Charles. 2001. *Evil in Augustinian Tradition*. Cambridge: Cambridge University Press.

Murphy, Colleen. 2007. "Political Reconciliation, the Rule of Law, and Genocide." *The European Legacy* 12.7: 853-865.

Murphy, Jeffrie and Jean Hampton. 1988. *Forgiveness and Mercy*. New York: Cambridge University Press.

Murphy, G. Jeffrie. 2003. *Getting Even: Forgiveness and Its Limits*. New York: Oxford University Press.

Svendsen, Lars. 2001. *A Philosophy of Evil*. Champaign and London: Dalkey Archive Press.

Tutu, Desmond. 2002. *Cape Times* (April 17, 1997). In Trudy Grovier, *Forgiveness and Revenge*. London and New York: Routledge.

_____. 1996. *The Sunday Times* (of South Africa). In Beth S. Lyons. 1997. "Between Nuremberg and Amnesia: The Truth and Reconciliation Commission in South Africa." *Monthly Review*.

Verdeja, Ernesto. 2004. "Derrida and the Impossibility of Forgiveness." *Contemporary Political Theory* 3.1: 23-47.

Walker, Margaret U. 2006. *Moral Repair: Reconstructing Moral Relations after Wrongdoing*. New York: Cambridge University Press.

Chapter 7

Unconditional Forgiveness and Practical Necessity

Christopher Cowley

Introduction

Let us begin with the classic paradigm: an *offender* freely and knowingly commits an *offence* against a *victim*. The offender has no excuses or justification, nor does he believe that he does. How should the victim react? Her resentment is justified. She may take revenge on the offender, she may ignore the offence, or she may seek or invent excuses for it. Alternatively, she could decide to attempt to forgive the offender. (This may take time, and, psychologically, it may not succeed.) The question is: morally, should she try to forgive; that is, should she try to overcome her justified resentment?

There is a relatively clear debate in the Anglo-American literature between two accounts here. The 'conditionalist' (such as Kolnai, Murphy, and Griswold) will say that the victim should wait for the offender to fulfil certain conditions (especially apology and repentance) before deciding to try to forgive; to forgive in the absence of fulfilled conditions would involve the victim condoning the offence and denigrating herself. For forgiveness to be morally respectable, it must be guided and justified by norms, and these norms are publicly accessible. Therefore a perplexed third party observer can ask the victim why she forgave, and the victim needs to be able to justify the forgiveness by citing relevant and sufficient reasons, namely the fact that the offender has fulfilled the relevant conditions. There might still be room for debate between the observer and the victim about whether the offender has fulfilled the conditions to the right degree or in the right way, but the conditionalist will say that such a debate is informed and guided by the existence of relevant shared justificatory norms.

On the other hand, the 'unconditionalist' (Garrard and McNaughton, Derrida, and the Christian[87]) claims that the conditional account comes too close to a transaction; once the offender has fulfilled the conditions, there is no longer any point to forgiveness—except to "rubber-stamp" the deal. In many cases of apology, the offender will offer sincere and valid excuses, and if these excuses are recognised as such then what the victim can offer is to excuse the offender, rather than to forgive him. Whatever the nature of the apology, forgiveness becomes too easy, so that it involves no moral work that would merit the moral admiration that characterizes our response to forgiveness. Although the victim may use the *words* "I forgive you," this is not *real* forgiveness but a mere simulacrum—a socially useful simulacrum, of course.

Instead, real forgiveness involves precisely those situations where the offence is incomprehensible, inexcusable, or where the offender is blatantly unrepentant. Only in response to such an offence is admirable work involved in forgiving. In addition, the unconditionalist reminds us that forgiveness, like gifts, should be essentially elective. The bottle I bring to a dinner party is not a real gift but an entrance ticket; in contrast, a genuine gift cannot be obligated or expected, and so it is with forgiveness. The sincerely repentant offender cannot demand forgiveness, even when there is nothing left that he can do. (I am assuming that the victim's

---

[87] There is a debate within Christian theology about whether forgiveness should be taken as unconditional and obligatory. For the purposes of this paper, I will assume that the Christian is an unconditionalist, and this will be relevant to our discussion of the Gordon Wilson example later on.

resentment remains justified only on the basis of an offence that was genuinely harmful, unjustifiable and inexcusable.)

In a recent 2014 piece, Steven Gormley develops an interesting hybrid position between the conditionalist and the unconditionalist accounts. I want to describe it, and then develop it in ways that strike me as plausible (but which he might not agree with at all). In terms of the arguments as laid out above, his first step is inclined toward the unconditionalist account. However, he is troubled by the perplexed third party observer asking the victim why she decided to try to forgive. Gormley (38 *ff*) understands the victim as having two possibilities: either she *can* give reasons or she *cannot*. Both possibilities undermine the unconditional forgiveness, albeit in different ways. If the victim *can* give reasons, the implication is that she was withholding forgiveness until the grounds of these reasons obtained, and this suggests some sort of conditional account, even if the grounds of her forgiveness are different than those of the traditional conditionalist. For example, the victim may forgive the offender "for old times's sake." This decision does not depend on the offender repenting, but there is a condition that the offender nevertheless fulfils in a way that other offenders do not. The implication of this kind of conditionality is that if the condition was not fulfilled, the victim *could not* forgive; and if it was, then she *had to* forgive. I have italicized the modal verbs here to show that either way, she seems to be acting under an obligation, and has lost the electivity that is crucial to the unconditionalist account. (This will be important later, when I consider "practical necessity.")

However, if the victim forgives unconditionally, and is then interrogated by the third party, and the victim *cannot* give a reason for forgiving, the implication is that the act of forgiveness is at best whimsical or frivolous or arbitrary, at worst unintelligible. All the victim might say, lamely, is that "it felt like the right thing to do at the time." This might preserve electivity, but at considerable rational and moral cost.

Importantly, it would not be clear why the rest of us can or should *admire* such forgiveness.

So Gormley wants to support the unconditionalist account, but finds he cannot, as conceived above. So Gormley offers an ingenious solution (43 *ff*), based on Derrida. Derrida's account of forgiveness is obscure at the best of times, and I cannot claim to understand it sufficiently. But I think Gormley is right to highlight two key insights of Derrida's: 1) "forgiveness only becomes possible from the moment it appears impossible" (Derrida 2001, 33); and 2) "the secret of this experience remains" (Ibid., 55). Gormley expands this as the following two-step. Real forgiveness cannot be spontaneous. It has to begin with the first step, with a pause, for the victim to truly appreciate the offense *as* wrong, inexcusable, incomprehensible—and *prima facie* unforgiveable. But the pause also allows time for the victim to deliberate about what to do. Such deliberation invokes reasons, reasons that could in principle be given to a perplexed observer. The second step then involves the victim's realization that the reasons do not "add up" to a decision, be it a decision to forgive or to not forgive; and yet the victim forgives. Gormley concludes: "an act of pure, unconditional forgiveness necessarily involves a moment of non-knowledge, a gap between the reasons one appeals to and the decision to forgive" (2014, 44).

This compromise would allow enough room for reasons so as to preserve the rational intelligibility and moral justifiability of forgiveness under the conditionalist account, while also preserving enough of a gap to allow the electivity of forgiveness under the unconditionalist account. However, it is worth emphasizing: the gap of non-knowledge applies not only to the observer, but also *to the victim*. The victim can provide some reasons to explain the forgiveness, but if the observer persists and asks why *those* reasons were sufficient for forgiveness, then the victim has nothing further to say. This is not because the victim chooses to keep something hidden, it is because the victim does not herself know why these reasons were sufficient; neither the observer nor the victim can see into the gap.

This is more than agent-relativity of reasons: it is not a situation where, say, the "career man" takes the boss's request as a sufficient reason to break his promise to his young daughter, whereas the "family man" does not. In that scenario, both the "career man" and the "family man" can *fully* justify (or agent-relatively justify) their respective behavior with reference to the different values and priorities they bring to the decision situation. In Gormley's scenario, the reasons only gesture toward forgiveness, and the gap between the reasons and the decision is essentially "secret" and impenetrable to the victim herself.

I find Gormley's compromise solution very interesting and intuitively plausible. As it stands, however, it is not sufficiently developed. And like many compromises, the chances are that neither conditionalists nor unconditionalists will be happy with it! In order to develop it, I want to look a bit more closely at the two examples that Gormley himself deploys: those of Dietrich Bonhoeffer and Gordon Wilson.

Bonhoeffer and practical necessity

The following example is not directly about forgiveness, but it does show the "gap" in action. Dietrich Bonhoeffer was a German theologian and priest, and had been an active opponent to the Nazi regime since its beginning in 1933. In 1938 he left Germany for the United States. A year later, however, he decided to return to Germany, at considerable risk to his safety and life. The risks were well founded: he was eventually imprisoned in 1943, and executed in 1945.

Bonhoeffer had two main reasons for returning, and he gave these reasons to concerned American friends: first, he felt he could not abandon his countrymen during their hour of need; second, he could not look forward to helping Germany recover after the war if he had not himself suffered during it. However, while Bonhoeffer was utterly sincere in being motivated by these reasons, he himself admitted that they did not, on their own, "add up" to the decision to return:

> *...today's decision is ... full of anxiety, however brave it may appear. The reasons that one gives to others and to oneself for an action are certainly inadequate ... in the last resort we are acting from a plane that is hidden from us. (Gormley 2014, 44)*

If such a "plane" is "hidden," the question is whether Bonhoeffer's decision could be anything but whimsical or arbitrary or unintelligible. (Although the three terms mean different things, I will refer to them collectively as the "risk of arbitrariness" from now on.)

Gormley gestures toward Bernard Williams's concept of "practical necessity" to address this issue, and he does not explain it in much depth.[88] The important phenomenology is that Bonhoeffer felt that he "had to" return to Germany. There are four things to say about Williams's conception of practical necessity that will be relevant to our discussion.

The first thing is to distinguish it from other kinds of necessity: 1) physical necessity (e.g. being carried off in a straightjacket, since these are forces external to the body); 2) psycho-

---

[88] Bernard Williams wrote at least two articles on the subject, 'Practical necessity' (1981a) and 'Moral incapacity' (1995), such that each phenomenon is roughly the inverse of the other. Under necessity, I find I "have to" do something, while under incapacity, I find I "cannot" do something. Gormley actually describes the Bonhoeffer example under the concept of incapacity, but I prefer to use the concept of necessity because I will later be examining the possibility that forgiveness is a matter of necessity for the victim, as in "I had to forgive him". Interestingly, Williams's main example in 'Practical necessity' is that of Martin Luther, a figure facing a situation not dissimilar to Dietrich Bonhoeffer's in many ways.

logical necessity (e.g. addictions and compulsions, since these are forces internal to the body but external to the self); and importantly, 3) practical necessity is also to be distinguished from moral obligation. The latter (however conceived) is normally expressed in terms of an 'ought', and is therefore essentially overridable: it is perfectly coherent to say "I know I ought to X, but I won't," whereas it is not coherent to say "I know I must X, but I won't."

The second thing about practical necessity is that although there is the same gap between reasons and decision in which Gormley is interested, the decision is *not* arbitrary in a different sense: because it is entirely expressive of the agent's self, of her evaluative stance upon the world, and of her self-understanding as a particular agent living a particular life in that world. At the minimal level, this means that the decision must cohere with the rest of the agent's values, principles, and with the narrative history of the life she has lived. But practical necessity goes beyond mere coherence with the self, to expression of the self: it becomes the only way that this particular self can go on. Sometimes a decision of practical necessity will be spontaneous and unsurprising, as when someone will reliably refuse a bribe, and we are inclined to say of her "she would never take a bribe." Other times, as in the case with Bonhoeffer, deliberation and discussion gradually revealed what he had to do, perhaps to the surprise of some of his friends, and perhaps even to the surprise of himself.

Genuinely arbitrary decisions can be a product of a flip of a coin, just as much as a product of whim or mood; I decide to go for a walk just because I feel like it, and my decision includes an awareness that I could well have remained at home, and could turn back at any moment. Neither the coin flip nor the whim have anything to do with the agent's self or evaluative stance, and as such the decision to go for a walk is arbitrary. (If my going for a walk somehow resulted in harming someone through my negligence, e.g. leaving my infant child at home alone, I would have no defense.)

The third thing about Williams's practical necessity is about the nature of the experience. Bonhoeffer did not *decide* to return to Germany, since deciding presupposes an awareness of genuine choice; instead, Bonhoeffer *discovered* that he *had to return*. In purely physical terms, there was more than one option open to him, of course, and this is precisely what tormented his friends, who begged him (and gave him excellent reasons) to remain in the United States. But given who Bonhoeffer was at that moment, given the way he had shaped his life and the way his life had been shaped, given the evaluative stance and self-understanding that he brought to the "decision," then there was only one option available *to him*. A different person, with a different evaluative stance and self-understanding, may well have approached the "same" situation by discovering that she had to remain in the United States. I put 'same' in scare quotes precisely because the situation is not exhausted by the physical description of the available options: it also includes facts about the person contemplating those options, and in that sense Bonhoeffer and this other person faced different situations. Part of what I mean when I say "I know Smith" is that I know something of the kinds of situation where she would act under practical necessity (and, by extension, something of the kinds of situation where she would "never do" X.)

This point about discovery can be put another way. Normally, when deliberation leads to decision, the agent can behold the reasons (for and against a particular option) at arm's length, as it were. Whereas insofar as this decision/discovery *expresses* the agent's self, there is not enough "room" for the agent to "get behind" it in order to compare the options and the reasons supporting each. Bonhoeffer's discovery was non-arbitrary in a second, more familiar sense as well: he understood how risky the return to Germany would be. When a reflective, informed person takes such a risk, there is a *prima facie* case for seeing her as deeply focused during deliberation, and as making a deeply serious decision. Bonhoeffer was not making a detached decision about travelling or not travelling, he was making a decision about the rest of his life, a life that might very well be cut off sooner rather than later because of that decision.

All this is perfectly compatible with others, especially concerned colleagues or relatives in the United States, being perplexed and indeed angry with Bonhoeffer's decision/discovery. They might say, for example, that he is a gifted theologian, and has plenty more to contribute to theology over a lifetime in an American university, rather than indulging these boy-scout antics smuggling papers under the noses of the Gestapo. They might accuse him of some sort of hero complex, or martyr complex, of a self-absorbed thirst for adventure. They might also accuse him of failing in his duties to his colleagues and relatives in the United States, by throwing his life away in a futile cause, at a very real cost to them. Bonhoeffer was well aware of this cost, and of the impression that he might give, yet he still felt he "had to" go. He realised that his motives might be forever held up to scrutiny and found wanting. Perhaps the dilemma would have been a lot sharper if he had abandoned a child in the United States.[89]

The fourth and final thing to say about Williams's account of practical necessity is that the full force of the necessity may only be revealed in time. Once back in Germany, Bon-

---

[89] In this I am reminded of another of Bernard Williams's examples (1981b), that of a semi-fictional painter named Gauguin, who feels he "has to" abandon his family in 19th-Century Paris (where their future, without relatives and without a welfare state, Gauguin knew would be "grim") in order to travel to Tahiti to paint. Williams argues that our moral attitude to him and to the abandonment will depend on the luck of whether it turns out that he has enough talent and that he can get his canvases back to Paris intact to become artistically successful. In contrast, we tend to admire Bonhoeffer despite the failure of his efforts, perhaps even because of that failure. But if Bonhoeffer had abandoned a family, those family members would have a real cause for grievance, whatever their father's posthumous reputation.

hoeffer was well-connected enough that he could have escaped again, but he never tried. Indeed, even after his imprisonment in 1943 a sympathetic guard offered him the chance to escape, and he refused. So he had plenty of opportunity to change his mind by re-inhabiting his 1939 mindset and coming to the conclusion that he had made a mistake—and this might have been enough for him and others to judge that the 1939 decision had been arbitrary in some way (e.g. over-hasty, culpably ignorant, sentimental). The fact that he never did change his mind, as far as we know, corroborates our sense that he did indeed discover in 1939 what he had to do, and what he had to do was not arbitrary.

I have been trying to flesh out Gormley's use of the Bonhoeffer example to support the idea that a gap need not result in an arbitrariness that would damage the decision's rational and moral credentials. But this example is not about forgiveness (although it might touch on forgiveness when we look at the friends that Bonhoeffer left behind in the United States). It suggests an interesting possibility, however, which Gormley does not consider. Maybe the phenomenology of real forgiveness is not one of decision but of discovery, such that the victim declares that she "has to" forgive the offender? With this possibility in mind, let us move to Gormley's second example.

Gordon Wilson

Gordon Wilson was a draper and a deeply committed Christian, living in Enniskillen, Northern Ireland. At a Remembrance Day service in 1987 the IRA detonated a bomb that covered him and his daughter Marie in heavy building rubble, and eventually Marie died from her injuries. Apparently the IRA had been targeting a platoon of British soldiers that were due to attend the ceremony, but in the end did not. Later, Wilson told a BBC reporter:

> *But I bear no ill will. I bear no grudge. Dirty sort of talk is not going to bring her back to*

> life. She was a great wee lassie. She loved her profession. She was a pet. She's dead. She's in heaven and we shall meet again. I will pray for these men tonight and every night.[90]

The IRA bombers were never identified, and as an organization they did not apologise until much later (and there are questions about the author and the sincerity of the "apology"). So in terms of the debate between the conditionalists and the unconditionalists, there was a clear failure to fulfil any conditions, at least at the time of Wilson's statement. Wilson would therefore be vulnerable to the accusation that he was condoning the action, as well as showing insufficient respect for either himself or his daughter.[91] Gormley mentions another person, Daphne Stephenson, who was injured in the same explosion (2014, 27). Stephenson was asked what she thought of Wilson's response, and she said: "I wouldn't have had that attitude at all. The people who caused the explosion didn't ask to be forgiven and haven't shown any repentance whatsoever." Nevertheless Wilson seems to have forgiven, either with these words, if not earlier.

It is worth highlighting three things about Wilson's forgiveness. First, we may assume that Wilson understood exactly what had happened, and considered the bombing to be morally deplorable; it was not as if an unpredictable natural catastrophe had killed his daughter. Even if she had not been

---

[90] BBC, The Age of Terror: Clips, retrieved from http://www.bbc.co.uk/programmes/p010gppk [accessed March 2016], and cited by Gormley p. 27. The example is also cited by Garrard and McNaughton (2003).

[91] It is true that some acts of killing might be justified by their occurrence within a just war, and some people might view the Catholic struggle against the British 'occupier' in these lights, but this particular bombing against innocent civilians (most of them elderly) was clearly unjustified.

intentionally targeted, the bombers were guilty of gross recklessness.

Second, despite what the conditionalists might think, most people take Wilson's forgiveness to be morally admirable. Daphne Stephenson's declaration above is actually ambiguous here. It *could* mean that she herself hated the IRA for what they did, that she would never forgive them for her own injuries, and would never have forgiven them if her own child had been killed—maybe she was too polite to phrase it in those terms. On the other hand, it could also mean that she was only psychologically incapable of forgiving the IRA, much though she realises it would be the appropriate thing to do; in this respect her comments are compatible with an admiration for Wilson.

Third, although Wilson was injured, the important thing here is that it was Wilson's daughter who was killed. There is a question here of whether Wilson had the "standing" to forgive the IRA for the death of someone else; one might argue that only the victim can forgive, and one can speculate about what Marie Wilson would have thought of the IRA, and would have thought about her father presuming to forgive them on her behalf. Nevertheless, if we assume that Wilson loved his daughter, then we can also assume that his life was very much bound up in hers, such that any attack on her was also an attack on him; indeed, he would probably have suffered much more from her loss than from any wounds the bomb could have inflicted on him. I think that while some people (especially Christians) could imagine being tortured, and going on to forgive their torturer, it is much more difficult for a parent to imagine their *child* being killed, and then going to on to forgive the killer. I do not know if Daphne Stephenson was herself a parent, but perhaps this was also relevant to her inability to "have that attitude." Again, though, this seems to push our reactions even further to the extremes: on the one hand, Wilson's forgiveness becomes even more admirable; on the other hand, it becomes even more tempting to condemn him for "betraying" his daughter.

The most obvious person who could criticise Gordon Wilson's forgiveness was Wilson's wife Joan. For Marie was her child too. Indeed, in the fact that it was she who bore Marie, that Marie was of her flesh, it could be said that she was more her child than Gordon's, and therefore that decisions about forgiveness would belong more to the mother than to the father. Even if we accept equal parenting status, there is a tension here. On the one hand, forgiveness is a highly personal matter, and each person has to answer the forgiveness question for themselves. On the other, it is interesting that we never hear about Joan Wilson's attitude to the IRA murderers, either through her husband speaking of 'we' forgiving them (in the same way that he would be inclined to speak of "*our* child"), or at least through a reference to what 'my wife' thinks. Presumably she agreed with his decision: it would be intolerable to live with someone whom one thought of as having betrayed one's child.

Now let me bring in the perplexed observer (the BBC reporter), asking Wilson why he forgave. Wilson mentions the pointlessness of "dirty talk." He mentions his intention to pray for the bombers, which suggests that he pities them. We therefore have two reasons that point in the direction of forgiveness, but, I think, fall far short of sufficiency. In his discussion of the example Gormley does not explicitly suggest that Wilson acted on practical necessity, but this is what I interpret him as implying. Wilson first paused to contemplate the enormity of the offence. He then deliberated about whether to forgive or not. And he discovered that he "had to" forgive them. I admit that I am speculating at this point—I could find no evidence that he would have articulated the forgiveness under the modality of necessity; but I want to argue that this is the most philosophically compelling account of real forgiveness, that it is essentially unconditional and essentially about the discovery of a necessity; without the practical necessity, then it would be a matter of decision, and without sufficient reasons then such a decision would indeed risk being arbitrary, whimsical, frivolous or unintelligible.

There is one more difference between Bonhoeffer and Wilson that is relevant to Wilson's forgiveness, and that is the role of Wilson's religious beliefs. Both men were devout believers, but Bonhoeffer was more interested in his country and his compatriots when looking for reasons to return to Germany. Wilson made an explicit reference not only to praying for the IRA bombers, but he also reaffirmed his faith that he would meet his daughter again in heaven. In dealing with a question of forgiveness, Wilson's Christianity would have been directly relevant, and so this is worth examining more closely.

A Christian duty to forgive?

I have already expressed my reluctance to go too far into the theological debate about the Christian obligations. The first thing to say is that it is perfectly compatible for a Christian to forgive her offender while at the same time supporting all the efforts of the secular criminal justice system to apprehend, prosecute and punish him. (As far as I know, Wilson never demanded that the IRA bombers be shown mercy.)

Second, I want to reject a conception of religious faith that reduces it to a mere struggle over psychological obstacles (e.g. one's selfishness, fear, the seven deadly sins...). I mentioned this when I introduced the possible criticism by the fellow survivor, Daphne Stephenson. Although this might have been what was going on in Wilson's mind, this conception is not very interesting philosophically or morally. Instead, I'm going to assume he was deliberating about whether or not to forgive, just as Bonhoeffer was deliberating about whether or not to return, *given* that they both had the strength of will to carry out their respective decisions or discoveries.

Third, it seems to be a clear command for Christians to "love your neighbour as yourself" and to "forgive us our trespasses, as we forgive those who trespass against us." Such commands are surely central to the Christian faith (in a way that, say, the prohibition against contraception is arguably not really central to the Catholic faith). On the one hand this would provide an intelligible and sufficient agent-relative reason to forgive: to put the matter as a crude caricature, we could then describe Wilson as "merely following orders." However, I want to reject this conception of religious faith not only because it threatens the electivity which I am arguing is essential to real forgiveness, but more broadly because it threatens the free will which is exactly what gives religious faith its value (God does not want merely servile obedience). Instead, it is better to understand the above expressions not as commands backed by threats, but rather as *definitions* of what a good Christian would do. And this leads me to the important point.

The best way of accommodating Wilson's religious faith in his discovery that he has to forgive is to see his dilemma as beginning *not* with the question "should I forgive?" but *one stage back*. I suggest that the murder of his daughter presented a deep challenge to his belief in God, and this is what he struggled with in the time between the offence and the forgiveness. Once he could reaffirm his belief in God, then the forgiveness followed on from that. By the time the BBC interviewer asks him the question, Wilson was able to re-affirm his faith: "I don't have an answer, but I know there has to be a plan. If I didn't think that, I would commit suicide. It's part of a greater plan, and God is good. And we shall meet again."

The problem now is that the reaffirmation of faith is essentially mysterious; indeed, just as mysterious as the acquisition of faith by a so-called religious experience. Almost by definition, there is very little that a believer can explain to a non-believer about her conversion, or about her reaffirmation, beyond a vague description of the experience. What seems clear is that reasons alone are never sufficient for religious belief, as the notorious failure of the so-called "proofs of God attest through the ages. There always has to be a nonrational leap for the final step. And this starts to sound like Gormley's description of forgiveness. The religious believer can offer certain reasons for believing in God, and knows that she has to offer some reasons if her belief is not to appear as mere superstition or self-consoling fantasy, and yet the reasons never come close to adding up to the final decision/discovery, and the final gap is and should be essentially mysterious to both others and the believer herself.

The non-believing observer will not understand this, and will apply standards of rational belief-formation in vain. For the conditionalist to challenge the Christian's unconditional forgiveness is to challenge the entire edifice of Christian belief. This is not the place to explore the relationship between rationality and religious belief. However, Wilson's decision to forgive could be criticised even by those who *accept* that Bonhoeffer's decision to return to Germany was not arbitrary because of the gap. For Bonhoeffer was literally risking his life to do what he felt he had to do, and this gave his decision/discovery the requisite moral seriousness and underpinned its authority in expressing his self-conception. The risks involved such a high degree of probability and severity as to override, in strictly rational terms, any positive reasons for returning to Germany (namely his obligation to help his compatriots in their hour of need). Only a self-expressing practical necessity could make that decision admirable and non-arbitrary.

For Wilson, on the other hand, there was no risk to his safety or life in his decision to forgive the IRA. He might meet the disapproval of Daphne Stephenson (the other victim of the same blast), or of his wife or of his daughter Marie's school friends, but that was hardly a great risk. But maybe this is again looking at the matter too late. Wilson's real problem, before the problem of whether to forgive, was the crisis of faith. For Wilson, a devout Christian up to this moment of great evil, this crisis carried the same existential risks to Wilson's soul as any threat to biological life.

The classic counter-example

So far I have been expanding Gormley's account of unconditional forgiveness as involving reasons that render the forgiveness partly intelligible while being insufficient to fully justify it, and I have been developing Gormley's suggestion that Williams's practical necessity could fill the gap between the reasons and the forgiveness in order to deflect the charge of arbitrariness. Gordon Wilson can give *some* reasons for having forgiven (e.g. the pointlessness of the "dirty talk"), but beyond these he might only say "I had to forgive them." In this final section, I want to deploy the classic counter-example of the conditionalists.

Imagine a husband who regularly and systematically abuses his wife over the course of years. Relatives and friends know enough about it to beg her to leave him and to report it to the police. But the wife refuses to leave, refuses to press charges, refuses to complain despite her evident injuries and distress. Whenever the police do come to the house, she denies there is anything wrong and explains away the bruises as resulting from her own clumsiness. Perhaps she explicitly uses the words 'I forgive you', perhaps the mere fact that she remains with him without complaining is itself an expression of forgiveness. Either way, we would surely want to say that she is *mistaken*, that her forgiveness merely condones the evil and evidences a failure of self-respect.

And yet it would seem that Gormley's and my unconditional account would allow just such an example. The wife can offer certain reasons: "he needs me," "he's under a lot of stress," "I married him, and committed myself for life" which are intelligible as reasons to forgive, but in this case they are not sufficient. And yet the wife has deliberated—perhaps after each new incident—and "discovered" that she "has to" forgive him. We could accept all that, but surely we should still think her mistaken. With Bonhoeffer, I might well think that he is mistaken, but in a different way: my belief is fully compatible with admiring his risky decision and the high ideals that motivated it. With Wilson, I might think that he is mistaken, but there is no sense that he is denigrating himself in the process. Not so with the battered wife, whose behavior I start to explain by reaching for various psychological concepts of impaired agency: adaptive preferences, learned helplessness, self-loathing. Such psychological concepts might even go so far as to undermine autonomy and thereby undermine the "forgiveness" (with scare quotes) which she evinces. No matter what she said, she would not be forgiving so much as resigning.

The social and psychological problem of battered persons who seem to consent to their own battery is very complicated, and again, I cannot do it justice here. But I think it fails as a counter-example to Gormley's and my unconditionalist account precisely because of the element of *repetition*. When the wife is battered for the first time and the husband does not show any sign of apology or repentance, I would claim she can still forgive—genuinely forgive—in accordance with the account I developed above. But this forgiveness should not be seen in a vacuum, cut off from the past and future. It is not as if the wife faces the same dilemma after the first battery as after the second battery. For after the first battery she has forgiven him; by committing the second battery, he has effectively rejected the forgiveness, and this renders it null and void, as it were. Forgiveness, like a gift, has to be given *and received* in order to work as forgiveness in the full sense.

For this reason, I do not think one can forgive only "in one's head"—sometimes called "therapeutic forgiveness" and a key part of the self-help industry. Forgiving in one's head is usually a matter of ignoring the matter, or explaining it away, or finding excuses, or getting over it etc.; whereas forgiveness is essentially bilateral.[92]

---

[92] I acknowledge there is a special case when one forgives the dead, which I do think is possible.

However, surely Wilson's forgiveness was not received? Or at least, there was no evidence to Wilson that the forgiveness had been received, just as there was no evidence at the time that the IRA were apologetic or repentant. Wilson's forgiveness was made very publicly, and so it must have reached the bombers sooner or later. I have to admit that if another IRA bomb then killed Wilson's wife, and he proceeded to forgive the IRA again, that he would be in the situation of the battered wife, and his forgiveness, insofar as it could be called forgiveness at all, would certainly be much less admirable.

Conclusion

Forgiveness therefore remains mysterious: but I hope to have discussed the *limits* of that mystery, limits that allow it a certain amount of the intelligibility and admirability that is essential to the forgiveness as we know it in our daily lives. It is not wildly mysterious to the point of whimsy and arbitrariness; but nor is it rigidly rule-governed and unmysterious as the conditionalists would have it. I think Gormley's compromise points us in the right direction, and I have tried to develop it further.[93]

---

[93] I would like to thank Steven Gormley, Sean Pierce and Court Lewis for comments on an earlier draft of this piece.

References

Garrard, Eve and David McNaughton. 2003. "In Defense of Unconditional Forgiveness." *Proceedings of the Aristotelian Society* 103.1: 39-60.

Griswold, Charles G. 2007. *Forgiveness: A Philosophical Exploration.* Cambridge University Press.

Gormley, Steven. 2014. "The Impossible Demand of Forgiveness." *International Journal of Philosophical Studies* 22.1: 27-48.

Kolnai, Aurel. 1973. "Forgiveness." *Proceedings of the Aristotelian Society* 74: 91-106.

Murphy, Jeffrie and Jean Hampton. 1988. *Forgiveness and Mercy.* Cambridge University Press.

Derrida, Jacques. 2001. *On cosmopolitanism and Forgiveness.* Translated by Mark Dooley and Michael Hughes. New York: Routledge.

Williams, Bernard. 1981a. "Practical Necessity." *Moral Luck.* Cambridge: Cambridge University Press.

———. 1981b. "Moral Luck." *Moral Luck.* Cambridge: Cambridge University Press.

———. 1995. "Moral Incapacity." *Making Sense of Humanity.* Cambridge: Cambridge University Press.

Chapter 8

The Double Intentionality of Forgiveness: A Non-reductive Account of Forgiveness in Ricoeur and Confucius

Man-to Tang

Introduction

Contemporary Western interpretations of forgiveness can mainly be divided into two kinds, namely a private personal account (e.g. Jeffrie Murphy and Jean Hampton) and an interpersonal account (e.g. Charles Griswold). The private personal account maintains that forgiveness is merely a private matter, an "internal struggle," and the interpersonal account maintains that forgiveness is an interpersonal process between two individuals. These two accounts seem incompatible, and cause the debate of the nature of forgiveness to splinter into two different conceptual directions. What is more, the incorporation of Chinese conceptions of forgiveness are rarely (if ever) included in the debate. This lack of incorporation is especially odd, since Chinese sources, especially within Confucianism, are abundant.

This chapter has two aims. First, I argue that both the private personal account and the interpersonal account of forgiveness are reductive, in the sense that the former reduce forgiveness solely to the acts of individuals, and the latter reduces forgiveness solely to the reconciliation between the wrongdoer and the victims. Both reductive accounts agree that forgiveness is a "change" from the present situation to a better situation: e.g. the overcoming of resentment or the restoration of relationship. Through Paul Ricoeur's hermeneutic account of forgiveness, we could understand that the act of forgiving is a re-evaluation of past suffering. This re-evaluation presupposes a remembering of the past event. He draws resources from Edmund Husserl's study of intentionality, namely the horizontal intentionality and the transverse (vertical) intentionality. Through the detailed analysis of the double intentionality, the unilateral and bilateral dimension of forgiveness could be explained. Thus a non-reductive account of forgiveness could then be developed. Secondly, I argue that a hermeneutic account of forgiveness could foster a possible comparative study between forgiveness of the East and the West in the future, based on the Confucian term '*shu*'—translated as 'forgiveness'. *Shu* lacks an elaborate and systematic philosophical account in Confucius's thought, but I will show that it suggests that forgiveness is having a certain type of attitude. It is my hope that such an examination will spur further East-West dialogue about the nature of forgiveness.

I. Two reductive accounts of forgiveness

a. Private personal accounts

Private personal accounts have a common feature that forgiveness is an internal private matter or struggle. There are two ways in which this struggle might be resolved: 1) forgiveness is achieved by "moving on" or "forgetting"; and 2) forgivingness is the overcoming or "letting go" of resentment for a moral reason (e.g., to regain self-respect).

Let us look at the first account: forgiveness-as-forgetting. Years ago, American President Ronald Reagan was asked about his opinion towards Japan's invasion of China, occupation of Korea, and attack on Pearl Harbor during World War II. He answered:

> *Well, I think we'd be going into past history there. And, of course, those were tragic times.*

And we think there was a different philosophy than is governing Japan today. And I think the fact that we have been able to forget or forgive—whichever you want to use—that period, and become the good friends that we are today, I think, is what we should be more interested in. I would rather not rehash the war feelings that I'm sure were felt on both sides and that led to that tragedy. (1982, 1041-2)

Reagan agrees that the period of World War II was a tragic time, but what we have to do is move on. The way to move on is "to forgive and forget," which as Regan suggests, equates forgiveness with forgetting. If correct, then forgiveness can only be a private personal matter, since only individuals themselves can forget, or work towards forgetting. No other person has the power to make victims forget.

Most philosophers, however, emphasize that forgiveness is not equivalent to forgetting. They suggest forgetting is neither a sufficient nor a necessary condition for forgiveness. There are three major counter-arguments. First, Charles Griswold maintains there are some cases when we stop resenting, and even (re)accept the offender as a friend, without forgetting the wrong deeds (2007, 40). If it is possible to stop resenting and not forget, then forgetting is not a necessary condition for forgiveness. Second, Margaret Holmgren argues there is no conditional relationship between the two. For example, "The wife who is battered by her husband one night should not forget the incident entirely if she forgives her husband, as she must remember to take steps to protect herself in case he does it again" (2012, 40-1). She goes on to suggest that when we forgive, we normally remember what has happened in the past, and it may be important for us to do so. Finally, Jeffrie Murphy provides a conceptual distinction between the two that forgetting is not even sufficient for forgiveness. Forgetting "just happens to us; that is, it is totally non-voluntary," but forgiveness "is properly regarded as a moral virtue," which is "a desirable disposition of character to possess" (1990, 23). Forgiveness is a voluntary act, while forgetting is involuntary, and to assume an identical relationship between the two commits a "categorical mistake." So, one could forget, and yet, not forgive a wrongdoer, which shows forgetting is insufficient for forgiveness.

Having made clear why forgiveness is not equivalent to forgetting, we may look at the second personal account. Unlike Joseph Butler's influential account of forgiveness, as "the foreswearing of resentment," Jeffrie Murphy and Jean Hampton argue that forgiveness is something more (Ibid.).[94] For Hampton, in "Forgiveness, Resentment and Hatred," forgiveness involves overcoming "the point of view of the other as 'the one who wronged me'" (Ibid., 38). The "points of view" referred to by Hampton are "retributive emotions," like indignation, contempt, and hatred. To forgive is to overcome resentment through the liberation from the burden of moral debt and the establishment of a new perspective—that the wrongdoer is inherently decent" (Ibid., 87).

For Murphy, "Forgiveness is not the overcoming of resentment *simpliciter*; it is rather this: forswearing resentment on moral grounds" (Ibid., 24). By 'moral grounds', Murphy discusses the concept of being selfish. If someone has the desire to promote his own mental health, then his motive is "purely

---

[94] It is debateable whether Murphy's interpretation of Butler is faithful to what Butler really wants to say. See, for example, (Newberry 2001) and (Dillon 2001). Different from Murphy's and Hampton's account of Butler's forgiveness-as-overcoming resentment, Charles Griswold argues that forgiveness-as-overcoming resentment, *simpliciter*, allows for a form of vengeful manipulation. Thus, instead of overcoming resentment, forgiveness is better to be defined as the overcoming of revenge, along with a moderation of, and an commitment to let go of, resentment altogether (2004, 54).

selfish" and "not moral at all" (1982). 'Selfish' is a property employed when one's own interests are emphasized, whereas 'moral' is a property employed when not only one's own interests, but others as well, are emphasized. Moral grounds must be plural because there could be many unselfish reasons. These moral reasons "must be compatible with self-respect, respect for others as moral agents, and respect for the rules of morality or the moral order" (Murphy 1990, 24). Thus Murphy's understanding of forgiveness requires not only the overcoming of resentment, but also moral grounds/reasons compatible with self-respect.

Why does forgiveness relate to respect-as-a-moral ground? In Murphy's view, on the one hand, the wrongdoing consists of a disrespectful message that expresses one of the following: "I [wrongdoer] can use you for my purposes;" or "I [wrongdoer] am here up high and you are down there below" (Ibid., 25). These communications undermine the self-esteem of the victim, because the wrongdoer treats the victim as a mere means through the wrongdoing. Such a communication is illustrated nicely in an article from a September 2015 issue of *The Mirror*, which says the following of accused rapist Gavin Julienis: "He allegedly told the victim that 'she is the type of mental b**** to say that it's rape'" (Vaughan 2015). Not only does his alleged action (raping) express a disrespectful message that he can use her body merely for his sexual satisfaction, but he actually verbalizes his moral message by taunting the victim.

Murphy's goal is to merge together the definition of forgiveness with the justification of forgiveness. For Murphy, we cannot define forgiveness and then ask what moral reasons make it appropriate" (1990, 23). Murphy maintains that because "forgiveness involves the overcoming of certain passions (resentment, hatred) when they are inappropriate," which makes us focus on the victim's negative emotions toward the wrongdoer, a true account of forgiveness will both define forgiveness and provide reasons for when overcoming such passions are appropriate (Ibid., 33). Although there are methods for overcoming negative emotions that would not count as forgiveness (e.g., we have not forgiven the wrongdoer if we simply take a pill or undergo hypnosis to eliminate our resentment in order to better get on with our lives), Murphy wants to make a sharp distinction between true forgiveness and these types of "non-forgiveness" (Ibid.).

Therefore, if a victim forgives an offender, it is necessary for the victim to describe why he is willing to forgive the offender. The question "how is forgiveness justified?" does not aim at whether one has enough "reasons" to persuade someone to forgive, but aims at giving the victim himself a certain justification of reasons. The overcoming is to go beyond the resentment by one's own efforts, as it is an "internal struggle" that the victim distance herself from the disrespectful message through another message, repentance. It follows that the forgiveness must be "individual and personal in a way that legal guilt and responsibilities are not," as other individuals could never provide reason for why the victim should/ought forgive the offender (Ibid., 33). Murphy's doctrine, then, commits a reductionist account of forgiveness, in the sense that he reduces forgiveness down to a mere a private matter, as though it is merely an "internal struggle."

Michele Moody-Adams, to a certain extent, agrees with the personal account of forgiveness. She says, "The difficult, but morally praiseworthy task for forgiveness is always unilateral, and thus genuine forgiveness is unilateral forgiveness. Forgiveness is a non-obligatory, unilateral revision in judgement that may make reconciliation possible, but that is properly and essentially distinct from reconciliation" (2015, 162). So, for Moody-Adams: 1) forgiveness is always unilateral; and 2) forgiveness is properly and essentially distinct from reconciliation. Although forgiveness "can be a constructive force in personal relationships, families and political communities," it is not a tool to lead to the reconciliation of the victim and the wrongdoer.[95] She objects that such a feature would make forgiveness an obligatory moral behavior, but "forgiveness cannot be obligatory…"—it "is not a panacea for societies damaged by violence, oppression, or war" (2015, 164). Social and political situations aroused by mass suffering are "too complex for forgiveness to provide the sole, or even primary, solution to the problem" (Ibid., 178).

Interestingly, both Moody-Adams and Ricoeur use South Africa's Truth and Reconciliation Commission as an example to show that forgiveness cannot resolve political guilt. What it can do is let victims express what they experienced and how they felt. Ricoeur argues "there is no politics of forgiveness," because on the one hand, it is impossible to institutionalize forgiveness, as no non-victim can represent (i.e., take the place of) the victim, and forgive the wrongdoer in their stead;[96] and on the other hand, political institutions have no relevant moral relationship to the wrongdoing, so any moral act of forgiveness is unbinding (2004, 488). Rather than incorporate politics into forgiveness, which amounts in

---

[95] Instead of connecting forgiveness with reconciliation, Moody-Adams uses the term 'civic grace' for the political commitment of reconciliation. She states that "civic grace is rooted in the value we place on commitment to a common life. Civic grace commits us to being prepared to extend good will to political opponents and to assume that disagreement does not have to be equivalent to disrespect. It demands a willingness to relinquish political resentments and bitterness in service of common ideals and goals. It also commits us to seeking compromise and reconciliation in response to division and disagreement, consistent with basic respect for the dignity of fellow citizens" (2015, 179).

[96] Ricoeur asks an important question, "on what authority can a political leader in office or the current head of a religious community presume to request forgiveness from the victims, with respect to whom he or she was not personally the aggressor and who themselves did not personally suffer the harm in question?" He does not offer any answer, as he believes no authority can be presumed.

total failure, the personal account of forgiveness simplifies and reduces the complexities of forgiveness to the prerogative of single individuals.

b. An interpersonal account

The alternative to a personal account is an interpersonal account. The essential feature of the interpersonal account is to emphasize the relationship and reconciliation of victim and wrongdoer. For instance, in *Forgiveness: A Philosophical Exploration*, Griswold defines forgiveness as an "interpersonal process whose success requires actions from both parties." It is not simply a private matter or an "internal struggle." "Rather it is an appeal to human *solidarity*, the concern for the well-being of those who one feels are in the same condition as oneself" (2007, 65). Forgiveness is supposed to repair the moral relationship between victim and wrongdoers, in order to achieve the well-being of all parties involved.

For Griswold, "forgiveness comes with certain conditions or norms," and presupposes a conditional *social relationship* in which the wrongdoer and victim are mutually dependent (Ibid., 47). Forgiveness is possible if and only if the victim has a certain relationship with the wrongdoer, and this relationship must be "abnormal." Terms like 'victim' and 'wrongdoer' reflect the idea that the relationship between the two individuals is damaged or "abnormal." Otherwise, we would not call someone "victim" or "wrongdoer," they would simply be "friends" or "colleagues." Thus forgiveness supposes, on the one hand, an abnormal relationship between individuals, which on the other hand, presupposes there was once a normal relationship between the individuals. Due to these relational features, a victim cannot simply forgive a wrongdoer unconditionally; both parties must work to satisfy certain conditions that qualify as what Griswold deems "paradigmatic" forgiveness (Ibid., 56).

Paradigmatic forgiveness "…is not just a matter of fighting back, but of experiencing the appropriate sentiment (anger or resentment) that expresses one's regard for *self as one-not-*

to-be-treated-in-this-manner [emphasis added]. To give up *that* sentiment is perhaps (on the best construal) to stand up for oneself 'on principle'…" (Ibid., 65). By 'on principle', Griswold does not mean that the victim should overcome her sentiment through the obeying of a certain moral principle or rule. Rather, it asks the victim to reframe herself *as if* not-yet-have suffered. When this is achieved, we have achieved "affirmative reconciliation," which is the outcome of ideal or paradigmatic forgiveness. Affirmative reconciliation entails the "renewal of any previous ties of affection," such as friendship. More generally, affirmative reconciliation can imply a situation in which "previously antagonistic partners find a way to rebuild and even flourish together" (Ibid., 111).

Opposed to Griswold's paradigmatic forgiveness and its emphasis on affirmative reconciliation, Margaret R. Holmgren argues that "many factors govern the wisdom of maintaining particular personal relationships, and it is simply a mistake to believe that forgiveness must always result in the restoration of these relationships" (2012, 42). Holmgren's criticism is that the reconciliation of the victim and the wrongdoer is not *always* a necessary or a sufficient condition for forgiveness; that in some cases, forgiveness does not aim at any reconciliation. As Holmgren quotes Geoffrey Scarre, it is mistake to view forgiveness as the restoration of "some valued status quo ante," since there are cases of forgiveness (e.g., relationship with a stranger) where there is no such relational status to restore. It is because the wrongdoer and the victim, in some cases may not know each other, and in others the victim is dead or in a coma, that forgiveness must not require the restoration of a relationship. If Holmgren's account of Scarre is correct, then Griswold's strict interpersonal account fails to adequately explain significant morally relevant instances of forgiveness and reconciliation. Hence, the interpersonal account (like the personal) is insufficient by itself.

II. Double intentionality and a hermeneutic account of forgiveness

Paul Ricoeur does not completely refute the personal or the interpersonal account, but he does criticize how the two accounts fail to take into account the significant conceptual points made by each other. On the one hand, he draws resources from Hannah Ardent that forgiveness is a faculty inherent in plurality, because it rests on experiences that no one can have in isolation and which are based entirely on the presence of others (2004, 487). On the other hand, the bilateral and reciprocal dimension of forgiveness are inadequate to understand how forgiveness could overcome the resentment and suffering of a victim, simply through the restoration of some valued relational status.

Ricoeur maintains that the nature of forgiveness is so difficult to understand because it involves two levels of discussion: 1) the vertical or transverse structure and its horizontal correlation; and 2) the difference of "height" between forgiveness and an admission of fault (Ibid., 479). This section will address the first level of discussion, which is the basis of the second level of discussion.

The vertical structure refers to the *historical dimension* of a person, while the horizontal correlation refers to the *social dimension* of a person. Humans are relational beings, and as such, part of a society. We live and interact with other people. This is what is called 'the horizontal correlation'. In addition, a person exists for a certain period of time. He "has" a past history, and this history is what is called 'the vertical structure'.

The distinction is based upon Edmund Husserl's analysis of memory. The foundational structure of memory entails "a double intentionality." The first intentionality is what we call "memory of the perceived object," and serves to constitute the object remembered. The second intentionality serves as the unity of the lived experience, what we call our memories. Husserl calls the first object-oriented intentionality 'horizontal intentionality', while the second is called 'transverse (vertical) intentionality' (1991, 390-392). In Ricoeur's phrase, the first intentionality mentioned relates to memory (*le souvenir*) as the thing intended, and the second intentionality relates to memory (*la mémoire*) as intention (2004, 22).

The intentionality of memory (*le souvenir*) as the thing intended is two-fold: in a memory, there is a "nexus between the 'what' of memories and the 'who' of memory" (Ibid., 460). When I am remembering a past event in my lived experience, I do not only recall what I experienced from the past (the object of my lived experience), but I also unthematically and implicitly recall who experienced the past (the past subject who originally experienced the recalled event in a living present). For example, I can remember the breakfast I had yesterday. At the present moment, I recall what I ate for breakfast, e.g., eggs, bacon, and ham. I also recall who ate the breakfast, and how I responded to eating such a breakfast. Both aspects are recalled as part of the single event that I experienced yesterday. So, any time I recall an experience, I must also necessarily recall myself as the subject of that lived experience.

When I think of eating breakfast yesterday, the "I" of yesterday is re-presented in the present, as a different "I." This implies that self-recognition is given to me at a distance, because the past subject is remembered and is constituted by the present remembering subject at a temporal difference (de Warren 201, 599-600). So, there is always a temporal difference between the present "I" who is remembering and the "I" who is remembered.

This framework can be applied to the relationship between the wrongdoing and the wrongdoer. The wrongdoer is "wrong" and the wrongdoing is "wrong," and as such, the individual wrongdoer is both acting badly as an individual and receives an evaluation of his action as wrong. This negative evaluation has a certain "depth"' that it is always a reflection after the action. Through this sort of analysis, Ricoeur finds the "what" of memory and the "who" of memory cannot be suppressed by memory (*le souvenir*), since the thing intended is a lived experience from the past, and is always about recalling both "what he did" and "that he did it." As a result, the wrongdoing cannot be separated from the wrongdoer in the memory as the thing intended.

Such an account supports Jacques Derrida's criticism of a common misunderstanding of forgiveness: the attempt to separate the guilty person from his act, by forgiving the subject of the present who is different than the subject of the past who committed the act. Such an explanation implies that the wrongdoing is an "irreversible" fact, and since the past cannot be changed, actions are everlasting in both the wrongdoer and the victim.

As such, Ricoeur agrees with Arendt that we could forgive, if we were only able to "re-evaluate" ourselves (2004, 489). The perception of a wrongdoing involves an evaluation. Expressed in terms of the double intentionality, forgiveness—the act of forgiving—relates to *two* objects. Firstly, the wrongdoer is constituted as the primary object, as the subject responsible for wrongdoing. Secondly, the wrongdoing is constituted as the secondary object. As illustrated by Arendt, "what was done is forgiven for the sake of who did it" (1998, 241). Ricoeur's idea is that the wrongdoer "acted" a wrongdoing, which is an irreversible fact. The act of forgiving is a re-evaluation of an irreversible fact. It is what Arendt calls the "predicament of irreversibility." To achieve this goal, we must first unbind the wrongdoing (the past action) from the wrongdoer (the present agent), then adopt a different perspective that attaches a different meaning to the past wrongdoing. Such an account of forgiveness explains just how the meaning of a past event can be changed without actually undoing, ignoring, avoiding, rationalizing, or forgetting it. Ricoeur's double intentionality is the condition of possibility for this re-evaluation, through which the meaning of the past event is differently constituted. Yet it requires two apparent conditions: 1) the recollection of one's own life-story; and 2) the agreement of the victim and the wrongdoer.

III. A hermeneutic account of forgiveness as a non-reductive account of forgiveness

Now we come to the second level of our discussion: the difference of height between forgiveness and an admission of guilt. This level of discussion assumes the soundness of Ricoeur's account of double intentionality, and describes the relationship between both intentionalities through the act of forgiving.

The re-evaluation requires the agreement of the victim and the wrongdoer, so Ricoeur states that "the forgiveness resulting from the mutual recognition of the two antagonists who admit the limits of their viewpoints and renounce their partiality denotes the authentic phenomenon of conscience" (1995, 343). He recognizes the first stage of the relationship through the act of forgiving is reciprocal. The agreement can be founded in two speech acts, that is to say, the wrongdoer requests for forgiveness, while the victim responds (offers or rejects) to the request. He states, "Recognizing the reciprocal dimension of the relation between the request for and the offer of forgiveness constitutes only a first stage in the complete reconstruction of this relation" (2004, 482). It is the conditional forgiveness, which is an exchange on the market level.[97] Ricoeur further explains that:

> *This stage, however, was necessary in order to make apparent the dimension of otherness in an act that is fundamentally a relation. We*

---

[97] Ricoeur uses the height of forgiveness, but not 'higher' and 'lower'. Throughout his analysis, he does not explicitly argue which forgiveness (conditional or unconditional) is more valuable or better. His distinction is based upon the spirit of the Abrahamic tradition of forgiveness. Unconditional forgiveness, which is similar to what God does, is an exchange on the non-market level; whereas conditional forgiveness is an exchange on the market level.

> *attached this relational character to the vis-*
> *`a-vis that confronts two speech acts, that of*
> *admission and that of absolution: "I ask you*
> *for forgiveness." "I forgive you." These two*
> *speech acts do what they say: the wrong is ac-*
> *tually admitted; it is actually forgiven. (2004,*
> *482)*

It shows that the reciprocal relationship appears at this stage of forgiveness. However, it is possible to conceive that unconditional forgiveness is God-like and is an exchange on the non-market level. On the one hand, similar to how the interpersonal account understands forgiveness, forgiveness is always bilateral and aims at the restoration of the relationship. The relationship is based upon the model of exchange, which takes for granted the obligation to give, to receive, and to give in return. On the other hand, unconditional forgiveness tends to mask the reciprocity of the exchange that forgiveness spans as an interval between the high and the low, between the great height of the spirit of forgiveness and the abyss of guilt. The asymmetry between the horizontal correlation of conditional forgiveness and the vertical distance of unconditional forgiveness is constitutive of the forgiveness equation. Thus, in order to faithfully understand the equation of forgiveness, the apparent incommensurability between the unconditionality of forgiveness and the conditionality of the request for forgiveness must be understood and taken into account (Ibid., 485).

Ricoeur continues that, "...this suggestion deserved to be pushed to its limit, to the point where even the love of one's enemies can appear as a mode of reestablishing the exchange on a nonmarket level. The problem then is to recover, at the heart of the horizontal relation of exchange, the vertical asymmetry inherent in the initial equation of forgiveness" (Ibid., 458-9). Then what remains to be taken into account is the vertical distance between the two poles of forgiveness. To understand the vertical distance, a very question has to be answered: "What about the invisible force that unites the two speech acts of admitting and forgiving?" His answer is "love" (Ibid., 506).

In this sense, Ricoeur's hermeneutic account of forgiveness is far from simply an action, but is an attitude. Through forgiveness-as-love, the victim and the wrongdoer agree to give up their own perspective and re-open their heart again. Against Gadamer's doctrine of the fusion of horizons (one's own perspective), "horizon does not mean only the fusion of horizons but also the receding of horizon, incompletion" (Ibid., 413). Rather than reinforcing my previous perspective and meaning towards the wrongdoing and the wrongdoer, the victim realizes his perspective is incomplete. On the one hand, "we" are the capable being. On the other hand, "we" are culpable being. "Under the sign of forgiveness, the guilty person is to be considered capable of something other than his offenses and faults, so that the subject of an action must also be able to be released from it through forgiveness" (Ibid., 459).

Throughout the discussion of both the forgiveness on a market level and the forgiveness on a non-market level, Ricoeur shows that there is a difference of "height" between forgiveness and an admission of guilt. The *forgiveness in a market level* and its admission of guilt require a certain justification or reason, as it requires the agreement of the victim and the wrongdoer. Nevertheless, the *forgiveness on a non-market level* and its admission of guilt does not require any justification or reason, as it is a God-like unconditional forgiveness.

Therefore, both the interpersonal account and personal account are correct in a certain extent, but inadequate to give a faithful account of the complexity of forgiveness on both a market level and a non-market level. On the one hand, the personal account of forgiveness is correct because the victim is "internally" struggling, in a certain circumstance. If the victim forgives the wrongdoer, he justifiably aims at giving himself a certain justification or reason. But if the victim forgives the wrongdoer for the sake of a certain justification or reason, the act of forgiveness seems to be "impure." The personal account could capture the paradox of forgiveness. The paradox of forgiveness is based upon the struggle between the human-like conditional forgiveness and the God-like unconditional forgiveness. However, Ricoeur shows that the personal account of forgiveness is inadequate because the internal struggle is possible if and only if there is the difference of "height" between forgiveness and an admission of guilt. The difference of "height" is a description of the complexity of forgiveness in market and non-market levels. The personal account pays attention to the internal struggle only, but does not pay attention to address how the struggle is possible. Therefore, what is reduced in the personal account is the condition of possibility for the human forgiveness and the God-like forgiveness/the conditional and the unconditional forgiveness/the forgiveness on a market level and a non-market level.

On the other hand, the interpersonal account of forgiveness is correct because the act of forgiveness requires the agreement of the victim and the wrongdoer, in a certain circumstance. If the victim forgives the wrongdoer, he aims at the reconciliation between the two. But if the victim fails to reconcile with the wrongdoer, the victim can still forgive the wrongdoer, or the victim forgive the wrongdoer, their relationship could remain "broken." The interpersonal account could capture the hope of forgiveness. The hope of forgiveness is ultimately to reconcile the broken relationship between two finite beings (human beings). However, Ricoeur shows that the interpersonal account of forgiveness is inadequate because the reconciliation is possible if and only if there is the difference of "height" between forgiveness and an admission of fault. Unlike the personal account, what is reduced in the interpersonal account is not only the condition of possibility but also the forgiveness on a non-market level. Since it lacks the account of personal forgiveness, it cannot understand why forgiveness involves an internal struggle.

As a result, a hermeneutic account of forgiveness could adequately capture and account for both insights in both the personal and interpersonal accounts without reducing to the other. A hermeneutic account of forgiveness re-opens different horizons of forgiveness, namely both the human-like horizon on a market level and the God-like horizon on a non-market level.

IV. Confucius on forgiveness: 'Shu'

In ancient China, there are many Chinese terminologies related to forgiveness, for example, *Kuan, Rong, Shi, Mian, She*, and *Rao*. *Kuan* (寬) refers to generosity, a willingness to pardon, and is often used by people of a higher social status or hierarchical party, e.g., the emperor. *Rong* (容) refers to an individual act of pardoning, through which guilt is admitted. *Shi* (釋) refers to an act of pardoning as well, but is specifically used to release a certain social crime. It implicitly implies the restoration of the relationship between civilians and the criminal, that is to say, to let the criminal back to the community. *Mian* (免) refers to the decision to let someone avoid punishment for his wrongdoing. *She* (赦) also refers to the decision to let someone avoid the punishment of his wrongdoing, but like *Kuan* (寬), is specifically used by someone of higher social status or hierarchical party. *Rao* (饒) refers to the decision to let someone avoid the punishment of his wrongdoing, but is specifically used by equals of a higher social status, e.g., a noble to another noble.

Making clear these terminologies, Christoph Harbsmeier correctly claims that forgiveness is a socially role-governed behaviour (2011, 18). However, if we pay attention to all these terms, we find that they could somehow describe or refer to some nature of forgiveness: e.g. willingness to pardon, the act of pardoning, and the decision to let someone avoid punishment. All these are contained within different patterns and acts of forgiveness within different social standings/status. There appears to be no privileged term for, or standardized form of, forgiveness in Ancient Chinese texts. The one source of texts that contains a mention of 'forgiveness', however, is Confucius. Confucius singles out the term '*shu*' as a privileged term in his thought. Most sinologists and philosophers translate '*shu*' as 'forgiveness'. This section aims at arguing that a hermeneutic account of forgiveness can make sense of why the notion of *shu* in Confucian thought is correctly understood and translated as 'forgiveness'.

Shu has a core role in Confucius's thought. We may consider the *Analects* of Confucius:

The Master said, 'Zeng! My way is bound together in a single thread.'

Master Zeng replied, 'Yes'.

After the Master left, the disciples asked, 'What did he mean?'

Master Zeng said, 'The Master's way, only zhong and shu.' (Tan 2013, 88)

The notion of *shu* is a key notion in the Master Confucius's "way." Confucius has a way of life, and the "way" is only *zhong* and *shu*. *Zhong* is the attitude someone has when he performs his duties as best as he can. How, then, should we understand the meaning of *shu*?

Another passage expresses further the notion of *shu* through the conversation between Confucius and his student Zigong:

Zigong asked, "Is there one word that can guide a person's entire life?"

> The master replied, "It is Shu! Do not impose on other what yourself do not desire." (Ibid.)

Most often, the concept of *shu* appears to be a negative imperative, as it is about what we should not do unto others and is phrased negatively, "do not…" For instance, Tan and Harbsmeier argue that *shu* is a negative version of the Golden Rule: "Do not do to others what you do not desire to be done to yourself" (Ibid.; and Fricke 2011). Nevertheless, instead of taking *shu* as a negative version of the Golden Rule for granted, I suggest *shu* presupposes a self-understanding, similar to Ricoeur's double-intentionality. For instance, Zu Xi suggests the following interpretation: that "extrapolating from oneself is *shu*" (Fricke 2011, 22). Along these same lines, there are various other supporting translations of *Shu*. D. C. Lau translates *shu* as using oneself as a measure to gauge the likes and dislikes of others. Roger Ames translates it as "putting oneself in the other's place." Antonia Cua translates it as "reciprocity." And Edward Slingerland translates it as "understanding."

All of these definitions center on self-understanding. Self-understanding in *shu* consists in imagining oneself to be in the place of how the other is there. To imagine oneself to be in the place of how the other is there, it is necessary for one to give up his limited perspective and re-open his horizon. Through giving up his limited perspective and re-opening his horizon, an equal position between a self and another is reserved (Nivision, 1996, 66). Thus, according to Fricke, "*shu* is not only about doing things to people. It is about doing things or not doing things to people 'down there'" (2011, 24). Nivision describes this as "mental likeness," an ideal status of "how I should behave toward you, or some other "like myself," behaving with "reciprocal considerateness" (Tan 2013, 89). The reciprocal considerateness does not entail any commitment of the restoration in interpersonal account, but it is a re-opening of one's own understanding.

I endorse that *shu* be translated as 'forgiveness'. On the one hand, although Harbsmeier emphasizes *shu* is a moral virtue, *shu,* at least for Confucius, is a way of life. It is more likely to be an attitude, which means an openness of one's heart, rather than something merely about following moral rules. On the other hand, although Tan does not follow Harbsmeier's translation, he still grasps the key of the notion. He interprets *shu* as "the idea of helping others as wholeheartedly as you would when helping yourself" (Ibid.). *Shu,* as the idea of helping others as helping yourself, captures the hope of forgiveness seen in Ricoeur. It does not only refer to the act of self-understanding or helping others, but also refers to the "idea" of inter-related others.

One practical question we might ask, then, is how it is possible to help others as wholeheartedly as helping oneself? It seems that if we help others with a certain justification or reason, then the help is not wholeheartedly in accordance with the horizon of God-like unconditional forgiveness in a non-market level. However, Confucian *shu* is not that radical, as it does not require a God-like unconditional horizon. What it requires is for each person to act as "wholeheartedly" as *you* "can." Wholeheartedness will depend on the degree of your "humanity." Metaphorically speaking, if you can help yourself with 60 dollars, then you should help others with 60 dollars. If you can help yourself with 100, then you should help the others with 100.

The notion of *shu* "directs me to notice, when someone else 'down there' is to be hurt by my act, whether I would be willing to accept the hurt myself; if I would not, I am to hold off, if I can" (Nivision 1996, 67). In this sense, the discussion of Confucian *shu* does not only capture the complexity of forgiveness, but also offers an answer towards the paradox of forgiveness: we are only capable of offering our human-like conditional forgiveness on a market level, and beyond our own individual level, we are not required. Since we are human, we forgive as wholeheartedly as 'we' can. Nevertheless, we could (should) have the idea of God-like unconditional forgiveness on a non-market level, as *shu* always requires a re-opening one's own self-understanding. The always re-opening could mean an opening of a finite human horizon towards an infinite heaven (God-like) horizon in an infinite effort. So, we should aspire to forgive beyond our capabilities.

VI. Conclusion

Confucius and other Ancient Chinese sources provide fruitful resources for Western philosophical discussions of forgiveness. On the one hand, these resources offer a plentiful understanding of Chinese culture and history. On the other hand, these resources, especially *shu* in Confucius's thought, can clarify Western conceptions of forgiveness, and merits further philosophical reflection. Through a comparative study, we would find that forgiveness is not merely a parochial practice in Western culture, but also in Eastern culture. The exploration of forgiveness in East and West could further enhance the comparative study and mutual understanding of cultural similarities and differences.

References

Arendt, Hannah. 1998. *The Human Condition*. Translated by Margaret Canovan. Chicago: University of Chicago Press.

de Warren, Nicolas. 2012. "The Forgiveness of Time and Consciousness." *The Oxford Handbook of Contemporary Phenomenology*. Edited by Dan Zahavi. Oxford: Oxford University Press.

Dillon, Robin S. 2001. "Self-forgiveness and Self-respect" *Ethics* 112.2: 53-83.

Fricke, Christel. 2011. *The Ethics of Forgiveness: A Collection of Essays*. Edited by Christel Fricke. London: Rutledge.

Griswold, Charles. 2007. *Forgiveness: A Philosophical Exploration*. Cambridge: Cambridge University Press.

Harbsmeier, Christoph. 2011. "Forgiveness and Forbearance in Ancient China." *The Ethics of Forgiveness: A Collection of Essays*. Edited by Christel Fricke. London: Rutledge.

Holmgren, Margaret R. 2012. *Forgiveness and Retribution: Responding to Wrongdoing*. Cambridge: Cambridge University Press.

Husserl, Edmund. 1991. *On the Phenomenology of the Consciousness of Internal Time (1893-1917)*. Translated by John Brough. Dordrecht: Kluwer Academic Publisher.

Moody-Adams, Michele. 2015. "The Enigma of Forgiveness." *Journal of Value Inquiry* 49.1-2: 161-180.

Murphy, Jeffrie and Jean Hampton. 1990. *Forgiveness and Mercy*. Cambridge: Cambridge University Press.

Newberry, Paul A. 2001. "Joseph Butler On Forgiveness: A Presupposed Theory of Emotion." *Journal of the History of Ideas* 62.2: 233-244.

Nivision, David. 1996. *The Way of Confucianism: Investigations in Chinese Philosophy*. Chicago: Open Court Press.

Reagan, Ronald. 1982. *Public Papers of the Presidents of the United States: Ronald Reagan*. Washington: United States Government Printing Office.

Ricoeur, Paul. 1995. *Oneself as Another*. Translated by Kathleen Blamey. Chicago: University of Chicago Press.

_____. 2004. *Memory, History, Forgetting*. Translated by Kathleen Blamey and David Pellauer. Chicago: University of Chicago Press.

Tan, Charlene. 2013. *Confucius*. London: Bloomsbury.

Vaughan, Henry. "Man accused of raping teenager allegedly to told her 'you are the type of b**** who calls this rape," *Mirror*, http://www.mirror.co.uk/news/uk-news/man-accused-raping-teenager-allegedly-6376287. Accessed 17 December 2015.

Chapter 9

Christian Love and Unconditional Forgiveness:
A Response to Glen Pettigrove

Gregory L. Bock

Introduction

In *Forgiveness and Love* (2012), Glen Pettigrove explores the connection between forgiveness and love and argues that it is morally permissible to forgive the unapologetic and undeserving, but he stops short of endorsing a principle of unconditional forgiveness, which would make forgiveness a moral absolute. This chapter explores the connection between forgiveness and the Christian concept of love found in the New Testament, and concludes that forgiving the unapologetic and undeserving is not just morally permissible but also required.

The Possibility of Forgiveness

Before arguing for the moral permissibility of forgiving the unapologetic or undeserving, Pettigrove addresses the question of whether it is even (non-morally) possible to forgive someone who is unapologetic (2012, 106-10).[98] He defines

---

[98] It is not entirely clear why he argues for the possibility of forgiving the unapologetic in chapter six because it does not seem essential to the argument for the moral permissibility of forgiveness. *Ought* implies *can*, but moral permissibility does not. Nevertheless, the

forgiveness as the end of hostilities and the start of (or return to) active concern for the well-being of the wrongdoer. This kind of definition is monological—to use Charles Griswold's term—emphasizing the disposition or action of the one wronged (Ibid., 107). Griswold and others defend dialogical, or two-sided, versions of forgiveness that emphasize the necessary conditions of the wrongdoer as well, such as repentance. However, Pettigrove argues persuasively against dialogical versions.

First, Pettigrove says forgiveness can be distinguished from reconciliation. He uses the example of a student who vandalizes his teacher's house. The teacher could decide not to allow this to affect her attitude and behavior toward the student, even if she never sees the student again. If the student returns one day to apologize, it makes sense for her to say, "I forgave you for that offence years ago" (Ibid., 108). Pettigrove thinks that making reconciliation an essential component of forgiveness would make it impossible for a victim to forgive a wrongdoer until the relationship is fully restored, but the wait between the time forgiveness is communicated and the relationship is fully repaired could take many years. In fact, this would preclude the teacher from saying "I forgive you" until the student has completed the repairs on the house. However, it seems natural for the teacher to first say "I forgive you" and then accept the student's offer to repair the house, if indeed the student offers at all. As Pettigrove says, to make repairing the house a necessary condition for forgiveness in this case is to make an "accidental feature of the situation essential" (Ibid.).

Second, Pettigrove considers the view that wrongdoing entails a violation of trust and that the restoration of trust requires repentance. He argues that this view fails because

---

aim of my essay is partly to establish an *ought*, so I find the argument for the possibility of forgiveness helpful.

while some acts of wrongdoing entail a loss of trust, others do not. For example, one can be betrayed by a close friend, or one could be mugged by a stranger. The former is a violation of trust, but the latter is not. Pettigrove says, "As some wrongs are done by wrongdoers against victims with whom they had no relations in the first place, it is difficult to describe their wrong in terms of a breach of trust and, likewise, difficult to describe forgiveness as entailing the restoration of a (previously non-existent) trust" (Ibid., 109).

Third, Pettigrove considers the view that any case of wrongdoing is the breaking of an agreement, and that an agreement, once broken, needs to be reestablished by both parties, which would be impossible if one party were unapologetic. Pettigrove thinks that this relies too heavily on a contractualist model of ethics and involves an unacceptable asymmetry. First, he says the ethics of contracts only covers some of our moral situations, that there is more to the moral life than just agreements between individuals. Second, he says such a view entails the following asymmetry: that an agreement is established by two parties but can be dissolved by only one. He thinks that when one party to a contract fails to fulfill her obligations as part of the contract, this does not dissolve the agreement but provides grounds for the wronged party to sue the other. Since the agreement has not been dissolved, it does not require two parties to reestablish it. For these reasons, Pettigrove rejects the arguments against the possibility of forgiving the unapologetic.

The permissibility of forgiveness

Pettigrove then considers two objections to the moral permissibility of forgiving the unapologetic: condonation and self-respect. The condonation objection states that forgiving the unapologetic is immoral because it constitutes condoning the actions of the wrongdoer. The self-respect objection states that forgiving the unapologetic is immoral because it entails a lack of self-respect on the part of the victim when the proper response is anger. This lack of self-respect may be in regards to the victim or to the victim's community.

Pettigrove responds to both these objections by showing that forgiveness functions in the same way as both punishment and apologies, and since the latter two are permissible, so is the former. Punishment functions in the following ways: it 1) condemns wrongdoing; 2) affirms the moral worth of the victim; and 3) channels and reduces feelings of resentment. Apologizing functions in the same way. It condemns wrongdoing, calling it what it is. It affirms the victim's moral worth, and it reduces negative feelings. Forgiveness does the same. First, it identifies the action as wrong—otherwise, there would be nothing to forgive. Second, it is a self-respecting action insofar as forgivers are often admired by others in the community. Third, it reduces hostile emotions.

In Chapter Seven, Pettigrove considers and rejects the argument that forgiveness is only morally permissible if the wrongdoer deserves it, or has met certain conditions such as the following conditions proposed by Griswold: "accepting responsibility for the action, repudiating that action, experiencing and expressing regret for one's misdeed, acknowledging the harm that one's wrongdoing has (or might have) caused the other, and convincing the other that one is capable of and committed to doing better in the future" (Ibid., 124). In order to answer this objection and demonstrate that forgiving someone who is "undeserving" is morally acceptable, he develops a non-theological concept of grace and links it to forgiveness. Relying heavily on Seneca, Pettigrove defines an act of grace as an "intentional act of unmerited favor" (Ibid., 127), and the virtue of grace as the "inclination and spontaneous readiness to promote others' interests and bring them joy, which is not determined by the merit (in the strong sense) of those toward whom it is directed" (Ibid., 133-4).

Defending the value of grace, Pettigrove gives two examples. First, he explains that we naturally show grace to the ones we love, promoting their interests and bringing them joy without consideration of merit (Ibid., 136-7). Second, he tells a story of a caring Sunday school teacher named Ora who graciously volunteers his time and energy teaching an extremely difficult and disrespectful child in his class, persevering even when the average person would have quit. As the story goes, Ora has a profound impact on the child who grows into a responsible adult and decides to live his life showing grace to others just as Ora did for him. Such examples show that grace plays an important part in our relationships and that we admire those who excel at it.

In addition, we admire grace when it manifests itself in forgiveness, even to strangers and enemies. Pettigrove identifies several moral exemplars who are praised in part because of their gracious forgiving:

> *We can point to exemplars, whose readiness to forgive those who have not merited forgiveness is part of what we admire about them. Indeed, many of the exemplars who come to mind—Jesus, Stephen (whose stoning was witnessed by Saul of Tarsus), Abraham Lincoln, Mahatma Gandhi, Martin Luther King, Jr, Nelson Mandela—do so precisely because they were willing to forgive before the wrongdoer had acknowledged his wrongdoing, often even before the wrongdoer had stopped wronging them. (Ibid., 138)*

Some of these figures sacrificed their lives in offering forgiveness, and we admire them for their strength of character and the results their gracious forgiveness had on the world. Nevertheless, not everyone would link grace and forgiveness.

Pettigrove responds to several attempts to connect forgiveness and merit instead. First, he discusses a point made by Griswold that a wrongdoer is apt to interpret forgiveness as a sign that the victim is condoning the wrongdoing (Ibid., 142). Related as this is to the condonation objection above, I will not spend much time on it. Pettigrove counters Griswold with statistical evidence that shows that very few people, in fact, confuse forgiveness with condonation. As Pettigrove says, "Most adults understand the conceptual difference between forgiving an act and endorsing it" (Ibid.).

Second, he considers an argument that resentment, not forgiveness, is the morally appropriate and natural response to wrongdoing. As a natural response, there seems to be a tight fit between resentment and being wronged, but Pettigrove, citing Robert Roberts, argues for a looser fit, saying that emotions are "concern-based construals," and as such, there is some interpretive flexibility depending on the features of the situation. According to Pettigrove, linking a belief that one has been wronged to any number of other beliefs could change the construal of the situation and one's response to it. For example:

> *If Abe's judgment that he has been wronged by Charles is coupled with the belief that he is likely to have future dealings with Charles, then he may respond with feelings of caution and with calculations regarding how he might avoid being wronged in a similar fashion in the future. If it is coupled with the belief that Charles' vice, if it goes unchecked, is likely to ruin Charles' career, then Abe may respond with feelings of pity or compassionate concern. (Ibid., 145)*

In spite of this looser fit, it might be said that not showing resentment toward the wrongdoer represents not taking the wrongdoing seriously enough. However, Pettigrove argues that if resentment is required, then this would mean that moral exemplars like Martin Luther King, Jr. are not, in fact, admirable, contrary to our moral intuitions. In defense of preserving our intuitions, Pettigrove says, "[The moral exemplars] responded to wrongs done them without sustained resentment but also without lowering their moral standards, or denying the moral standing of the offender, or assuming that they (i.e. the exemplars) deserved to be treated badly" (Ibid.).

Third, there is the concern that linking forgiveness and grace makes forgiveness unresponsive to reasons or arbitrary. For an action like forgiveness to be rational and praiseworthy, it should be based on moral reasons, but this seems to be what is missing with grace. There are no reasons for it; it is given freely without conditions. However, Pettigrove gives a number of examples in which forgiveness can be linked to grace and not to merit and still be sufficiently responsive to reasons. He says it is possible to forgive because: 1) it is better for oneself, for example, one's health; 2) one has compassion on the wrongdoer who may have been hurt or humiliated; 3) the victim realizes that resentment will not do any good; 4) remaining unreconciled to the wrongdoer is not worth it to the victim; and 5) the one who has been wronged recognizes that forgiveness will enable the wrongdoer to be happy again (Ibid., 147-150).

Pettigrove's case for the moral permissibility of forgiving the unapologetic or undeserving is compelling, but he makes clear in Chapter Eight that he does not support a stronger principle of unconditional forgiveness, one that would make forgiveness an absolute. As he says, "I have argued that many [acts of forgiving the unapologetic or undeserving] are morally acceptable, but this is still a far cry from the claim that all such actions are permissible. Thus, for all I have said, there may still be conditions that must be met before a particular act of forgiving is morally acceptable" (Ibid., 152). He presents three conditions that would limit the moral permissibility of forgiveness: 1) the psychology of the forgiver; 2) the psychology of the wrongdoer; and 3) the social environment. Before I respond to his conditions, we will examine what he says about the forgiveness and love.

The connection between forgiveness and love

Pettigrove explores the connection between forgiveness and love and argues that "(1) the central cognitive element of love is a necessary condition of forgiveness; (2) the volitional aspects of forgiveness and love are also quite closely related; however, (3) the connection between forgiveness and love's affective dimension is both looser and much more complex" (Ibid., 74). I will look at each of these separately.

First, love's cognitive dimension is the lover's perception that the object of her love is good. While forgiveness—insofar as it views the other as a wrongdoer—seems opposed to love's cognitive dimension in this way, Pettigrove argues that having at least a "not wholly rotten" view of the wrongdoer is necessary for forgiveness. The wrongdoer must at least be viewed in the positive sense of having some redeemable value. As he says, "Normatively it would be problematic to have or foster pro-attitudes toward or commitments to the interests of someone entirely devoid of value" (Ibid., 97).

Second, the volitional dimension of love is a commitment to the other's well-being. Similarly, the volitional dimension of forgiveness is a commitment to not be angry with the wrongdoer, so there is in both cases a commitment involved. However, he notes that the one forgiving may not be committed to the other's well-being but be motivated by her own or someone else's well-being. In addition, Pettigrove thinks that loving someone is compatible with being angry with or not forgiving her, which means love is not a sufficient condition for forgiveness. However, he also says, "A refusal, *over the long term*, to forswear hostile reactive attitudes and to commit oneself to the other's well-being is not consistent with the volitions of love" (Ibid., 99; emphasis added).

Third, the affective dimension of love is multifarious. There are many affective states of love just as there are many affective states related to forgiveness. Love deals only in positive "pro" emotions, but forgiveness deals in both positive and negative ones, reducing the latter and cultivating the former. Because of these differences, the relationship between forgiveness and love is, as Pettigrove says, naturally "messy." To complicate the picture even more, positive and negative emotions may be present at the same time.

Pettigrove's analysis of the connection between forgiveness and love highlights its complex nature, but his account of love is, as he acknowledges, incomplete. It is also somewhat vague. Perhaps this is why he defends only the permissibility of forgiving the unapologetic and undeserving and not a stronger obligation to do so. A better approach, I propose, would be to use a more specific concept of love for analysis, so it is to this project that I now turn.

Love and forgiveness in the New Testament

In the New Testament, the Greek word for God's love is *agape*, which means "unmerited, self-giving love" (Hoehner 2001, 708). This is in contrast with other forms of love in Greek, including *eros* and *philia* which mean desire and affection respectively. The Apostle Paul describes the unique properties of *agape* in his first letter to the Corinthians: "Love is patient, love is kind. It does not envy, it does not boast, it is not proud. It does not dishonor others, it is not self-seeking, it is not easily angered, it keeps no record of wrongs. Love does not delight in evil but rejoices with the truth. It always protects, always trusts, always hopes, always perseveres" (I Corinthians 13:4-7).[99] The contrast between *agape* and other forms of love is most evident in the passage where Jesus of

---

[99] All biblical references are to the New International Version.

Nazareth asks Peter three times if he loves him. This conversation occurs after Peter's three denials of Christ, and the irony is obvious. Jesus, using the Greek word *agape*, asks Peter if he loves him. Peter responds meekly that he does love Jesus, but here Peter responds with the term *phileo* instead, knowing that the extent of his love has recently been tested and shown wanting. The usage of the two terms in this passage seems to indicate that the biblical concept of *agape* is not a different kind of love altogether but is the wholeness and completeness of love (John 21:15-18).

Agapic love, or Christian love, is grounded in the nature of God. The New Testament says, "Dear friends, let us love one another, for love comes from God. Everyone who loves has been born of God and knows God. Whoever does not love does not know God, because *God is love*" (I John 4:7-8; emphasis added). The term for love here is, again, *agape*, and this passage indicates that love is part of God's essential nature. As Wayne Grudem says, "We see evidence that this attribute of God was active even before creation among the members of the Trinity. Jesus speaks to his Father of 'my glory which you have given me in your love for me before the foundation of the world' (John 17:24), thus indicating that there was love and a giving of honor from the Father to the Son from all eternity" (Grudem 1994, 198-9). Gerald O' Collins explains the significance of this doctrine: "The Trinity's *koinonia* or absolutely blissful communion of love presents itself as the ultimate ground and goal of all other such relations-in-communion. In a world where sharing and community have often tragically broken down, the *perichoretic* existence of the tripersonal God invites us to live in communion with each other and with our God" (1999, 179-80).

The New Testament teaches that God's love for us is a father-like love. As 1 John 3:1 says, "See what great love the Father has lavished on us, that we should be called children of God! And that is what we are!" Romans 8:15 says we are his children and call him, "*Abba*," which is the Aramaic term for "daddy" used to denote a close personal relationship. The image of God as a loving father appears, among other places, in the Parable of the Prodigal Son. In this story, a rebel son leaves home with his inheritance, squandering it in "wild living." After he loses all his money, he shamefully returns home to beg for his father's mercy, but instead of being angry, the father is described as eagerly waiting his son's return. Luke 15:20-23 says, "But while he was still a long way off, his father saw him and was filled with compassion for him; he ran to his son, threw his arms around him and kissed him." The father then throws the son a grand homecoming party. This love is affectionate and forgiving.

In the parable, the father's love is steadfast and unconditional, enduring in spite of the son's disobedience. This is how it ought to be in father-child relationships. A good father does not say to his children, "If you do such and such, I will love you, and if you are bad, I will love you no longer." Rather a good father loves his children simply because they are. So it is with God's love toward us, his prodigal children. As Romans 3:23 says, "All have sinned and fall short of the glory of God, and are justified freely by his grace through the redemption that came by Christ Jesus." Grace is unconditional love, a love that according to the New Testament involves rescue because our prodigality has led us to a place where we are unable to save ourselves. Ephesians 2:4-5 says, "Because of his great love for us, God, who is rich in mercy, made us alive with Christ even when we were dead in transgressions—it is by grace you have been saved."

God's love is normative for human action. As the Apostle Paul writes: "Be imitators of God, therefore, as dearly loved children and live a life of love, just as Christ loved us and gave himself up for us as a fragrant offering and sacrifice to God" (Ephesians 5:1). Love is not simply one norm among many; it is the guiding norm of Christian ethics. As Jesus says, "'Love the Lord your God with all your heart and with all your soul and with all your mind.' This is the first and greatest commandment. And the second is like it: 'Love your neighbor as yourself.' All the Law and the Prophets hang on these two commands" (Matthew 22:37-9). This means that love is given priority in New Testament ethics and that all other norms are to be understood as ways of loving God or one's neighbor. In his letter to the Galatians, Paul applies this teaching to a matter pertaining to adherence to the Mosaic Law: "The entire law is summed up in a single command: 'Love your neighbor as yourself'" (Galatians 5:14). For this reason, he explains, the Galatians are free from the requirements of the Law and now must only obey the law of Christ, which is to love. This is also what St. Augustine means when he says, "Love, and do what you will" (2016).

Jesus teaches not only that we ought to love our neighbors but also that we ought to love our enemies. He says in Matthew 5:43-48 that we should love our enemies as God does. Martin Luther King Jr. says,

> *Jesus eloquently affirmed from the cross a higher law. He knew that the old eye-for-eye philosophy would leave everyone blind. He did not seek to overcome evil with evil. He overcame evil with good. Although crucified by hate, he responded with aggressive love... Generations will rise and fall; men will continue to worship the god of revenge and bow before the altar of retaliation; but ever and again this noble lesson of Calvary will be a nagging reminder that only goodness can drive out evil and only love can conquer hate. (King 2010, 35)*

Loving one's enemies means forgiving them. Colossians 3:13 says, "Bear with each other and forgive one another if any of you has a grievance against anyone. Forgive as the Lord forgave you. And over all these virtues put on love, which binds them all together in perfect unity."[100] As Miroslav Volf says, "In the Christian account of things, we forgive because we love—specifically, because we love our debtors, our offenders, and even our enemies" (2005, 189). A refusal to forgive is a refusal to love as God loves us. Since God's love is unconditional, so is forgiveness.

The cognitive dimension of Christian love is necessary for forgiveness. God sees good in his children and loves us because we are his children, but he also recognizes our wickedness and forgives us. In his eyes, we are both sinful and redeemable, and we are to view our neighbors in the same way, flawed but "not wholly rotten." As King says:

> *We must recognize that the evil deed of the enemy-neighbor, the thing that hurts, never quite expresses all that he is. An element of goodness may be found even in our worst enemy. Each of us is something of a schizophrenic personality, tragically divided against ourselves. A persistent civil war rages with all of our lives. Something within us causes us to lament with Ovid, the Latin poet, "I see and approve the better things, but follow worse," or to agree with Plato that human personality is like a charioteer having two headstrong horses, each wanting to go in a different direction, or to repeat with the Apostle Paul, "The good that I would I do not:*

---

[100] See also Ephesians 4:32

but the evil which I would not, that I do.
(2010, 35)

If God sees something redeemable in the wrongdoer, then we must, too. The act of *unforgiveness*, on the other hand, can often be attributed to an ungodly view of the other and oneself, an inflated perception of self-righteousness. This leads to an us-versus-them mentality, where we think others are to blame, but we are without fault. *They* are the offenders, and *we* are the victims. Therefore, we demand retribution. However, on this view of the situation, the other is dehumanized as an embodiment of evil. The good in the other is obscured by wrongdoing, and the bad in ourselves is forgotten under the mantle of victimhood. Nonetheless, the reality is that we share something in common with the offender—a sinful nature.[101] On this particular occasion, it may be true that we are the victim, but yesterday we were the wrongdoer, and even now sin defiles our demand for justice. We hate the wrongdoer and desire excessive punishment to fall upon his head. The evil that we judge in the other is the same evil that festers in our hearts. If we are honest with ourselves, we recognize that we are also the offender, maybe not on this particular occasion but many times before, maybe not this particular sin, but we are capable of even worse sins in our minds. As Jesus says in the Sermon on the Mount, "You have heard that it was said to the people long ago, 'Do not murder, and anyone who murders will be subject to judgment.' But I tell you that anyone who is angry with his brother will be subject to judgment" (Matthew 5:21-22). On the other hand, if we see the wrongdoer as God sees us, as

---

[101] This refers the New Testament teaching mentioned above that everyone has sinned. The doctrine of original sin is a traditional Christian teaching, but it is not necessary for the point I am making here. All that is required is the acknowledgement that "everyone has sinned and fallen short of the glory of God."

both sinful and redeemable, then compassion is possible. If our sins have been forgiven, then we must also forgive others.

The volitional dimension of Christian love is also necessary for forgiveness. Pettigrove, in contrast, thinks that forgiveness might be offered merely for one's own sake, not for the sake of the offender or out of concern for his well-being. He admits that forgiveness may sometimes be offered out of love for the wrongdoer, but it need not be (2012, 98). This view, however, seems incompatible with the other-centered nature of Christian love. While it may be psychologically possible to reduce hostile attitudes without any reference to the other's well-being, this is just anger management. Christian forgiveness is rooted and understood in the unity and context of love for others.

The affective dimension of Christian love is also necessary for forgiveness. Some have objected to this saying it is enough to forswear hostility toward wrongdoers; we need not have loving feelings toward them. King seems to hold this view. He says, "We should be happy that [Jesus] did not say, 'Like your enemies.' It is almost impossible to like some people. 'Like' is a sentimental and affectionate word. How can we be affectionate toward a person whose avowed aim is to crush our very being and place innumerable stumbling blocks in our path?" (2010, 46) It is unclear whether King means to totally separate loving one's enemies from having affection toward them, but a total separation does not seem to be the view of the New Testament. Admittedly, this depth of love is impossible if it depends upon our own strength, which may be all King is saying; however, the New Testament teaches that our strength to love comes from God. As Volf says, "Christ is not just outside us, modeling forgiveness and urging us to forgive. Christ lives in us and is himself, as Luther wrote, 'the basis, the cause, the source of all our actual righteousness.' From Christ we receive the power and the willingness to forgive. Christ forgives through us, and that is why we can forgive" (2005, 200). According to the New Testament, believers are empowered by the Holy Spirit to live in obedience to God's commands, and the evidence that the Spirit is, in fact, present in the life of the believer is the manifestation of *agape*, affectionate love, even toward one's enemies (Galatians 5:22).[102]

Pettigrove's conditions

With this understanding of the connection between love and forgiveness, we now return to Pettigrove's three conditions for the moral permissibility of forgiveness. First, he says the psychology of the forgiver is relevant to the permissibility of forgiveness (2012, 153). He says that it may not be right for the victim to forgive at present because of her lack of self-esteem or because of her need to experience resentment at this stage in her moral development. He says, "So even though there is a preferable course of action that could be taken by some ideal agent, for less ideal agents with the psychological make-up in question, in certain circumstances it may be preferable that they angrily resist evil than that they forgive evildoers, since forgiving *for them* would entail that they no longer resisted evil" (Ibid., 152). Therefore, for someone who is morally immature, there may be an obligation of unforgiveness.

In response to this, it is unclear why anyone would need to refrain from forgiveness to reach moral maturity. In fact, it seems that the opposite is true, that learning how to forgive is a condition for one's moral development. A child may not be able to forgive in the way that an adult does, but this is no reason to encourage the child to stew in resentment. According to Aristotle, we learn virtue by practicing it just as we learn to play a musical instrument through practice (Aristotle 1999, 19; 1103a30). We may not get it right in the beginning, but mastery only comes through proper instruction and

---

[102] Again, *ought* implies *can*.

practice. In the same way, someone grows in moral maturity not by refraining from the practice of morals but by engaging in it. It may be natural to move through stages of resentment on the way to forgiveness, but it does not follow from this that unforgiveness, rather than forgiveness, is normative.

According to King, unforgiveness is destructive to the soul. He says, "Like an unchecked cancer, hate corrodes the personality and eats away its vital unity. Hate destroys a man's sense of values and his objectivity" (2010, 48). Moreover, if a person is reluctant to forgive others, this may indicate that she has not accepted God's forgiveness, or it may mean that she fails to view herself from the perspective of God's love. The remedy for this is not to refrain from forgiveness or conclude that unforgiveness is morally permissible but to realize that the strength needed to forgive one's neighbor can be found through faith in God's love for us.

Second, Pettigrove says the psychology of the wrongdoer is relevant to the moral permissibility of forgiveness (2012, 154). He says that some offenders may not realize that they are in the wrong. For them to realize the harm they have done, visible resentment may be necessary; in other words, the victim may have an obligation to refrain from forgiveness until the wrongdoer is made aware of this fact.

In response, it is unclear that there is ever a situation in which only anger can accomplish this goal. It seems that visible sadness could do the same. In addition, making the wrongdoer's awareness a condition of forgiveness might have the regrettable consequence of making the victim a prisoner of resentment. She might feel obligated to persist in anger until the wrongdoer repents, which may never happen. Perhaps the victim will never cross paths with the offender again, or perhaps the victim and offender live in the same house. Either way, the wrongdoer may have a callous heart and may always be blind to the harm he has inflicted.

Jesus says that we must always forgive wrongdoers even if they persist in their wrongs. Matthew's gospel says, "Then Peter came to Jesus and asked, 'Lord, how many times shall I forgive my brother or sister who sins against me? Up to seven times?' Jesus answered, 'I tell you, not seven times, but seventy-seven times'" (Matthew 18:21-22). Jesus demonstrated this kind of forgiveness on the cross when he said, "Father forgive them, *for they do not know what they are doing*" (Luke 23:24; emphasis added). Jesus was crucified by men who were not aware of their wrongdoing. King comments on this passage: "We must recognize that Jesus was nailed to the cross not simply by sin but also by blindness. The men who cried, 'Crucify him,' were not bad men but rather blind men" (2010, 35). Jesus still forgave them even though it is possible that anger (or fire from heaven) might have made them aware of their wrongdoing.

Pettigrove's third condition is the social environment. He says that in some cases of systemic injustice, the lack of social support may require victims to refrain from forgiving. In other cases, community support will mitigate the need for resentment because "there may not be a claim out there in social space that still needs to be cancelled" (2012, 154). However, where society does not adequately acknowledge the wrongdoing, there may be an obligation of unforgiveness. He describes three factors that will affect the moral permissibility of forgiveness in cases of systemic injustice. The first factor is whether forgiveness is compatible with continuing to resist the wrongdoing. He believes they are not always compatible. The second factor is whether the principle of forgiveness is considered a threshold concept or an ideal. If forgiveness is an ideal, something to reach for but not immediately attain, then it is possible that other concerns may be more pressing such as focusing on one's personal well-being or removing one's family from harm's way. The third factor is the potential that the victim will be pressured to forgive as a way of maintaining the status quo of systemic injustice.

Regarding the first factor, a Christian can continue to resist evil while forgiving those who are complicit in it. King's nonviolent resistance is a good example of this. He taught both resistance and forgiveness. Perhaps this was possible in part because of the Christian teaching to hate the sin and love the sinner. As King says, "We love every man because God loves him. At this level, we love the person who does an evil deed, although we hate the deed that he does" (2010, 46). For King, love is a kind of resistance, the only thing that can conquer evil. Hate and violence only breeds more of the same, but love can turn an enemy into a friend. This kind of love is a defiant love. King says, "Throw us in jail, and we shall still love you. Send your hooded perpetrators of violence into our community at the midnight hour and beat us and leave us half dead, and we shall still love you. But be ye assured that we will wear you down by our capacity to suffer. One day we shall win freedom, but not only for ourselves. We shall so appeal to your heart and conscience that we shall win *you* in the process" (2010, 51).

Regarding the second factor, Pettigrove's meaning is unclear. He may mean that moral ideals are supererogatory. A person may follow them if she likes but, is under no obligation. Or, he may mean that ideals are fine but they are like secondary norms, obligatory unless something more pressing arises, which often occurs. Forgiveness for a Christian is a primary norms, as Jesus's teachings demonstrate, and even if forgiveness is an ideal, it is not supererogatory. It is something to aim for now like an Aristotelian virtue, and it is normative for everyone regardless of his or her level of maturity as discussed above. Moreover, it is compatible with concurrently looking after oneself or one's family.

Regarding the third factor, it is indeed possible that forgiveness may occasionally be pressed upon victims in order to perpetuate an unjust status quo. Of course, systemic injustice should be resisted and wrongdoers should repent, but if the Christian message is right, forgiveness is the way of resistance. Therefore, it is a supreme irony that any wrongdoer would encourage forgiveness because forgiveness is the necessary ingredient to end wrongdoing. This is God's way of redeeming sinful humanity. According to Volf, "Forgiveness overcomes evil with good. Forgiveness mirrors the generosity of God whose ultimate goal is neither to satisfy injured pride nor to justly apportion reward and punishment, but to free sinful humanity from evil and thereby reestablish communion with us" (2005, 161).

Conclusion

In this essay, I have examined Pettigrove's arguments for the permissibility of forgiving the unapologetic and undeserving. In addition, I have explored his analysis of the connection between forgiveness and love and considered his reasons for limiting the moral permissibility of forgiveness. I have argued that on the Christian account, love is unconditional even toward one's enemies. God loves us in spite of our sin and forgives us because of our sin. We in turn are called to imitate this love, loving and forgiving unconditionally.

References

Aristotle. 1999. *Nicomachean Ethics*. Cambridge: Hackett Publishing.

Augustine. "Homily 7 on the First Epistle of John." Accessed 12 April 2016. http://www.newadvent.org/fathers/170207.htm.

Grudem, Wayne. 1994. *Systematic Theology*. Grand Rapids, MI: Zondervan.

Hoehner, Harold W. 2001. "Love." *Evangelical Dictionary of Theology*. Edited by Walter A. Elwell. Grand Rapids, MI: Baker Academic.

King, Jr., Martin Luther. 2010. *Strength to Love*. Minneapolis: Fortress Press.

O' Collins, Gerald. 1999. *The Tripersonal God: Understanding and Interpreting the Trinity*. Mahwah, New Jersey: Paulist Press.

Pettigrove, Glen. 2012. *Forgiveness and Love*. Oxford: Oxford University Press.

Volf, Miroslav. 2005. *Free of Charge: Giving and Forgiving in a Culture Stripped of Grace*. Grand Rapids, MI: Zondervan.

Chapter 10

Buddhism and the End to Forgiveness

Christopher Ketcham

Introduction

The question that this chapter will explore is how the idea of forgiveness was considered in early Theravada Buddhism. My thesis is that there is a different understanding for the unenlightened student of Buddhism who exists in the state of *dukkha* (unsatisfactoriness and suffering) and one who is enlightened (in the ethical state of *nibbana* in the Pali language, or *nirvana* in Sanskrit). However, these early texts lay down fundamental precepts of Buddhism that are the subject of this chapter, which I suggest, are fairly (but not universally) consistent throughout the different Buddhist belief systems.

There is, however, not just one form of Buddhism. There are as many branches of Buddhism as there are branches of Christianity. This chapter will consider the earliest form of Buddhism represented in the first written texts about Buddhism called the Pali Canon. These anonymous texts were written two hundred years or so (200-300 BCE) after the Buddha died in the fifth century BCE, so we have no way of confirming that these were derived from direct quotes from the Buddha. However, these early texts lay down fundamental precepts of Buddhism that are the subject of this chapter, which I suggest, are fairly consistent throughout the different Buddhist belief systems.

The chapter is divided into two parts. Part I, *Defining Forgiveness and the Need for Forgiveness* will first explore different Western definitions of forgiveness. Second, I will consider why forgiveness is necessary, and for that I will turn to Hannah Arendt and her theory of the irreversible act. While any act is irreversible, Arendt suggests that a person who commits an untoward act will become stuck in the consequences of that act unless forgiven by another. One cannot forgive oneself, she says. Arendt's purpose of forgiveness is an "unsticking"—to let the person move on in life.

In Buddhism, unsticking is an act of a "person," achieved by following the process of the Noble Eightfold Path, which ends *dukkha* (unsatisfactoriness) and produces enlightenment.[103] This unsticking changes the nature of forgiveness for the enlightened one.

Both Arendt and the Buddha are trying to end a type of uncertainty. For Arendt it is the ending of uncertainty of being stuck in the wrongful act and not being able to escape. Forgiveness by others is Arendt's means to escape. Arendt will be contrasted with the Buddha who saw *dukkha* as the unsatisfactoriness of the uncertainty of impermanence manifested in the cycle of rebirth. The end to impermanence in Buddhism also means the end to bad actions or bad *kamma* (karma).[104]

For both Arendt and Buddhism, the irreversible act cannot be undone. However, Arendt offers that forgiveness by another unsticks the wrongdoer from the uncertainty of being able to move forward. The wrongdoer's public Promises then move the forgiven wrongdoer forward.

---

[103] The Buddha did not believe in a separate soul or self. We are made up of five separate processes called *khandhas* or heaps that never coalesce into a permanent self or soul. However, he did not deny that we are persons even though we are not static beings who have an unchanging self. In this context I use the word 'person' as there is no phrase in English to denote the Buddhist notion of *khandhas*.

[104] Pali language terms will be used in this paper because Pali Cannon books in this derivation of Sanskrit were first translated into English. Some more commonly used Sanskrit words (i.e. karma) will be shown in parenthesis.

While forgiveness can be offered by the unenlightened student of Buddhism to the wrongdoer who asks, what the Buddha offers is unconditional compassion to the other to unstick the other from the uncertainty of *dukkha*. He then shows the other the Promise of the Noble Eightfold Path with the caveat that the other must commit to its rigor. This is why I will offer the idea that Buddhism ultimately seeks an end to forgiveness by replacing it with unconditional compassion. Even though they use different approaches, I will suggest that Arendt and the Buddha both are seeking an end to uncertainty.

In Part II *Buddhism and The Idea of Forgiveness* I explore basic precepts of Buddhism that will help frame the idea of forgiveness from a Buddhist perspective. These will include *kamma* (karma), rebirth (*saṃsāra*), enlightenment or nirvāna (*nibbāna*), the idea of no separate permanent self (*anātman*), and unsatisfactoriness (*dukkha*). I will then consult *suttas* (lessons) attributed to the Buddha from the Pali Canon involving the idea of forgiveness. Specifically I will review: 1) the Buddha and his rehabilitation of the murderer Angulimala; 2) the exhortation to forgive after being apologized to in the *Book of Disciplines*, and, 3) a new translation by Jayarava Michael Attwood from the original Pali where the Buddha responds to the 'confession' of the King Ajātasattu who committed an act of regicide against his own father.

Part I: Defining forgiveness and the need for forgiveness

There is no agreed upon definition of forgiveness in Western literature. Forgiveness is generally understood as a process that leads to a change in attitude towards another person. Major theoretical differences include issues involving who the players are in an act of forgiveness, and whether forgiveness is a means, an end, or both.

The Paul Hughes entry on 'forgiveness' in the *Stanford Encyclopedia of Philosophy* says: "From the ancient Greeks through the Hebrew and Christian Bibles to the present day, forgiveness has typically been regarded as a personal response to having been injured or wronged, or as a condition one seeks or hopes is bestowed upon one for having wronged someone else" (2015). Hughes explains the ends of forgiveness, "The standard definition of forgiveness makes clear that its main purpose is the re-establishment or resumption of a relationship ruptured by wrongdoing. The notion that forgiveness is teleological is also a central element of forgiveness both in contemporary philosophical accounts, which frequently stress the moral and non-moral purposes to be achieved by it, and within the Christian religious tradition, which links forgiveness to human redemption by God (2015). Given the broad parameters of resumption of relationship, *many* Western theories have been proposed. There is no consensus in the west as to how forgiveness should be defined. Hughes also notes that, "There is disagreement over the meaning of forgiveness, its relation to apparent cognates, the psychological, behavioral, conceptual, and normative dimensions of forgiveness, and when and under what conditions forgiveness is morally permissible, required, or wrong" (2015).

Michael E. McCullough, Kenneth I. Pargament and Carl E. Throensen explore some of the definitions others have proposed:

> *1) They quote R.D. Enright and C. T. Coyle who define forgiveness as, "a willingness to abandon one's right to resentment, negative judgment, and indifferent behavior toward one who unjustly hurts us, while fostering the undeserved qualities of compassion, generosity and even love toward him or her." (2000, 8)*

In this definition the forgiver not only lets go of negative feelings for the other, but also turns towards the other compassionately.

> 2) McCullough et al., define forgiveness as "...prosocial changes to one's motivations toward an offending relationship partner..."(Ibid.)

Forgiveness in this theory is contextual, meaning that one's attitude towards the offending partner changes according to social convention. This can vary from society to society.

> 3) McCullough et al. quote T. T. Hargrave and J. N. Sells who offer a two-part definition: 1) allowing one's victimizer to rebuild trust in the relationship through acting in a trustworthy fashion; and 2) promoting an open discussion of the relational violation so that the offended partner and the offender can agree to work toward an improved relationship." (Ibid.).

Hargrave and Sells want the victim to permit the victimizer to make amends. Once that is accomplished, dialogue is the process used towards mending the relationship. While this theory has strong potential for significant violations of interpersonal trust, perhaps it is too involved for a simple issue such as trespassing into an other's right of way by mistake.

One difficulty with defining forgiveness is that different disciplines—theology, psychology, healthcare, philosophy, law and politics, to name a few—all have different approaches to the concept of forgiveness. Donald W. Shriver addresses forgiveness from a political purpose approach: "Forgiveness in human affairs has purpose, not only the purpose of healing wounds internal to the person but wounds external in social relation" (2001, 153). In the macro-sense, forgiveness is certainly a social process.

Both Hannah Arendt and Rodney Petersen note that in theology forgiveness comes into to its own through Jesus's teachings (Petersen 2001, 3 and 8; Arendt 1958, 238). Petersen adds that in medicine forgiveness is, "a powerful psychotherapeutic tool..." Peterson also noted that holding onto anger increases stress and medical problems (2001, 8).

Charles Griswold gives what he calls an ideal *context* of forgiveness within philosophy, as "...a moral relation between two individuals, one who has wronged another, and who (at least in the ideal) are capable of communicating with each other" (2007, xvi). Griswold does, however, acknowledge that there are derivations from the ideal in the context of forgiveness, including "...forgiving wrongs done to others...third party forgiveness...forgiving the dead or unrepentant...self-forgiveness...God's forgiveness...and, forgiving God" (Ibid.). Griswold requires that all affected parties engage in the forgiving process but notes that the number of participants in the process becomes more complex when one includes third parties, society, the dead, and God.

Philosopher Joanna North engages a nine step ideal process of forgiveness which is different for the injured party versus the wrongdoer (1998, 30). North calls her *process* ideal because she sees it as something we should aspire to. This is an active process involving two persons. She says, "Forgiveness is a matter of a *willed* change of heart, the successful result of an active endeavor to replace bad thoughts with good, bitterness and anger with compassion and affection" (1998, 20; emphasis original). Again, North requires two to forgive. As I will demonstrate with Arendt, her idea of forgiveness can only be given by another. For Arendt, it is up to the forgiven to find a way forward through the use of the Promise, but this is not a requirement to be forgiven.

Philosopher Joram Haber says, "...that when an agent forgives, he forgives a wrongdoer *for* an injury received," that "...the forgiveness is *unilater*al," and that the wrongdoer does not have to be involved in any way, only the forgiver (1991, 11; emphasis original). Haber explains in contrast with

Griswold's ideal, it only takes one to *express* forgiveness. Haber is more concerned with the performative act of forgiveness than defining it. Haber outlines the required steps in *expressing* forgiveness:

1. X did A;
2. A was wrong;
3. X was responsible for doing A;
4. S was personally injured by X's doing A;
5. S resented being injured by X's doing A' and
6. S has overcome his resentment for X's doing A, or is at least willing to try to overcome it. (Ibid., 40)

Haber turns to John L. Austen's theory of performative utterances, to outline the required conditions for the same. These include, accepted conventional procedure, appropriate persons involved, correct and complete execution by all parties, participants have thoughts and feelings associated with the procedure, and the participants must maintain the conduct they performed in the procedure going forward in time (Ibid., 41).

In review, some understand forgiveness as a means towards achieving an equilibrium in a relationship. Once the giving up has occurred, the move forward in personal relationships is accomplished through dialogue. Others see an active engagement in a process that is a means towards an end: forgiveness. For some the process is unilateral; for others the process involves two or more participants. Ultimately, there is no consensus whether forgiveness is a means or an end. The only apparent consensus in the Western literature as to what forgiveness means is that it is generally understood as a process that leads to a change in attitude towards another person.

In this context, it is important to understand what the circumstances are that underlie the purported *need* for forgiveness in the first place. For that I turn to Hannah Arendt's concept of the irreversible act to provide one important theoretical approach. Arendt's approach not only is provocative, but also lays the groundwork for a more robust discussion of forgiveness through Buddhism, especially in what I believe is their shared idea that it is important to eliminate the "uncertainty" of being stuck without a way forward.

a. Arendt and the irreversible act

Hannah Arendt's theory of forgiveness begins in the irreversible act. For example, simply conducting our lives we trespass innocently every day. Walk down a crowded sidewalk. One simply cannot avoid bumping into an occasional person. Arendt says about trespassing and other wrongdoing, "…it needs forgiving, dismissing, in order to make it possible for life to go on by constantly releasing men from what they have done unknowingly" (1958, 240).

The faculty of forgiving, says Arendt "…serves to undo the deeds of the past whose 'sins' hang like Damocles' sword over every new generation…" (Ibid., 237). The deed cannot be undone because it is irreversible. However, being stuck in the shadow of the deed is what forgiveness undoes. Our conscience often clings to ideas and conceptions we have about ourselves and others. This insight is also one the Buddha had, that one of the unsatisfactory processes of the conscience is to cling to guilt, sorrow, and anger over deeds that we have committed that are untoward. Forgiveness by another informs us that we can let go. However, this letting go is only part of the process.

Forgiveness, according to Arendt, has a companion faculty and that is the Promise: "…binding oneself through promises, serves to set up in the ocean of uncertainty, which the future is by definition, islands of security without which not even continuity, let alone durability of any kind, would be possible in the relationships between men" (Ibid., 237). The public Promise provides direction against the chaotic and uncertain future. However, both the faculty of forgiveness and the Promise require others:

> *Both faculties, therefore, depend upon plurality, on the presence and acting of others, for no one can forgive himself and no one can feel bound by a promise made only to himself; forgiving and promising enacted in solitude or isolation remain without reality and can signify no more than a role played before one's self. (Ibid., 237)*

However, says Arendt, both the faculty of forgiveness and the Promise depend upon pluralities and others. We cannot forgive ourselves, as Arendt says, "...because we would lack the experience of the person for the sake of whom one can forgive" (Ibid., 243).[105] We must Promise in public because a Promise made just to oneself cannot be enforced.

Arendt contemporary, Emmanuel Levinas, said, which I paraphrase, "...we can never know the infinitely alterior other" (1979, 34). Therefore, we cannot know of what effect our trespass or act has had on the other. The act of forgiving ourselves, according to Arendt, is inadequate because we cannot understand the full nature of the harm to the other that requires forgiving, which is also consistent with Levinas's infinitely alterior other.

Arendt says, "The discoverer of the role of forgiveness in the realm of human affairs was Jesus of Nazareth" (1958, 238). Her idea is that the realm of forgiveness is between

---

[105] Robin S. Dillon found it troubling that forgiveness of the other could be virtuous but "self-loathing and interminable self-punishment for some long-past wrong seems incompatible with respect for yourself as a being with the intrinsic worth Kant called 'dignity'..." (Dillon 2001, 53). The scope of this chapter does not permit a more comprehensive discussion of self-forgiveness in Western literature. However, this discourse should be engaged further by others.

humans in society. We forgive each other and this precondition is necessary to earn God's forgiveness (Ibid., 238).

Buddhism has no God, so there is only the interpersonal to consider. Nor do we possess a separate and distinct self or soul that is permanent and unchanging. We live in a condition of existence called change. Consider this concept through the idea that even your memory of a memory becomes a new memory.

Can we forgive ourselves for harming ourselves? Arendt explores forgiveness in context of the public sphere. However, if I injure myself, likely, I am also injuring another or society. Attempted suicide, for example, costs society in medical bills and in pain to one's family and friends. Overeating and not taking care of oneself are other instances where society may be harmed. Can the Promise alone help the one become unstuck from an injury one does to oneself that has not otherwise caused actualized harm to society? I must offer the Promise publicly, which means I must admit that I have harmed myself. Without forgiveness for injuries I cause to myself, the Promise can be given, but I am still stuck in the untoward act I have committed on myself. Therefore, the personal wrong to oneself requires forgiveness by another in order to unstick the self-wrong, and the public Promise to move forward.

For Arendt, only the other can forgive me. While we can imagine that the individual other who has been wronged understands better the extent of the wrong than any other, neither the wrongdoer nor the societal other can understand the full nature of the wrong. Society then must approximate through laws what wrong is and punish and/or offer forgiveness based upon that approximation. Whether the societal notion is forgiveness, mercy, or whether it is essential to the idea of justice is beyond the scope of this chapter. Explicating the notion of "societal forgiveness" would be a good subject for additional research.

The notion of power contained in Arendt's idea of forgiveness is considerable. Arendt's contemporary, Jacques

Derrida was concerned that Arendt's idea of forgiveness might convey too much power to the forgiver. Derrida comments, "If, as [Vladamir] Jankélévitch and Arendt claim (I have given my reservations on this subject), one only forgives where one can judge and punish, therefore evaluate, then the putting into place, the institution of an instance of judgement, supposes a power, a force, a sovereignty" (2001, 59).

The harmer has exerted power to commit the harm. The reverse is also true because the harmed one has power over the wrongdoer to give or withhold forgiveness. If forgiveness is withheld by the other or others, the unforgiven remains stuck under the shadow of the irreversible act, the wrongdoing that is never forgiven. The stuck one cannot move forward. Without forgiveness, the associated faculty of Promise cannot move the individual forward because the past *is* the future, no matter how sincerely the Promise is given.

Arendt is not the last word on the need for forgiveness. However what Arendt does is explain how people can become stuck in reliving the past over and over again; and if there is no way out, the person cannot move forward. Arendt suggests that forgiveness is personal, "Forgiving and the relationship it establishes is always an eminently personal (though not necessarily individual or private) affair in which what *was* done is forgiven for the sake of *who* did it" (1958, 241, emphasis original). As a result, in the act of forgiveness, power is brought back down to a kind of equilibrium between persons.

Yet behind Arendt's unsticking is the power of the other, and only the other, to forgive. Derrida yearns for, as he says, "What I dream of, what I try to think as the 'purity' of a forgiveness worthy of its name, would be a forgiveness without power: *unconditional* but *without sovereignty*" (2001, 59; emphasis original).

b. Buddhism and letting go

In Buddhism, self-healing from the damage one has done in this life and past lives involves the Promise to follow the process of the Noble Eightfold Path. However, despite the fact that most who begin the path do so with considerable assistance from experienced Buddhists, the public Promise is not required. Therefore, the public Promise is not a necessity for the Buddhist paradigm.[106]

The Buddhist idea of letting go closely approximates the purity of forgiveness that Derrida seeks. Letting go in Buddhism releases the tension of power directed towards specific emotions or other persons. Letting go produces an unconditional space where one—anyone—can offer compassion to another, whether forgiveness is offered or not. Examples in part II of this chapter and others from the Buddhist Pali Canon demonstrate that the Buddha is most interested in first, offering wrongdoers compassion to remove fuel that burns the passions, and then a way forward through the process of the Noble Eightfold Path. As such his objectives are not all that different from Arendt—become unstuck; move forward.

Buddhism considers forgiveness in context of the Buddhist process of letting go. Patrick Boelyn-Fitzgerald distinguishes between complex definitions and simple definitions. The complex are more like those discussed in the idea of forgiveness in Western literature. The simple, Boelyn-Fitzgerald says is, "letting go of anger" (2002, 83). I will agree with Boelyn-Fitzgerald that letting go of anger is a fundamental process the Buddhist convert learns by walking the Noble Eightfold Path, a process that can lead to enlightenment. However, in enlightenment, anger itself has been extinguished and there is no longer a question of letting go of anger. This is not the only complicating factor. While the

---

[106] Monks, however, are required to make frequent confessions.

repair of relationships is fundamentally a good thing, there is the fact that once the wrong is committed, the wrong produces *kamma* (karma, the accumulation and accounting of actions from current and past lives which serves to direct into what realm of existence the being will be reborn), which is not something that can be undone. *Kamma* flows from rebirth to rebirth based upon the cumulative activities of past lives. One who is born again carries forward all of the *kamma* accumulated from past lives. *Kamma* is irreversible and as such represents a powerful incentive to perform good acts.

Part II: Buddhism and the idea of forgiveness

As there is no one definition of forgiveness, there is no monolithic Buddhism. There are many versions of Buddhism practiced around the world. However, according to Wing Cheuk-Chan, there is general agreement that to be classified as Buddhist, a sect must embrace three *dammas* (*dharmas* in Sanskrit: universal truths): dukkha (unsatisfactoriness, suffering), *anitya* (impermanence) and anātman (no self; no soul) (1999, 228).

The Buddha uses compassion to find ways to help you remove the fuel from the fires of the passions in order to let go of that which you have come to think you possess.[107] This is

---

[107] The illusion of possession extends to possessing other persons or beings (e.g. animal) or property itself. The idea of possession goes beyond being associated with to totalizing the object or other and making it part of you. By possessing you produce violence to the other through converting, even if only cognitively, into a static object. The act of possession produces anxiety that others will take this possession away and forceful actions to retain this now static object or possession for one's self (which of course is another illusion). The Buddha saw that the act and continuity of possession inflames the passions and only serves to continue and even increase *dukkha* in the world.

not forgiveness in the traditional Western sense, but is rather like Derrida's idea of a construct of forgiveness that is unconditional, without power, and without sovereignty. This is forgiveness without the power of possession behind it, whether of possession itself and/or of that which might be possessed. It is a complete letting go of anger and of any possessive sovereignty over the other. While beyond the scope of this paper, this notion of unconditional forgiveness without power and sovereignty may lead to a better understanding of how a collective or societal idea of forgiveness might be described.

The Buddha explains that you can find the level of equilibrium where power is no longer an issue. He then offers his Noble Eightfold Path in the form of a Promise to help you move forward. While the Promise of the end of *dukkha* lies with the Noble Eightfold Path, the Buddha himself makes no promise. He cannot make that promise because he cannot know how you will perform. Many will promise to follow the path but few will achieve enlightenment. However, if you faithfully follow the path, even if you do not ultimately succeed in becoming enlightened in this lifetime, your good *kammic* efforts will carry forward for you into your next (perhaps higher) rebirth.

While the Buddha understood the nature of *kamma*, and the centerpiece of his process of the Noble Eightfold Path guides persons towards their achievement of the ethical state of *nibbāna* (nirvāna), his lessons teach compassion towards all living beings.

The wisdom of letting go meets the ethics of compassion for the other in Buddhism. The "Buddhist turn," beginning with the Buddha himself, is to recognize that there is more to the achievement of wisdom than wisdom itself. Wisdom for wisdom's sake was the general objective of the monks of *other* belief systems during the Buddha's time. The Buddha's turn was not to remain alone in joyful enlightenment as had his contemporaries, but to go public to teach others the way towards enlightenment while maintaining his own meditative practices. The path of wisdom, at least for the Buddha, is both an ethical path and a knowledge path, which means the end to ignorance.[108]

To begin the journey towards wisdom one steps onto the process of the Noble Eightfold Path. The Noble Eightfold Path is a system of living. Through meditation and other practices honed over time, one begins to shed the clinging, craving, and attachment that bring unsatisfactoriness (*dukkha*) to the person and the world. Anger is a cause of *dukkha*. Anger is a clinging to the idea that a wrong has been committed against me or society itself. It burns like a fire until it the fuel is removed—if it can be removed.

In contemporary philosophical discussions of forgiveness, as Patrick Boelyn-Fitzgerald points out, much of what have been offered are complex processes tied to the event, the wronged, and the wrongdoer. On the other hand, of Buddhism, Boelyn-Fitzgerald says:

> *An act of simple forgiveness is an act of letting go of anger. If we do this whenever anger arises in our minds, then eventually the anger will burn itself out. If we forgive enough, then eventually we will be able to forget. This sense of forgetting is not passive. It is the consequence of a habitual response. (2002, 490-1)*

I will agree with Boelyn-Fitzgerald that a conditioned approach (i.e. the process of the Noble Eightfold Path) to letting go of anger is something that can be practiced. Effective utilization of this practice can ultimately remove the fuel that

---

[108] It is beyond the scope of this chapter to discuss the idea of knowledge and the end to ignorance for the enlightened one.

produces the fire of the anger towards the other that arises from the event that caused it. The enlightened one has left behind anger and while the injury may sting, anger is no longer part of the process of experience for the enlightened one.[109]

What the unilateral letting go of anger does *not* do is provide succor or assistance to the other, the wrongdoer. For this, the Buddha teaches compassion for the other. This is helping the other become unstuck from performing future wrongful acts; while understanding that no one can undo what has been done.

Buddhism is not power-centric in the sense that there is no sovereign God or state or even empowered other who has the categorical power to forgive. Granted there are rules of conduct for monks, but these are designed to help one travel the Noble Eightfold Path towards the change in consciousness that is *nibbāna*. There is, of course, the power of mutually agreed upon conduct in the monastery. One can be sent away from the association of monks for specific infractions and chronic inattention to the conduct and processes associated with the *damma* (doctrine).

Buddhism is not like the Abrahamic religions where God has a part to play in ethics. For example, in his Talmudic reading about the other, Levinas points out that, "It is well understood that faults toward one's neighbor are *ipso facto* offenses toward God" (1994, 16; emphasis original). Levinas,

---

[109] The enlightened one (Arahant) who still lives is like a charred log with fuel remaining that does not burn and the dead Arahant is without fuel remaining. Says the Buddha, "While the Arahant [Tathágata] is still alive, he/she still experiences the process of the five aggregates, but they do not burn with the fires of passion, aversion, or delusion. When the Arahant passes away, there is no longer any experience of aggregates here or anywhere else. (Note 1, §44, p.29, from the Thanissaro Bhikkhu translation of the Itivuttaka in the chapter, The Group of Twos. Content in brackets added.)

while he saw the offense to the other to be also an ipso facto offense against God, he also saw, "An earthly tribunal is necessary to create justice among men!" However, "The drama of forgiveness involves not two players but three" (Ibid 18). God is the third player for Levinas. There is no God, as a third player in Buddhism, nor any God who can forgive.

Early Buddhist doctrine assumes that *kamma* is unconditional; *kamma* is and cannot be undone by any means. Neither the other nor any devā (a mortal god in the early Buddhist sense) can undo or change *kamma* by any act of forgiving. Buddhism understands (as does Arendt) that any act is irreversible.

The Buddha was a product of his times in northern India. Two precepts that the Buddha borrowed (but modified) from emergent Indian beliefs were *kamma*, and the cycle of rebirth and death (*saṃsāra*). The issue associated with wrongdoing is *kamma*. *Kamma* results not only from a completed act, but a contemplated act. *Kamma* is; and is not revocable. *Kamma* can be good or bad.

The Buddha understood that everything has a cause which he calls dependent arising (*paṭiccasamuppāda*). There is a chain even matrix of causes for all things. *Kamma* includes an accounting for these causes over the course of one's lifetimes. In other words, both our good and bad deeds are recorded, carried forward, and ordered by the *kammic* forces. These forces ultimately determine the level of existence we will be born into in our next rebirth. However, we cannot know the future nor can we understand the implications of what we do today will have on our future lives. We do know that actions produce good and bad *kamma*. However, predicting what each action will mean for a future rebirth is a bit like trying to predict the weather where one is today three years in the future from past weather patterns. Nor can we know ultimately what the effect of the commission of one bad *kammic* act will have against the backdrop of one who otherwise leads a generally ethical existence.

Kamma is not something that is judged by an external entity as Mark Siderits explains:

> *Karma is not a set of rules that are decreed by a cosmic ruler and enforced by the cosmic moral police. Karma is understood instead as a set of impersonal causal laws that simply describe how the world happens to work...A true causal law has no exceptions. Likewise, the laws of karma are understood not as rules that can be either obeyed or broken, but as exceptionless generalizations about what always follows what. (2007, 9)*

Kamma cannot be undone but it is always the result of a prior cause. The irreversible act and *kamma* consider that nothing done can be undone, and both can include good and bad acts.

The Buddha also asks: how could there be a separate and distinct and unchanging self when we are all about change? Our minds are always thinking; our bodies are always changing—of what purpose would be a separate and distinct self that cannot change? There is no separate self or soul (*anātman*), says the Buddha. While the idea of *anātman* has been the subject of considerable discussion in Buddhism, what is important for the idea of forgiveness is that people can change. They are not locked into a being that is stuck in one mode.

Unlike the Abrahamic religions where one has only one life to live, Buddhism gives more opportunities to improve one's level of existence until one can become enlightened and will not be reborn again. Knowing that there is an empirical mechanism involved in rebirth is not as important as understanding that the Buddha saw *saṃsāra* (the cycle of rebirth and death) as being the inevitable consequence of unsatisfactoriness, of *dukkha*. Rebirth then is something that must be ended if an individual desires to achieve nibbāna (enlightenment). The state of enlightenment is an ethical state. If enlightenment is the goal of Buddhism, a brief explanation of Buddhist ethics is in order.

It follows that if we know what will produce good *kamma* versus bad *kamma*, to live an ethical life we should do the things that will produce good *kamma*. However, humanity is a messy business. Damien Keown explains that Buddhism recognizes this and unlike utilitarianism, "...does not define right independent from the good" (2001, 177). Keown says that it isn't strictly the act itself that defines its rightness, "It is the preceding motivation (cetanā) which the determines the moral quality of the act and not its consequences" (2001, 178). I might be motivated by road rage to ram the car in front, but the other driver avoids my aggression and no damage occurs. Even though the consequence is not an accident, the motivation behind the action was not rightful. On the other hand, a drunk driver swerves into my lane and I take evasive action but it is inadequate to save my passenger from being killed. The motivation of avoiding the other driver was rightful even though the result is injury and death.

What will the thousands of trespasses that Arendt envisions we make each day ultimately have on our rebirth? A lot will depend upon motivation. For example, you step around the corner and bump into a person. You did not intend to bump into that person. Intention in Buddhism is critical to understanding whether the act will produce bad *kamma* or not. However, should you intentionally trip someone—a form of trespassing—that will likely generate bad *kamma*.

From Indian society and mainstream religions, the Buddha reframes the ideas of rebirth (*saṃsāra*) and *kamma* in the context of *anātman* (no separate self and soul). However, what sets him on his journey of discovery is the problem of *dukkha*. It is important to reflect on what *dukkha* means in the Pali and how the Buddha probably understood the term. *Dukkha* has no easily explained meaning in English. *Dukkha* has been explained as suffering, ill, unsatisfactoriness, and lack. Says T. W. Rhys Davids, no one of these by itself is a good fit because *dukkha* involves not only the physical but the mental (1921-1925, 363). *Dukkha*, Michael C. Brannigan says, is "dislocation" that includes both physical pain and mental anguish (2010, 52). Padmasiri de Silva adds, "disharmony, anxiety and unsatisfactoriness" but he cautions that *dukkha* is not angst (1976, 20). Sue Hamilton explains that, "…it is important for proper understanding of what *dukkha* means to realise that it is being used to make a truth statement and not a value judgment…In particular it is not stating that human experience is unpleasant" (2000, 13-14). As Ketcham summarizes, "Therefore if *dukkha* is a truth statement, assigning the Western concept of 'evil' to it would not be appropriate. *Dukkha* simply is" (2015, 116).

The Buddha understands that every sentient being experiences *dukkha*. *Dukkha* is ultimately the clinging and craving to being itself, hence the problem of rebirth as becoming a being all over again—this is a state of impermanence. The Pali texts speak of three types of dukkha:

1. Ordinary suffering *dukkha-dukkha* (like the pain from a fall or a bug bite.)

2. *Viparināma-dukkha* is the suffering that occurs during change or disappointment (*Viparināma*) (Rhys Davids 1921-1925, 695, Viparināma). (What this implies is that change is a condition of unsatisfactoriness in that it is related to impermanence—the cycle of death and rebirth. Change is not something that necessarily produces physical pain but it does produce mental anguish. Growing pains would be included in this category—could be both physical and mental. We see this kind of mental anguish with Martin Heidegger's idea that we are a being towards death.)

3. *Samkhāra-dukkha* is the suffering of the mental formations from the process of the aggregates (*khandhas*) and, "…is the suffering which is inher-

ent in conditioned existence (samkhāra-dukkha)" (Collins 1996, 140). (This form of *dukkha* explains that Conditioned things are impermanent and not *nibbāna* therefore a conditioned thing is unsatisfactory. A condition thing does not fit the English definition of suffering which is more like *dukkha-dukkha* and *Viparināma-dukkha* which is why unsatisfactory is a better term for the aggregation of the three types of *dukkha*. Conditionality is encapsulated in the idea of dependent arising.)

The Buddha explains that in the process of becoming enlightened, he has gained wisdom about the cause of *dukkha*, but needs a way to explain it to others. His revelations begin with the four noble truths of Buddhism which identify both the problem of *dukkha* and that there is a cure for *dukkha*. Then, he outlines the cure for *dukkha* in a process which he calls the Noble Eightfold Path. The path towards enlightenment begins with the understanding that there are four noble truths, and that all things are dependently originated.

The four noble truths (*cattaro ariyā saccā*) of Buddhism are:[110]

1. All living things suffer (*dukkha*);
2. The cause of suffering (*dukkha*) is craving (*samudaya saccā*). *Samuyada* is the rise or origin, origin of *dukkha*, a bursting forth; *saccā* is truth;
3. It is possible to end suffering (*dukkha*): (*nirodha saccā*), oppression, suppression; destruction, cessa-

---

[110] Terms defined from: Rhys Davids 1921-1925).

tion, annihilation (of senses, consciousness, feeling & being in general: *sankhārā*);[111]

4. Suffering (*dukkha*) can be cured by following a path (*magga*), the Noble Eightfold Path (*Atthangika-ariyā-magga*).

The normal state of sentient beings is in *dukkha*, which is unsatisfactoriness: the state where we cling the desire to be reborn again in the cycle of rebirth and death called *saṃsāra*. The Buddha sets about to end *dukkha* but needed a way forward from being stuck to and attached to conditioned things (by nature impermanent) that maintain a person in *dukkha*.

The Noble Eightfold Path is a process, not a set of rules or rituals. The Buddha through Keown explains, "Purity is not attained through views (*diṭṭhi*), learning or knowledge, nor through rules and rituals [the lord] said" (2001, 47). Morality, insight and proficiency in meditation are *all* required for purity or enlightenment. Keown explains, "If too much emphasis is placed on morality there is danger of falling into the error of 'attachment to rules and rituals'" (Ibid.). The release of attachment (clinging and craving) to the cankers (*āsavas*) and to being itself is one of the basic tenets of Buddhism.

Craving (*taṇhā*) is seen as the fundamental cause of suffering. Keown explains: "From *taṇhā* arises grief, from *taṇhā* arises fear. For him who is totally free from *taṇhā* there is no grief, let alone fear" (Ibid., 65). The Noble Eightfold Path leads to the end *taṇhā* and the end of *dukkha*.

---

[111] The Pali-English dictionary says of *Sankhārā*: "*Sankhārā* includes the ideas of: "preparation, get up…coefficient of consciousness and life… the sum of the conditions or properties making up or resulting in life or existence; the essentials or "element" of anything…" (Rhys Davids 1921-1925, 736-737). This brief quotation is not an exhaustive representation of the idea of *Sankhārā*.

The elimination of the *dukkha*-causing aspects of existence that removes all the ills of *dukkha* leads to the end of rebirth. Hamilton explains, "And it is this process that one needs to understand." First, we must understand the continuity of this process so that the process can be modified. Second, this begins with understanding ourselves, our cognitive processes. If we can better understand how we think, we can begin to unravel the contingent processes that need to be interrupted. So the first goal of Buddhism is to understand how we think (2000, 30). Following the Noble Eightfold Path can lead one towards the end of *taṇhā* and the end of *dukkha*.

Nibbāna results from following the Noble Eightfold Path. Not all who follow the Noble Eightfold Path fastidiously will become enlightened. As T.W. Rhys Davids points out, "The ethical state called Nibbāna can only rise from within. It is therefore in the older texts compared to the fire going out, rather than to the fire being put out." (1921-1925, 405). Many say that the fuel for the fire is removed in *nibbāna* even though the embers of existence still glow.

Steven Collins says, "...the enlightened person is deep, immeasurable, unfathomable like the great ocean" (1996, 163). Says Collins, "...nirvāna is a genuine Existent, not a conceptual one" (1996, 164). In fact, in enlightenment there is a change of consciousness itself. Collins remarks that this wisdom is not momentary, "Rather, it is supposed to be a continuous form of awareness present throughout any and every activity, achieved by and embodied in the practice of mindfulness" (2010, 42).

In achieving *nibbāna*, one does not ask for forgiveness from others but stops contributing bad *kamma*. To enter the ethical state of *nibbāna*, one is not forgiven for past sins or bad karmic acts. One, in principle, makes a promise to the *kammic* forces not to continue these acts in the future.

What is not explainable is how the karmic forces engage with the individual to make enlightenment possible. The forces are an independent process even though they are co-determined with all of existence. It would be expedient but not correct to suggest that the *kammic* forces (as both independent from and co-determined with existence) are somehow giving the student of Buddhism forgiveness for letting go of those faculties which produce *dukkha* and ultimately bad *kamma*. One cannot escape one's *kamma*. Unsticking is the recognition that my clinging to these prior acts produces *dukkha* and that *dukkha* can be defeated by my following the Noble Eightfold Path. The Promise in Buddhism is a process that can lead me forward to a future existence in the ethical state of *nibbāna*. This is not necessarily a public Promise as Arendt requires. However, most students of Buddhism learn the process through active participation with more practiced teachers. On the other hand, the Buddha himself discovered the Promise of the Noble Eightfold Path on his own.

What is clear in Buddhism is that clinging to anger and resentment associated with the injury associated with wrongful or harmful acts committed by another is no longer evident in an enlightened one. The enlightened one does not merely let go of anger as may an unenlightened Buddhist student does as part of the journey along the Noble Eightfold Path. Rather, anger does not form in the enlightened one even after being injured by another. The enlightened one might feel physical pain from an injury by an other or feel compassion for others who injure the enlightened one, but anger and resentment are no longer the case. Says Floyd Ross, the real test of compassion comes when a brother is attacked and even then, "he is not to harbour enmity towards his abusers" (1953, 111).

The Buddha suggests that enlightenment also requires a change in consciousness itself: "Then that idea, (that consciousness), of lusts, that he had before, passes away. And thereupon there arises within him a subtle, but actual, consciousness of the joy and peace arising from detachment, and he becomes a person to whom that idea is consciously present. 'Thus is it that through training one idea, one sort of consciousness, arises; and through training another passes away. This is the training I spoke of", said the Exalted One" (T.W. Rhys Davids 1899, 182).

Buddhism explains that the unenlightened are stuck, stuck in the world of *dukkha* (unsatisfactoriness) because we cling to (causal) impermanence which is the cycle of birth and death (*saṃsāra*). To become enlightened, in other words, to move forward in a more certain manner, into a state (a different form of consciousness) where impermanence is no longer an issue and deathlessness is the goal, one must follow the Buddhist Noble Eightfold Path.

a. Arendt and the Buddha

Arendt does not require the wrongdoer to ask for forgiveness for it to be given. Neither does the Buddha. However, the Buddha, as the other, does not grant himself the power to give forgiveness or not. He offers compassion without restriction. Examples from the Pali Canon in this chapter's next section, *Forgiveness in the Pali Canon*, will show how the Buddha offers others a way out of being stuck, the unsatisfactoriness of impermanence and uncertainty.

Getting unstuck is Arendt's purpose for forgiveness. Getting unstuck from clinging, craving, and attachment to things and being itself is the purpose of the Noble Eightfold Path. Both the Buddha and Arendt are trying to move people forward—to live better lives. Freed from unsatisfactory attachment to Arendt's irreversible act, the forgiven can begin to make public promises to move forward. The Promise of Buddhism (not necessarily publicly given) is that if one promises to follow the process of the Noble Eightfold Path, one will journey towards becoming unstuck from the irreversible acts of bad *kamma*. In Buddhism one does not forgive oneself for past acts and one is not forgiven for these irreversible act. What one must do is to promise to follow a path that does not produce more bad *kamma* going forward. In both Arendt and Buddhism, the hinge for change is becoming unstuck even though both approach the task through different means and processes.

b. Forgiveness in the Pali Canon

How the Buddha reacts to the confession of wrongdoers and to the efforts of wrongdoers to achieve enlightenment provides an important insight into how Buddhism addresses relationship building and/or repairing in a world where bad *kamma* is ever-present.[112]

There are instances in the Pali Canon of the Buddha helping those who have committed terrible crimes become ardent followers of his *damma* (teachings). These are not like the miracles performed by Jesus in the Christian Bible. Rather, more like Jesus's sermons, it is the way the Buddha speaks and turns situations into lessons that help others begin to journey down a more enlightened path.

In *Angulimalāsutta* (Discourse with Angulimala) from the Pali text of the *Middle Length Sayings*, Buddha walks along a country road where shepherds and villagers warn him away because the killer Angulimala who wears a garland of fingers is near. The Buddha keeps walking and Anguilimala sees him and delights that Buddha is alone. He tries to follow the Buddha, but the Buddha uses his psychic power to keep his distance (a mystical act, perhaps, but not really a miracle). Amazed that he cannot catch the Buddha, Angulimala calls

---

[112] In the Parable of the Saw, the Buddha eschews anger for compassion even when someone injures you grievously. He says to Phagguna, "Phagguna, get rid of those desires that are worldly, those thoughts that are worldly; and you, Phagguna, should train yourself thus: 'Neither will my mind become perverted, nor will I utter an evil speech, but kindly and compassionate will I dwell with a mind of friendliness and void of hatred.' (The I. B. Horner translation of the Middle Length Sayings of the Buddha, The Parable of the Saw Pali Text Society, Lancaster UK, 2007 § 124-125, p. 161." This is not forgiveness, but the condition under which an enlightened one would respond to an injury caused by another.

out to the Buddha for him to stop. After a short conversation, Angulimala throws away his weapons and honors the feet of the Buddha (foot washing was a common ritual of respect) after which the Buddha says, "come on monk" to Angulimala. Angulimala becomes a monk, but his reputation precedes him and while walking alone with his alms bowl, he is pummeled bloody by townsfolk. Angulimala endures and by all accounts learns the *damma* well. Anguilimala may be a perfect metaphor for the Buddha's idea of compassion. As Hamilton says, "Compassion lies in seeing and effecting what will best help someone to help themselves; and this is in fact the most profoundly constructive thing that one can do for another person" (2000, 213).

Second, there are his lessons to the monks. In one of his teachings in *The Book of Disciplines* Volume IV, the *Mahāvagga*, §26, the Buddha says, "Monks, when you are being apologised to you should not not forgive. Whoever should not forgive, there is an offence of wrong-doing." What is the Buddha telling his monks? Is he saying your forgiveness will lessen *dukkha*; will change the *kammic* result of the action; is a polite gesture that is basically good manners? I suggest that the lessons in the *Mahāvagga* are lessons in good behavior specifically directed towards monks. If pressed I believe he would not have agreed that forgiveness would change the *kamma* that produced the act or intention that precipitated the giving of forgiveness.

Would forgiveness mitigate *dukkha*? It might, as Arendt suggests, unstick the wrongdoer from the wrong so the wrongdoer can move on. On the other hand, the Buddha would not have forgiven what has become a permanent act of kamma, rather he would have used skillful means to help one who Arendt would forgive to move forward using the process of the Noble Eightfold Path to not produce bad *kamma* in the future. While unsticking the individual is the important outcome both Arendt and the Buddha are striving for, the Buddha does so by looking into the future in the form of a Promise to not produce more bad *kamma*; Arendt begins in the past in a Christian act of forgiveness of bad sins which then requires the wrongdoer's public Promise to refrain from wrongful acts in the future. The Buddha teaches his unenlightened monks to forgive, because they have not yet let go of anger that may require an act of forgiveness to dissipate the passion that anger produces.

However, if the individual is enlightened, *dukkha* has been defeated, and forgiveness is no longer necessary. Forgiveness is replaced by unconditional compassion. The complex nature of the Buddha's world is that he is both an intellectual force and spiritual presence, but even he cannot spread his hands like a healer and enlighten everyone with his touch. Sometimes compassion is the only thing that is needed to encourage another to embrace the *damma*. Compassion is what might have changed Angulimala. This is a subtle compassion: calling Angulimala "monk" gives the man, otherwise excluded from society through his own actions, admission back into society in order to begin again.

In other instances, some who cross the Buddha's path have real questions they struggle with. Others think that they can stump the Buddha with their questions or statements about how things are, primarily from belief systems that the Buddha has found lacking. In both instances he offers his thoughts to counteract the wrong-headed ideas of challengers, and provide answers to questions that truly vex others. From the first few days after he becomes enlightened until his death more than forty years later, the Buddha gives lessons, and teaches many numbers of monks on how to compassionately help others not only to achieve *nibbāna*, but also the ways of reducing *dukkha* in order to live a more ethical life towards a higher rebirth for those who cannot endure the rigor of the Noble Eightfold Path.

The pragmatic Buddha understands that there is a need for householders in society as well as kings and monks. I believe he knew he personally could not help all achieve *nibbāna*. However, he does the best he can for some towards that end, and creates an order of monks who will proselytize the Buddha's *damma* and work towards eliminating *dukkha* for all.

This is why I suggest that Buddhism's enlightenment means an end to forgiveness. Forgiveness is not necessary for one who has let go and for whom the commission of bad *kamma* is no longer possible. Compassion replaces forgiveness and the enlightened one does not commit any acts that might encourage another to forgive one. Forgiveness, though not unconditional compassion, I believe helps others who are not yet ready to walk down the Noble Eightfold Path to begin to explore the possibilities for compassionate being for others.

There is one more *sutta* which deserves attention in the context of forgiveness. The Buddha in his lesson on forgiveness in the *Mahāvagga* does not suggest that his monks give out gratuitous forgiveness. He does not advocate walking through a village saying to anyone you meet, you are forgiven. His *Mahāvagga* lesson says, when someone apologizes to you for an infraction or perceived infraction either against you or another, offer forgiveness.

To exemplify that the Buddha would not give gratuitous forgiveness, I turn to King Ajātasattu and his conversation with the Buddha. King Ajātasattu has killed his father. Jayarava Michael Atwood carefully considers the passage of the so called confession of King Ajātasattu in relation to traditional translations of the Pali into English. His first question is whether King Ajātasattu is simply confessing, or is he also apologizing, attempting to make amends for the murder he had committed. If he is merely confessing, Atwood asks, which I paraphrase, "would the Buddha forgive King Ajātasattu, or would he offer his thoughts on how King Ajātasattu might avoid doing such an evil deed in the future" (2008, 281)? In the end, Atwood concludes that, yes, King Ajātasattu has confessed, but has not apologized. As a result, the Buddha does not offer forgiveness, only compassion and a way forward. Atwood's revised translation is thus:

> *You definitely, O King, fell into transgression when you foolishly, in confusion, and unskillfully deprived the good and just king of his life. Since, having seen your transgression as a transgression, you Dhammicly counteract it, we accept that. One who, having seen his transgression as a transgression, Dhammicly counteracts it, grows in the discipline of the Noble Ones, O King, and will restrain themselves in future. (2008, 299)*

If King Ajātasattu had in his confession apologized and offered to make amends for his transgression, the Buddha as he exhorted his monks to do, would have forgiven him, much the same as he forgave Angulilama by calling him "monk," not to erase the bad *kamma* the king had earned, but to help him forward towards becoming unstuck so that he could walk a more righteous path. However, his "forgiveness" in the form of skillful means would come from someone who has let go of anger. His 'forgiveness' is transformed from erasing negative *kamma* towards unconditional compassion towards the other to help unstick the other from performing future actions that produce bad *kamma*.

The Buddha tells his monks to offer forgiveness when asked. However, he himself, has moved away from 'forgiving' as such to offer unconditional compassion and ways to help the other become unstuck through a process of moving forward in much the same manner as Arendt does with the Promise. I suggest that the compassion that the Buddha offers is not an act of Arendtian forgiveness; it is first an acceptance of the other as who the other is. Second, while an acceptance of the other both as other and through the use of the act and actions of hospitality is a welcoming, it is also responsible, through the use of skillful means to help the other find ways out of *dukkha*. In this context, his compassion is not gratuitous but is part of a lesson that both unsticks the other and can, if the lesson is listened to, moves the person forward towards ending *dukkha*. Sometimes this moving forward is as simple as saying to Angulimala, "come along, monk." However, the Buddha is not offering the Promise, the other must make the Promise and this is consistent with Arendt. In the case of the Buddha, many offered their promises directly to him, but the public Promise is not required.

The Buddha's consistency in what he says suggests that he not only lives what he teaches, but that he has very definitive ideas of what are the right ways of treating others compassionately. He does not give gratuitous forgiveness, but he always tries to find a way to help another who suffers *dukkha* to find a way forward which many call "skillful means." This compassion to help others find a way forward, regardless of whether someone asked to be forgiven or not, I suggest is similar to but not exactly like the "Promise" that Arendt suggests begins to help the forgiven to find a way through the chaos of the uncertain future. Forgiveness in the Arendtian sense and in most other Western definitions involves judging another (and the wrong) before it is given. The difference is that the Buddha's forgiveness is unconditional because it does not begin in a place of judgment, only compassion.

While his goal is to end *dukkha*, and thus end the need for forgiveness through enlightenment, the Buddha is a pragmatist. He could offer forgiveness to another who apologizes and this is a lesson he teaches his monks. However, he understands that forgiveness is never enough in and of itself because the true way forward is through the Noble Eightfold Path. By his *suttas* and lessons in the disciplines, he prepares monks for their own enlightenment. He cannot explain exactly what they will find once they achieve *nibbāna*, but he knows that the state is an ethical state and a state where not only is *dukkha* defeated, but also ignorance. In that state, the Arahant knows that the path forward ultimately is not only to forgive the others but also to help others make their own effort to find a way forward towards enlightenment.

c. The Promise

However, can one call this effort "Promise"? The issue with the Promise is that it serves to attach the person to the goal. One may cling to this goal to producing the outcome required of the Promise. The Promise can even cause craving for the actions required to achieve the conditions of the Promise. These forms of attachment are all things that produce *dukkha*.

For example, can one desire *nibbāna*? I will agree with Collins, that, "…it would be better to talk of the aspiration to nirvana rather than the desire for it, of purposive action as intentionally oriented towards its goal rather than as desiring it" (1996, 186). Any Promise would need to be phrased as a goal that can be aspired to rather than something to which the person attaches.

I will briefly deconstruct Arendt's "Promise" in order to gain understanding of its applicability to Buddhism. First, for Arendt the Promise is a partial solution to unpredictability because it: 1) helps the person master the problems of uncertainty about the future; and 2) addresses the inability of the individual to rely upon oneself or have faith in oneself in a society of others (Arendt 1958, 244). Arendt says:

> *The function of the faculty of promising is to master this twofold darkness of human affairs and is, as such, the only alternative to a mastery which relies on domination of one's self and rule over others; it corresponds exactly to the existence of a freedom which was given under the condition of non-sovereignty.* (1958, 244)

The "Promise" of *nibbāna* is both freedom from *dukkha* and the knowledge of and giving of unconditional compassion in a world of others. *Nibbāna*'s "Promise" is something that is aspired to and gained only through a transformation of consciousness itself. There is no sovereign in Buddhism and the 'contract', as such, which underlies all activities of sentient beings is with the *kammic* forces, which, if understood from the change of consciousness that is *nibbāna*, is the ethical: meaning the enlightened one no longer contributes to bad *kamma*. Collins, through D.C. Davis, says that Buddhism addresses, "the collective problem ... [which is] the reconciliation of limited satisfactions and unlimited human desires within a social context ..." (1996, 294). Buddhism is not a utopia in the strict sense of the word, but like the Promise contributes to social theory rather than to a specific ideal society (Collins 1996, 293-294). Collins, again through Davis, explains:

...there is no Buddhist utopia. That is, there is no imagined human society of the normal productive and reproductive kind where, in his words, "the collective problem [is solved] collectively, that is by the reorganization of society and its institutions, by education, by laws and by sanctions." (Collins 1996, 557)

In no sense does Arendt suggest that the Promises engaged in by persons in society produce an ideal society.[113] Arendt does not go as far as Buddhism to suggest the need for a change in consciousness itself, but she sees the Promise as being something that is earned from existing in a society where freedom is obtained through the Promise and not the

---

[113] In the introduction to *The Human Condition*, Margaret Canovan makes this clear by explaining, "But she emphatically denied that her role as a political thinker was to propose a blueprint for the future or to tell anyone what to do" (Arendt 1958, viii).

actions of an individual ego acting on his/her own (Arendt 1958, 245).

Nibbāna is a shedding of the ego for existence without the cankers (*āsavas*). *Nibbāna* is also the defeat of ignorance which is the reduction of uncertainty. The Buddha continues to walk the Noble Eightfold Path of his own enlightenment while also offering compassion and his *suttas* (lessons) in the *damma* which are towards helping others avoid the uncertainty of living the *dukkha* of impermanence.

Conclusion

The way forward for Buddhism is ultimately not forgiveness as Arendt proposes. However, forgiveness serves to unstick the unenlightened so that a wrongdoer can learn the way forward. There is no exactly corresponding Arendtian Promise in Buddhism to wrest the future from chaos. However, following the Noble Eightfold Path is a process that leads the person past unsatisfactoriness and the impermanence that is *dukkha*. While one cannot conflate the Arendtian Promise and the Buddhist Noble Eightfold Path as conveying identical meaning, I offer that an end for both is towards the reduction of uncertainty.

Acknowledgements

I want to thank Dr. Joshua Mason Assistant Professor of the West Chester University of Pennsylvania Philosophy Department for his questions, critiques, and ideas on the subject of Buddhism. I would also like to thank Dr. Cassie Striblen Associate Professor also of the West Chester University Philosophy Department for her thoughtful edits and insightful ideas associated with Hannah Arendt's concept of forgiveness.

References

Arendt, Hannah. 1958. *The Human Condition*. Chicago: University of Chicago Press.

Attwood, Jayarava Michael. 2008. "Did King Ajātasattu Confess to the Buddha, and Did the Buddha Forgive Him?" *Journal of Buddhist Ethics* 15: 278-307.

Boleyn-Fitzgerald, Patrick. 2002. "What Should 'Forgiveness' Mean?" *The Journal of Value Inquiry* 36.4: 483-498.

Brannigan, Michael C. 2010. *Striking a Balance*. Plymouth, UK: Lexington Books.

Chan, Wing-cheuk. 1999. "Mahayana Buddhism and Levinas: The Primacy of the Other." *Varieties of Universalism: Essays in Honour of J. R. A. Mayer*. Edited by Marco Zlomislic, David Goicoccechea and Zdenko Zeman. n.p.: Thought House Publishing Group.

Collins, Stephen. 1996. *Nirvana and other Buddhist Felicities*. Cambridge, UK: Cambridge University Press.

———. 2010. *Nirvana: Concepts, Imagery, Narrative*. Cambridge, UK: Cambridge University Press.

de Silva, Padmasiri. 1976. *Tangles and Webs*, Second Edition. W.A.D. Ramanayake Mawatha Colombo: Lake House Investments LTD.

Derrida, Jacques. 2001. *On Cosmopolitanism and Forgiveness*. Translated by Mark Dooley and Michael Hughes. London and New York: Routledge.

Dillon, Robin S. 2001. "Self-Forgiveness and Self-Respect." *Ethics* 112.1: 53-83

Griswold, Charles. 2007. *Forgiveness: A Philosophical Exploration*. Cambridge, UK: Cambridge University Press.

Haber, Joram Graf. 1991. *Forgiveness*. Savage, Md.: Rowman & Littlefield Publishers.

Hamilton, Sue. 2000. *Early Buddhism: A New Approach: The I of the Beholder*, Volume 16. NY: Routledge.

Hughes, Paul M. 2015. "Forgiveness." *The Stanford Encyclopedia of Philosophy*. Edited by Edward N. Zalta. Stanford, CA: Stanford University. http://plato.stanford.edu/archives/spr2015/entries/forgiveness/. Accessed 24 May 2016.

Keown, Damien. 2001. *The Nature of Buddhist Ethics*. New York: Palgrave.

Ketcham, Christopher. 2015. "Meaning Without Ego." *Journal of the Philosophy of Life* 5.3: 112-133.

Levinas, Emmanuel. 1979. *Totality and infinity: An Essay on Exteriority*, Volume 1. Translated by Alphonso Lingis. Dordrecht, Netherlands: Kluwer Academic Publishers; an imprint of Springer Science & Business Media.

―――――. 1994. *Nine Talmudic Readings*. Translated by Annette Aronowicz, Volume 876. Bloomington, IN.: Indiana University Press.

McCullough, Michael E., Kenneth I. Pargament, and Carl. E. Thoresen. 2000. "The Psychology of Forgiveness: History, Conceptual Issues, and Overview." *Forgiveness: Theory, Research and Practice.* Edited by Michael E. McCullough, Kenneth I. Pargament and Carl. E. Thoresen. New York: The Guilford Press.

North, Joanna. 1998. "The 'Ideal' of Forgiveness: a Philosopher's Exploration." *Exploring Forgiveness.* Edited by Robert D. Enright and Joanna North. Madison, Wisconsin: The University of Wisconsin Press.

Petersen, Rodney. 2001. "A Theology of Forgiveness: Terminology, Rhetoric, & the Dialectic of Interfaith Relationships." *Forgiveness and Reconciliation.* Edited by Raymond G Helmick and Rodney Petersen. Philadelphia, PA: The Templeton Foundation Press.

Rhys Davids, TW & William Stede. 1921-1925. *Pali-English Dictionary.* Sri Lanka: Pali Text Society.

Ross, Floyd Hiatt. 1953. *The Meaning of Life in Hinduism and Buddhism.* Boston: Beacon Press.

Shriver, Donald W. 2001. "What is Forgiveness in a Secular Political Forum?" *Forgiveness and Reconciliation.* Edited by Raymond G Helmick and Rodney Petersen. Philadelphia, PA: The Templeton Foundation Press.

Siderits, Mark. 2007. *Buddhism as Philosophy: An Introduction.* Indianapolis, IN: Hackett Publishing.

Acknowledgements

I would like to thank Vernon Press and its wonderful staff for their work throughout the process of publishing the book. I would also like to thank all of the contributing authors for their hard work and patience during the editing process. Finally, I would like to thank my wife, Owensboro Community and Technical College (OCTC), the faculty and staff of OCTC who help, support, and are not afraid to answer my many questions (you know you are!), my students who inspire and teach me to be better, and my friends and family (including those who are no longer with me) who have supported all that I do.

Index

A

affective, 84, 93, 230, 231, 237
agape, xiv, 231, 232, 238
Angulimala, 245, 268, 270, 273
apology, 62, 80, 91, 125, 126, 170, 176, 181, 182, 191, 198
arbitrary, xiii, 183, 186, 187, 188, 190, 194, 196, 229
Arendt, Hannah, 131, 149, 179, 222, 277
Aristotle, 18, 24, 35, 36, 108, 111, 146, 238, 242
aspirational forgiveness, 27
awareness, 61, 99, 105, 106, 113, 187, 188, 239, 265

B

bankruptcy, xiii, 151, 158
Buddha, 243–46, 250, 254–57, 258–64, 266–74, 276–78

C

care ethics, xi, 40, 41, 43, 46, 47, 49, 50, 52–54, 56–62
cognitive, 78, 80, 87, 88, 92, 93, 230, 235, 265
compassion, 55–56, 99–100, 107–16, 118–19, 125–28, 229, 233–34, 245–48, 254–58, 266–76
conditional, 164–66, 175, 176, 182, 183, 203, 208, 213, 214, 216, 220
conditional account of forgiveness, 175
condonation, 225, 228
Confucius, xiii, 201, 202, 217, 218, 220–22
criminal, xi, 40, 41, 42, 46, 56, 58, 101, 113, 155, 163, 194, 217

D

Derrida, Jacques, 131, 179, 200, 277
Dostoevsky, Fyodor, 131
double intentionality, 210, 212, 213

E

electivity, 183, 184, 195
Emotion, vii, 68, 70, 96, 97, 222
epistemic bias, 21
eros, 231
exemplar, 112–14

F

Forgiveness, i, ix, x, xi, xii, xiii, xiv, 17–26, 30–37, 58–64, 76–81, 81, 90–94, 100–112, 114–21, 122–32, 133–41, 161–63, 168–71, 186–97, 209–14, 226–36, 251–62
French Revolution, 99, 109

G

gap between reasons, 187

G

Garrard, Eve, 179, 200
God, 91–92, 104–5, 112–15, 120–22, 126–31, 141, 153–59, 194–96, 213–20, 231–40, 241–42, 245–48, 252, 258
Gormley, Steven, 200
Grace, 233, 242
Griswold, Charles, 64, 179, 200, 222, 277
Grudem, Wayne, 242

H

healing, ix–xi, 33–34, 42–43, 67–68, 83–86, 87–95, 113–14, 169–71, 247, 254
hermeneutic, xiv, 210, 213, 215, 217, 218
hostile reactive attitudes, 230

I

injury, x–xi, 67–68, 71–79, 81–86, 91–95, 124–25, 165–68, 170–77, 248–52, 258–61, 266–69
injustice, x–xi, 32–33, 39–40, 59–60, 67–68, 72–81, 83–95, 162–66, 241
interpersonal forgiveness, xiii, 17, 19, 25, 32, 33, 35, 36, 151, 162, 166

J

Jesus of Nazareth, 91, 100, 141, 232, 251
Justice, viii, xi, 39–66, 137
justification, xi, 43, 46, 48, 49, 181, 205, 206, 215, 216, 220

K

King Ajātasattu, 245, 271, 272, 277
King, Jr., Martin Luther, 242
Kristeva, Julia, 132, 149

L

letting go, 167, 202, 250, 254, 256–58, 266
Levinas, Emmanuel, 277
love, x–xiv, 19–23, 50–51, 103, 108, 110–15, 119–29, 141–48, 153–55, 167–69, 194–95, 213–15, 223–26, 230–46

M

memory, viii, 83, 89, 100, 120, 124, 129, 165, 210, 211, 252
merit, 48, 182, 226, 227, 229
moral, ix–xv, 19, 26–31, 49–55, 59–79, 85–100, 104–30, 151–90, 196–209, 220–29, 238–48, 260–61

N

narrative, 82, 121, 187
New Testament, xiv, 107, 223, 231–34, 236, 237
Noble Eightfold Path, 244, 245, 254, 256–58, 263–67, 269–71, 273, 276
nonviolence, xi, 41, 50, 52
Nussbaum, Martha, 149

O

optimistic bias, 20

P

pain, xi, 40, 52, 67, 68, 72, 73, 77–85, 92, 93, 95, 106, 107, 115, 120, 124, 125, 128, 252, 262, 266

Pali, xiv, 243–45, 254, 261, 262, 264, 267, 268, 271, 278

permissibility, 223, 225, 229, 231, 238, 239, 240, 242

Pettigrove, Glen, 132, 242

phileo, 232

Philosophy, vii, viii, ix, 36, 37, 39, 41, 49, 63–65, 96, 97, 131, 132, 138, 145, 147, 149, 157, 179, 180, 222, 245, 276–78

pity, 101, 108, 110, 112, 113, 116, 118, 121, 128, 228

plurality, 140, 210, 251

political, viii–xiv, viii–xiv, 58–59, 99–102, 107–11, 115–30, 138–55, 165–73, 206–7, 206–7, 247, 275–76

political action, 100, 102, 121, 138–41, 143–46, 148

Power, 131, 132, 137, 138

promise, xiv, 100, 101, 103, 117, 118, 120, 124–26, 126, 128, 140, 144, 151, 170, 177, 185, 251, 256, 265, 267

public spaces, 102

pure, 159, 164, 165, 184

R

reasons for, xiii, 24, 68, 138, 171, 185, 196, 197, 205, 229, 242

reconciliation, x–xi, 22–23, 39–41, 50–62, 89–114, 124–37, 159–78, 206–24, 275–76

relationship repair, x, 17, 19, 22, 35

repentance, 90, 91, 151, 160, 164–66, 170–73, 175–78, 181, 191, 198, 206, 224

resentment, ix–xi, 17–35, 67–74, 81, 76–111, 151–55, 165–83, 201–11, 226–49, 266–67

resistance, 79, 172, 240, 241

restorative, xi, 39–50, 52, 56–59, 61, 87

retribution, xi, 39, 40, 50, 69, 74, 236

retributive, xi, 39, 40, 41, 50, 57, 58, 61, 84, 161, 167, 172, 204

Ricoeur, Paul, 132, 222

Roberts, Robert, 97

S

self-care, 29, 30, 31

self-esteem, 205, 238

self-respect, 23, 29, 30, 31, 168, 197, 202, 205, 225

Seneca, 226

servility, 24, 35

social work, 42, 44, 45

spaces of appearance, 100, 128

suffering, 77, 95–130, 156, 169, 202–11, 243, 255–64

supererogatory, 241

systemic injustice, 240

T

trust, 26, 28, 123, 125, 126, 170, 224, 247

U

unapologetic, xii, 223, 225, 229, 231, 242
uncertainty, 118, 140, 244, 245, 250, 267, 274, 276
unconditional account, 197
Unforgivable Evil and Evildoers, 151–60
unrepentant, xiii, 90, 106, 151, 156, 160, 164, 165, 182, 248

V

Volf, Miroslav, 242
volitional, 109, 111, 230, 237

W

Williams, Bernard, 97, 200
Wisdom, 69, 70, 97, 256

www.ingramcontent.com/pod-product-compliance
Lightning Source LLC
Chambersburg PA
CBHW072127290426
44111CB00012B/1805